CELTIC
BRITAIN

JOHN RHYS

Celtic Britain

First published in 1904 by SPCK, London

This edition published in 1996 by Senate,
an imprint of Tiger Books International PLC,
26A York Street, Twickenham,
Middlesex TW1 3LJ, United Kingdom

Cover design © Tiger Books International 1996

3 5 7 9 10 8 6 4 2

ISBN 1 85958 203 6

Printed and bound in Great Britain by
Cox & Wyman, Reading, Berkshire

CONTENTS.

CHAPTER I.

BRITAIN IN THE TIME OF JULIUS CÆSAR.

CHAPTER II.

BRITAIN DOWN TO THE CLAUDIAN CONQUEST.

CHAPTER III.

CHAPTER IV.

THE KYMRY.

CHAPTER V.

THE PICTS AND THE SCOTS.

CHAPTER VI.

THE ETHNOLOGY OF EARLY BRITAIN.

CHAPTER VII

THE ETHNOLOGY OF BRITAIN CONTINUED.

APPENDIX.

INDEX 327

MAPS, &c.

A coloured map of Britain, showing the relative positions of
    its chief peoples during the Roman occupation.

Ptolemy's " British Isles,"

Strabo's " Western Europe."

Wales in deaneries of the time of Henry VIII.

A plate with engravings of five coins, preceded by a brief
    letterpress description of each, pp. xv., xvi.

THE COINS.

(See p. xvi.)

No. 1 represents a gold stater of Philip II. of Macedon, with the wreathed bust of Apollo on the obverse, and a charioteer in a biga on the reverse : underneath is the name of Philip, ΦIΛIΠΠOΤ.

No. 2 is an early British imitation of the stater the coin is in Sir John Evans's collection, but the place of finding is unknown. Among other things it will be noticed that it has been attempted to make the charioteer into a winged figure of Victory, and that the two horses have been converted into one horse with eight legs.

No. 3 is also in Sir J. Evans's collection, and was found at Leighton Buzzard in 1849. Besides that the faces look the other way, it will be noticed that the place occupied by Philip's name on the original is in this instance devoted to a kind of ornamentation, which at a distance has somewhat the appearance of letters.

No. 4 is a coin of Addedomaros, a part of whose name is to be read AΘΘ‖D on the reverse. On the obverse the face has given way to the coiffure which has developed into a sort of cross.

No. 5 is a coin of the Parisi, and it is to be seen at the York Museum. The obverse is taken up by the coiffure, so that it shows no part of the face. The reverse represents a very peculiar horse, accompanied by the legend VEP CORF.

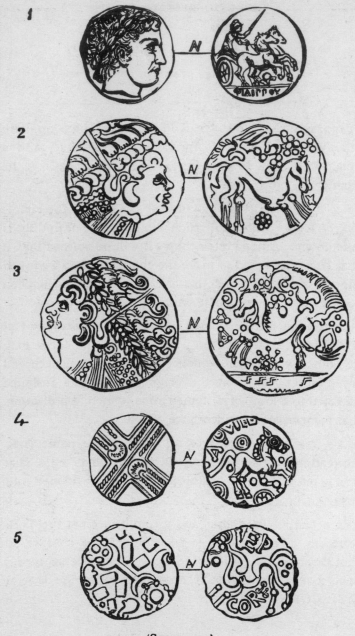

(See p. xv.)

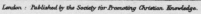
London : Published by the Society for Promoting Christian Knowledge.

SCALE OF ENGLISH MILES
0 10 20 30 40

A MAP OF
WALES
AS IT WAS IN DEANERIES
in the time of Henry VIII.

Stanford's Geogˡ Estabᵗ

London: Published by the Society for Promoting Christian Knowledge.

CELTIC BRITAIN.

CHAPTER I.

BRITAIN IN THE TIME OF JULIUS CÆSAR.

THE Celts form, in point of speech, a branch of
the great group of nations which has been
variously called Aryan, Indo-European, Indo-
Germanic, Indo-Celtic, and Japhetic, while the other
branches are represented by the Italians, the
Greeks, the Teutons, the Litu-Slaves, the Armenians,
the Persians, and the chief peoples of Hindustan.
The respective places of these nations in the geography of the Old World give, roughly speaking, a
very fair idea of their relative nearness to one another
as to language. Thus the gulf is widest between the
Celtic languages and Sanskrit or Zend, and narrowest
between Celtic and Latin, while it is comparatively
narrow between the Celtic and Teutonic languages,
among which is included English, the speech destined
in time to supersede the still living idioms of the
insular Celt. Now the Celts of antiquity who
appeared first and oftenest in history were those of
Gallia, which, having been modified by the French
into Gaule, we term Gaul. It included the France
and Switzerland of the present day, and much
territory besides. This people had various names.

One of them was *Galli*, which in their language
meant warriors or brave men, and seems to have
been always used by the Romans to designate them ;
but some of the Gauls in Cæsar's time preferred the
name which he wrote *Celtæ*. This may have been
synonymous with the other, and so it would appear
to have meant warriors, its origin, if Aryan, being
probably the same as that of the Old Norse *hild-r*,
war, battle ; but the word would admit of being
explained as originally of the same meaning as
Brittones, of which we shall have to speak later.
Recent writers, however, are of opinion that the
terms Galli and Celtæ argue an ancient distinction of race ; that the latter at first applied exclusively to the aborigines who were non-Aryans, while
Gaulish tribes only came in as the Aryan invaders of
their country ; and that these races only became
one nation by a long process of amalgamation. As
might be expected, ancient authors commonly mix
up the two names, and from that of the Celtæ of
yore modern writers have derived the terms Celt and
Celtic, which are employed in speaking of the family
in its widest sense. This would be a further extension of the meaning of the old word, as Britain was
considered to be outside the Celtic world. It was
an island beyond Celtica, or over against it, as the
ancients were wont to say.

It is a long time ago since the first Celts crossed
the sea to settle in Britain. Nobody knows how
long, but we should probably not be wrong in
supposing it to have been more than a millennium
before the Christian era. And when they did

come the immigration was not all over in one year or
even in one century. The invasions may, further, be
regarded as made by peoples belonging to both
branches of the Celtic family. For as the Teutonic
nations divide themselves into High Dutch, Nether
Dutch, and Scandinavians, so the Celtic family, as
far back as we can trace it into the darkness of antiquity, consisted of two groups or branches with linguistic features of their own which marked them off
from one another. To the one belonged the ancestors
of the people who speak Gaelic in Ireland, the Isle
of Man, and the Highlands of the North, a language
which existed also in Wales and Devon in the sixth
century, and probably later. The national name which
the members of this group have always given themselves, so far as one knows, is that of Gaoidhel, pronounced and spelt in English Gael, but formerly
written by themselves Goidel. So, as there is a
tendency in this country to understand by the word
Gael the Gael of the North alone, we shall speak of
the group generally as Goidels and Goidelic. The
other group is represented in point of speech by
the people of Wales and the Bretons; formerly
one might have added the Welsh of Cumbria, and till
the 18th century some of those of Cornwall. The
national name of those speaking these dialects came
sooner or later to be that of Briton; but, since that
word has no precise meaning, we take the Welsh form
of it which is *Brython*, and call this group Brythons
and Brythonic, whenever it may be needful to be
exact. The ancient Gauls must also be classified
with them, since the Brythons may be regarded as Gauls

who came over to settle in Britain Moreover, the
language of most of the country south of the Forth,
where English now prevails, probably differed little
at the time of the Roman conquest from that of the
Gauls of the Continent. This form of Celtic afterwards spread itself by degrees among the Goidels in
the west of the island ; so that the later Brythons there
cannot be regarded as wholly Brythons in point of
blood, a very considerable proportion of them being
probably Goidels using the language of the other
Celts. The Brythons formed the first group of
Gaulish invasions and they appear to have settled
here before the middle of the fourth century B.C.,
for Pytheas, to whom we are coming, gives indirect
evidence to their presence.[1] The next group of Gaulish
invasions was that of the Belgæ, which was recent
in Cæsar's time. As the language of the Belgæ was
not essentially different from Brythonic, their name
and individuality seem to have been eventually lost
in those of the Brythonic element. The Goidels were
undoubtedly the first Celts to come to Britain, as
their geographical position to the west and north of
the others would indicate, as well as the fact that
traces of them are difficult to discover on the Continent. They had probably been in the island for
centuries when the Brythons came and drove them
westward. The Goidels, it is right to say, had done
the same with another people, for there is no reason
to suppose that when they came here they found the
country without inhabitants. Thus we get at least four

[1] See Ch. H. Read's " Guide to the Bronze Age Antiquities
in the British Museum " (London, 1904) p. 22.

peoples to deal with—three Celtic and one pre-Celtic ; and a great difficulty in writing the history of early Britain arises from the circumstance that the ancient authors, on whom we have to rely for our information, never troubled themselves to make nice distinctions between these races, though they were probably in different stages of civilization.   We shall, therefore, proceed at once to give the substance of what they have put on record respecting this country, and make what use we can of ancient coins or other relics of the past to supplement that information about the island, seizing as we go on every opportunity of distinguishing between the different races peopling it.   When the reader has thus become acquainted with the leading facts, something will be added by way of a more detailed account of our ethnology.

No such islands as Britain and Ireland were known to Herodotus in the fifth century before the Christian era ; but some time afterwards one of the Scipios of Rome visited Marseilles [1] and Narbonne to find out whether trade could not be established with the region beyond Southern Gaul, so as to injure the Carthaginians, whose sailors used to bring tin, not only from Spain and certain tin-producing islands off the north-west of that peninsula, but also from Gaul.   The Roman could not, however, get any information about the north, but the idea of a voyage of discovery took form among the merchants of Marseilles, and the result was, that they fitted out an expedition accompanied by an eminent mathematician of that city, with whose name the reader should

[1] Strabo, Δ, 2, 1 (C. 190).

be familiar as that of one of the most intrepid explorers the world has seen. This was Pytheas,[1] who lived in the time of Alexander the Great and Aristotle, the latter of whom died in the year 322 B.C., while the year 330 is guessed as the date of the *floruit* of Pytheas. The publication of the history of his travels is supposed to have taken place soon after the death of Aristotle; and fragments of the diary of his voyage have been preserved to us in the works of various ancient authors. Pytheas sailed round Spain to Brittany, and thence to Kent and other parts of Britain; next he set out from the Thames to the mouth of the Rhine, and thence he rounded Jutland, proceeding east so far as the mouth of the Vistula: he turned back from there and possibly coasted Norway. Finally he returned to Britain and sailed thence to Brittany, whence he reached the mouth of the Garonne, and he found a route over land to Marseilles. Thus Pytheas was in Britain twice, and paid more attention to it than to any of the other countries he visited; but he does not seem to have been as far as the tin districts in the west, and it is remarkable that he gives no hint which would lead one to suppose that there was any communication between them and the Continent. That intercourse, as we are left to suppose, was confined to the southeast of the island, where the Channel was narrowest. Pytheas took a great many observations in Britain; but owing to the nature of the instruments which

[1] For a fuller account of Pytheas see Elton's " Origins of Eng. Hist." (London, 1882), pp. 13-40, and the extracts at the end of that volume.

were then in use, they are of no value. It is quite otherwise with regard to what he says of the inhabitants : he saw plenty of corn in the fields in the south-east, and he noticed that the farmers gathered the sheaves into large barns, in which the threshing was done. They had so little sun that the open threshing-floors of the brighter south would not have done in a land of clouds and rain like Britain. He likewise found that they made a drink[1] by mixing wheat and honey, which is the mead still known in certain parts of Wales ; and he is supposed to have been the authority for their use of another drink, which Greek writers[2] speak of as made of barley and used instead of wine. The name by which it was known to them is still the Celtic word for beer ; it was formerly *curmi*, and it now makes *cuirm* in Irish, and *cwrw* in Welsh. Thus we have ample evidence that in the fourth century before our era the Aryan farmer had made himself thoroughly at home in Britain. Now the expedition of Pytheas had been got up for practical purposes by his fellow-citizens, the Greeks of Marseilles, and it resulted undoubtedly in the extension across Gaul of their trade, directly or indirectly, to the corner of Britain nearest to the Continent. Some light, it may be added, is shed on this by the fact that the first coins supposed to have been struck in the island, though that happened long after Pytheas's time, were all modelled after Greek

[1] Strabo, Δ, 5, 5 (C. 201).

[2] Among others, Athenæus and Dioscorides ; see Diefenbach's Origines Europæeæ," s. v. *cervesia.*

coins made during his time. This points to a trade then opened with the north.[1]

Some two centuries later another Greek of note extended his travels to the island and visited Belerion,[2] as he called the district in Cornwall where tin was found. This was Posidonius, with whom Cicero studied at Rhodes. Besides his description of the people and their method of working the tin, Posidonius is supposed to have been the authority of Diodorus Siculus[3] for stating that the inhabitants of Britain lived in mean dwellings made for the most part of reeds or wood, and that harvest with them meant cutting the ears of corn off and storing them in pits underground, whence what had been longest in keeping was fetched day by day to be dressed for food. This appears to have been a way of preparing the cereal which was well understood in the 18th century in the Western Islands of Scotland, where one proceeded so skilfully to prepare the corn with the aid of a flame, that it might be dressed, winnowed, ground, and baked within an hour after reaping.[4] Posidonius would seem to have been speaking of a part of the country more remote than the south-east corner, to which the words of Pytheas probably applied. But we have

---

[1] See Evans's "Coins of the Ancient Britons," p. 24.

[2] Diod. Siculus's "Bibliotheca Historica," v. 21, 22.

[3] "Bibl. Hist.," v. 21, 22.

[4] See Elton's "Origins of Eng. Hist.," p. 33, where he quotes from Martin's "Description of the Western Islands of Scotland," published in 1703, a passage illustrative of this practice. See also, with regard to Ireland, Tylor's "Primitive Culture" (2nd ed.), i. pp. 44, 45.

now come down to a time when the Romans began to
acquaint themselves with the island in a very tangible
fashion.

Late in the summer of the year 55 B.C., Julius
Cæsar resolved to cross over to Britain,[1] from which
he understood the Gauls to have had repeated help in
their wars with him. The season for waging war was,
it is true, nearly over for that year, but he thought
it desirable to visit the island, to see the people, and
ascertain, so to say, how the land lay before him. So he
tried first to extract information from traders about the
size of the island, and the kind of people that lived
there, together with their mode of warfare and manner
of life ; also as to what harbours they had for a number
of ships of the larger size ; but it was all in vain, and
he says that no one but merchants readily crossed over,
and that they only knew the coast and the districts
opposite Gaul. He therefore sent Volusenus, one of his
officers, out in a war-ship, to get as much information
as possible respecting the coast of Britain, whence
he was to return as soon as he could. In the meantime Cæsar collected vessels from all parts, together
with the fleet which had been engaged the summer
before against the Veneti, to a port in the country of
the Morini, from which the passage to Britain could
be most readily made. News of this had been at
once carried across, and ambassadors from many
of the states in the island came to Cæsar, which
shows that there was a much readier and more inti-
mate communication between it and Gaul than Cæsar's
words would have led one to anticipate. The ambas-

[1] Cæsar, "De Bello Gallico," iv. 20-38.

sadors promised him hostages, and the submission of
their states to the Roman people. Cæsar, after making
liberal promises and exhorting them to continue of
that mind, sent them home, accompanied by Commios. This man was one of the Atrebates, whom
Cæsar had made king over that Belgic people when
they were conquered by the legions, and his rule was
afterwards extended to the Morini. Commios was
chosen for his supposed fidelity to Roman interests,
and because he had great influence in the south of
Britain, where a portion of the people of the Atrebates
had settlements. He had also, in Cæsar's opinion,
proved himself a man of valour and prudence. His
orders were to visit as many states as possible, and to
exhort them to embrace the alliance of the Roman
people; but no sooner had Commios landed, and his
business become known, than he was placed in bonds.
On the return of Volusenus with such information as
a man who had not ventured to land was able to procure, Cæsar embarked at midnight on the 24th of August
or one of the two succeeding days, with two legions
or about 12,000 men, in about eighty ships, together
with a number of galleys, leaving eighteen ships, detained at a neighbouring port by a contrary wind : these
were to follow with the cavalry as soon as they could.
Cæsar reached the British shore betimes in the morning ; but, finding the point touched an unfavourable
place to land in the face of the enemy that mustered
in force on the cliffs around, he coasted about seven
Roman miles to a spot where there was an open
beach and a level strand. The native cavalry and
charioteers, closely followed by the rest of the British

forces, were there in time to contest the landing of
the legions.   A severe engagement followed, in which
the Roman soldiers showed considerable hesitation,
and were thrown into much confusion by the British
charioteers, with whose movements they were not
familiar.   Gradually, however, as the Roman soldiers
got a firm footing, they forced the natives to retreat;
and Cæsar bewails the absence of his cavalry, which
he required to complete his victory.   Afterwards
ambassadors came to him to sue for peace, with Commios, released from bonds, at their head.   They laid
the war to the charge of the multitude, and begged
Cæsar to forgive those who knew no better: he met
this with the truly Roman complaint, that, after they
had sent ambassadors of their own free will to him
on the Continent, they had attacked him without
cause; but he granted their request with a demand
for hostages.   Some were given on the spot, and
others were to come from a distance in a few days,
while the leading men surrendered themselves and
began to send their troops home.

While this was going on, the eighteen ships bringing
the cavalry across appeared, when such a storm arose
that they were all forced in the face of night to turn
back to the harbour they had left, after some of them
had had a narrow escape from being wrecked on the
coast west of Cæsar's camp.   Moreover, as it was full
moon, there followed such a tide that the tempest filled
with water the war-galleys which had been drawn
up on shore, and dashed together the transport ships
that lay at anchor, so that many were wrecked or
made unfit for immediate use.   By dint of hard work

and by means of the timber and the bronze of the
vessels that had been wrecked, Cæsar was able to
get all but twelve passably refitted, while he sent to
Gaul for the things that were wanting. As soon as the
British chiefs saw what had happened to the Roman
cavalry and to the ships, and when they had reckoned
by the size of the camp how few soldiers it contained, they began to combine and secretly to muster
their forces again, as well as to stop sending in
hostages, hoping, as Cæsar thought, that they could
prolong the war into the winter, and thereby cut
off his whole army, as a caution to all future invaders. Their first move was to post cavalry and
chariots in good positions near the spot where alone
there was corn still standing, to which the Romans
must come. In due time one of the legions came,
and as soon as the men had set to work in the
fields a well-directed onslaught was made on them,
and it would have gone hard with the legion, as
it was attacked on all sides, had not Cæsar, who
was on the alert, brought them aid. The attack
then ceased, but he was only able to conduct a
retreat. Then bad weather is said by him to
have kept both sides quiet for several days, during
which the British forces seem to have received
reinforcements. They now advanced to Cæsar's
camp, which was by this time provided with thirty
horses which Commios had brought over : a battle
ensued, in which the Romans prevailed and slew a
considerable number of the enemy in their retreat.
After the soldiers had duly laid waste the country
around, and destroyed everything they could, am-

bassadors came the same day to sue again for
peace : it was readily granted, but Cæsar asked
for twice the number of hostages demanded the
time before ; for the general was getting impatient to
return to Gaul, the reason assigned being the lateness
of the season and the frail nature of his ships.
He had probably seen that he could not do much in
the island without a larger force, especially of cavalry.
He left shortly before the equinox, so that he had
been here nearly a month according to some calcu-
lations, or a little over a fortnight according to others,
but without having been able to advance a mile fiom
the place of landing. The hostages were to be sent
after him, and those of two states reached him, but
no more. Nevertheless, the Roman Senate, on learning by letter from him what he had achieved, thought
it right to decree twenty days of public thanksgiving.

Cæsar[1] gave orders that more ships and those of a
more suitable kind should be got ready for the ensuing
summer for a second campaign in Britain ; and such
was the eagerness with which the soldiers went to
work, that by the time he returned in June from
Illyricum and Italy, they had got nearly 600, new
and old, almost ready to be launched. Thus it would
appear that what they had seen of the island had
filled them with thoughts of valuable plunder : the
same feeling is proved also by the privateers, which
those who were able fitted out to accompany the
army across the Channel. Among other things it
was thought that British waters would be found to
produce abundance of precious pearls, an idea got

[1] " Bell. Gall.," v. 1-23.

rid of, no doubt, in time, though we read of British pearls adorning a corselet which Cæsar was pleased to dedicate in the temple of the Goddess of Victory at Rome. When all was ready he embarked at a place he calls *Portus Itius*, or the Ictian port, which was probably the harbour whence he had sailed before, with five legions and 2,000 cavalry : the number of vessels of all kinds was over 800, though 60 built on the Marne, in the country of the Meldi above the Parisii, had failed to join the expedition, owing to a storm which drove them back. This year Cæsar was resolved to begin in season : accordingly he set sail, as it is supposed, late on the 18th of July or, according to others, a day or two later, but by daybreak he found his fleet carried by the current past the South Foreland, and it was with great labour that he got back to the spot which he had ascertained the summer before to be the best place for landing : this work, together with the choice of a site for the camp, took up the rest of the day. During the night, however, he set out with all the army, except what force he thought needful to leave in charge of the camp and the ships moored near it, in quest of the enemy that had this time thought it of no use to contest the landing of such a force, but rather to take up an advantageous position inland. Cæsar, after marching about twelve miles in the night, came in sight of the Britons, and soon found them advancing to attack his men from a higher ground. On being repulsed by the Roman cavalry they withdrew into a place excellently fortified by nature and art, with all its entrances blocked up

with felled trees : it appeared to have been made
during one of their civil wars. The legions made
themselves in due time masters of it, but Cæsar
did not venture to pursue the enemy far that
day.   Next morning, as he was sending cavalry
and infantry after the retreating Britons, news arrived
from the coast that nearly all his ships had been
dashed to pieces on the shore during the night.   He
called back his men and marched to the coast, where
he found that about forty ships had been wrecked,
but that the rest might be repaired with great labour :
this was done, and they were hauled on shore to be
included within the lines of the camp.   About ten
days were taken up by this work, during which word
was sent to Cæsar's lieutenant in Gaul to have as
many ships as possible got ready and sent over.
When at length the general returns to seek the
enemy, he finds him mustering in much greater force
under the command now of a single leader named
Cassivellaunos, whose country lay north of the
Thames, being in all probability that of the people
called Catuvellauni.   This prince, though he had in
previous years been at constant war with the other
states, had now the sole command given him by the
consent of all, whence it would seem that they
acknowledged him to have been their ablest and
most tried general.   What gave Cæsar most trouble
would seem to have been the quick and sudden movements of the British cavalry and charioteers, who
fought bravely with the Roman cavalry ; they were as
dangerous when retreating as when advancing, for
when they got the cavalry of the Roman army away

from it, the combatants alighted and fought as foot
soldiers.   On one occasion the charioteers rushed
upon the Roman soldiers, when they were engaged
in fortifying their position, and fought so strenuously
with the outposts before the camp, that the first
cohorts of two different legions had to be called out ;
but when they had taken their places with small
spaces between them they were terrified by the
enemy's charioteers, who dashed through their midst
in safety and with the utmost boldness.   It was only
after one of the military tribunes had been killed, and
more cohorts had come forth, that the enemy retreated.   They never fought in close order, but they
arranged outlying detachments that harassed the
legions in relays.   The next day no less than three
legions were sent out together for the purpose of
foraging; but, owing to the Roman cavalry being then
better backed than before by the infantry, severe
losses were inflicted on the skirmishers : the British
auxiliaries, who had mustered in great number,
straightway withdrew; nor did Cassivellaunos after
that day hazard a battle on a large scale.   Consequently
Cæsar marched towards his territory and crossed the
Thames, somewhere above London with great difficulty, but with much alacrity on the part of the
soldiers, who had as yet had little chance of getting
much booty.   Cassivellaunos sent away most of his
forces, but retained about 4,000 charioteers to harass
Cæsar's march and to clear the country where he
was likely to come : his tactics greatly narrowed the
Roman area of devastation, and made the business
of burning and destroying much more laborious than

the soldiers could have wished; so their general speaks almost pathetically of their being only able to effect their purpose in the midst of the toils of marching.

This was, however, not to last long; for the powerful people of the Trinovantes, who inhabited the modern county of Essex and a part of Middlesex, from beyond the Lea to the Stour, sent in the meantime to Cæsar to ask for peace, a course which they were led to take, partly, no doubt, to escape the ravages of the Roman army, and partly perhaps to avenge themselves on Cassivellaunos, who had killed their king. The son of the latter, who was called Mandubratios, had succeeded in making his way to Cæsar in Gaul, and in securing his protection; the Trinovantes, therefore, not only asked Cæsar to accept their submission, but also to send Mandubratios to rule over them, and to save that prince from Cassivellaunos. Cæsar complied, and demanded forty hostages from them, together with corn for the army: they brought both, and their territory was protected from the soldiery. The work of conquest was now easy; for the example of the Trinovantes was followed by other tribes—namely, the Cenimagni, Segontiaci, Ancalites, Bibroci, and Cassi, while the invader was told that the stronghold of Cassivellaunos was not far off, where he would find a large number of men and cattle brought together. This he discovered to have been admirably fortified by nature and art, which latter in Britain consisted in making a defence of wood, with a rampart and trench drawn round it. But it was not long before the

Roman soldiers got possession of the place, together
with the large number of cattle it contained, while
many of the men were cut down in their flight. But
Cassivellaunos was not inactive either, and while these
things were going on in his own territory, he ordered the
four kings of Cantion, or Kent, together with a part
of Surrey, to storm Cæsar's camp by the sea, a thing
which they at once proceeded to do ; but they were
driven back with considerable loss, one of the
leaders being captured by the Roman soldiers. At
the news of this failure, and especially of the defec-
tion of the Trinovantes and the other states which
followed them, Cassivellaunos decided to sue for
peace through Commios, the Atrebat. Rumours
from Gaul, not to his liking, had reached Cæsar, and
because he had his former views as to the lateness of
the season, he seized the opportunity of bringing the
war to a close at once by demanding hostages and
fixing the sum which Britain was to pay as a yearly
tribute. He also gave Cassivellaunos strict orders,
which cost the giver little, to keep his hands off
Mandubratios and the Trinovantes. Since it was
near the equinox when Cæsar left, his stay here must
have been about two months. Of course he did not
depart empty-handed, for he took with him not only
the hostages, but also a great number of captives, the
sale of whom was to fill Roman coffers with gold.

From Cæsar's departure in the year 54 B.C. down
to the invasion of the island under Claudius in A.D. 43,
that is to say, for pretty nearly a century, we know
very little of its history, except what may be made
out by means of the coins, which began to be stamped

with letters soon after Cæsar's conquest of Gaul. The coinage of Britain had, in the first instance, been modelled after that of Gaul, which in its turn can be traced to the Phocæan Greeks of Massilia or Marseilles, through whom the Continental Gauls became acquainted in the latter part of the fourth century before Christ with the gold stater of Philip II. of Macedon. This was a fine coin, weighing about 133 grains and having on one side the head of Apollo wreathed with laurel, while the other showed a charioteer in his chariot, with Philip's name underneath. It was imitated by the Gauls fairly well at first, but as it got farther removed from the original in time and place, the figures degenerated into very curious and fantastic forms. It has been calculated by Sir John Evans, the greatest authority on the subject, that the inhabitants of the south of Britain must have begun to coin gold pieces of this kind from 200 to 150 B.C.,[1] and the information he has collected makes it probable that this took place first in Kent; next followed the coinage of the other tribes inhabiting the south of England, as far as the borders of Dorsetshire. It is also worthy of remark that coins of several types are found to have been current on the south coast, concerning which it is hard to decide whether they should be regarded as belonging to Gaul or to Britain. Money appears to have circulated as far as Cornwall, though there is no satisfactory evidence that any tribe west of the Durotriges of Dorset had a coinage of its own. Between Dorsetshire and the Worcestershire Avon, there was probably more than one tribe that had

[1] Evans's "Coins of the Ancient Britons" (London, 1864), p. 26.

an early coinage. So had the Catuvellauni, whose
territory stretched in a north-easterly direction from
the Thames to the neighbourhood of the Wash, and
also the Trinovantes, who lived between them and
the North Sea in Essex and Middlesex. But there
is no satisfactory evidence that any tribes north of
these, not even the Eceni, who occupied what is now
Norfolk and Suffolk, had a coinage of their own when
Cæsar landed in this country; nor does it appear
that any British tribe whatever had then begun to
have its coins lettered. It is not certain that silver
or bronze coins had as yet been struck, though it is
probable that in any case they came into use
much later than gold ones. But Cæsar is usually
made to say that no money was current in Britain,
but only bronze or pieces of iron of a fixed weight
to supply its place. The passage,[1] however, is hope-
lessly corrupt, and the manuscripts differ greatly,
some of them ascribing to the Britons the use of
coins of gold, and some also of bronze. Whatever
Cæsar wrote there can be little doubt about the
gold currency: he appears, from the best manuscripts, to have mentioned it, though he saw little
of it, as may be gathered from the correspond-
ence[2] of one of his officers; and it is by no means
improbable that ingots of bronze or bars of iron may
have been used for money among the tribes who had
no coinage, and that Cæsar was aware of that fact
When he goes on to say that iron was found on the

---

[1] "Bell. Gall.," v. 12.

[2] That of Cicero's brother to Cicero; see "Monumenta Hist.
Brit.," pp. lxxxvii., lxxxviii.

sea coast of Britain, but that the supply was small, he probably alludes to the iron-mining in the weald of Kent and Sussex, which Prof. Boyd Dawkins believes to have been carried on before Cæsar's landing, as it certainly was during the Roman occupation, and for many centuries afterwards.[1]   There is no reason, however, to suppose that the great wealth of the country in iron oré had been discovered by Cæsar's time, and the little already found had possibly been pointed out by some one who had seen iron worked on the Continent.   Cæsar tells us that the bronze used in the island was imported, which would be good evidence that copper was not yet worked here, bronze being a compound of copper and tin.   The importation of bronze (aes) and exportation of tin would accordingly have formed at this time the most important items in the trade of Britain; but there is reason to doubt that the inhabitants of this country depended to any considerable extent on the importation of bronze,[2] and we seem to be forced either to doubt the accuracy of Cæsar's information, or to explain his use of the term aes as referring to certain bronze works of art made in the workshops of the Mediterranean.

We have now come to an age when the coins of

[1] The last forge appears to have been blown out only in the year 1825, though the growing scarcity of fuel had driven several of the ironmasters to South Wales as early as the time of Henry VIII.   See a paper by Prof. Boyd Dawkins in the Transactions of the " Internat. Congress of Prehist. Arch." for 1868, p. 188.

[2] See Read's Guide to the " Bronze Age Antiquities in the British Museum " (London, 1904), pp. 23, 71.

Britain began to appear with letters on them. This
is found to have taken place first in Kent, or else
a little to the west on the southern shore, where
the Belgic tribes kept up an active communication
with Gaul. Here we find one or two coins of
Commios, and a great many of three princes who
called themselves Sons of Commios. Who this
Commios was is not known, but he and his sons
seem to have held sway in much the same part of
Britain as that in which the Commios of whom Cæsar
speaks had so much influence; and, on the whole, it
is not improbable that the latter is also the Commios
of the coins. He appears to have gone back with
Cæsar to Gaul, as we find him left with some cavalry
to keep watch the following year over the Menapii,
who seem to have lived on the coast between
the Morini and the Rhine. This duty was entrusted him while the general set out against the
Treveri; but in 52 B.C. so strong was the desire of
the Gauls to drive out the Romans, that Commios
became one of the leaders against the latter :
so dangerous was he considered, that Labienus,
Cæsar's lieutenant, tried to have him killed by
treachery, but he got away, though severely wounded.
He is said some time afterwards to have had a very
narrow escape from Cæsar himself, which he effected
by betaking himself to his ship, and having its sails
spread as though he had it already afloat, which it
was not : the pursuit was given up, and he had time
to get away to Britain. He figures, however, in 51 B.C.
again as one of the chief organizers of opposition
to Roman rule in Gaul, and when the other chiefs

had given in their submission, he still held out.   There
was another attempt to murder him by means of
the same officer as before, but the latter had the
worst of it, and Commios escaped, whereupon he
sent in his submission to Antony, then acting under
Cæsar in Gaul, and made it a condition that he
should be allowed to go where he should not set eyes
on another Roman.   He seems to have been an
active man in the prime of life, and since we hear no
more of him it is not unlikely that he came over to
Britain, and that his hatred of the Romans had been
sufficiently proved to his kindred here to make them
forget his having once been one of Cæsar's tools,
if, indeed, they ever took an unfavourable view of
that part of his history.   We need not suppose that
his influence here had to be acquired all anew, as
the Atrebates and the other Belgic tribes of Britain
had probably been induced by him to join the league
which he and others had organized of their kinsfolk,
the Continental Atrebates, the Bellovaci, and other
powerful peoples.   As far as can be gathered from
the places where the coins in question were found, the
rule of the Commian family did not extend beyond the
district represented by Kent, Surrey, Sussex, Hants,
and, perhaps, a part of Wilts.   According to Sir J.
Evans, the lettered coinage of this part of the
island may be supposed to have appeared some time
before 30 B.C.[1]   At his death his territory seems to
have fallen to his three sons, Tincommios, Verica
and Eppillos, who are supposed to have exercised
a sort of joint rulership over it, while each had

[1] Evans's "Coins of the Ancient Britons," pp. 154, 155.

probably a district which was more completely
under his own control; that is to say, Eppillos
ruled over the Cantii, Tincommios over the Regni,
whose territory may, roughly speaking, be supposed
to have been that which became the Saxon kingdom
of Sussex, and Verica over the country of the Atrebates, who appear to have in all possessed what is
now Berkshire, a part of Oxfordshire reaching as far
north as Aldchester and Bicester, and a certain
portion possibly of Surrey. The names of the three
brothers are found together on one coin, but Tincommios, who seems to have been the eldest, appears to have died before the others, as some coins
occur with their joint names alone. There are
reasons for supposing Eppillos to have survived
Verica, of whose territory, together most likely with
that of Tincommios, he may have become sole ruler :
at any rate, he appears, so far as one can judge from
the abbreviated forms used on some coins, to call
himself king of Calleva, which is identified with
Silchester in Hampshire. There is no indication
that Commios or Tincommios called himself king
of any people in Britain, but Eppillos and Verica
certainly take the title on some of their coins, whence
it would seem that Commios had placed himself in
a position of authority in South Britain as the head
of a league organized for a special purpose, and that
he so far consolidated his power as to be able to
pass it on to his sons, while Eppillos and Verica
appear to have thought themselves safe in taking the
title of kings. That was probably not done without
opposition, and it is not impossible that Eppillos's

position among the Cantii was altogether acquired by
conquest, either in his father's time or soon after, as it
seems doubtful whether Cantion came within the circle
of the original influence of Commios, whose direct
connection would rather seem to have been with the
Atrebates and the other Belgic tribes west of Cantion.
We appear to fall in with one of the princes who were
beaten in the struggle with the Commian family, in one
or other of the British refugees who are said, on one of
the monuments[1] recounting the events of the reign of
Augustus, to have sought his protection. The coins
of Commios, and some of the earlier ones of Tincommios, continued the degenerate imitations of the
Macedonian stater without showing any Roman
influence; but it was not long after Augustus became
emperor, that Tincommios copied the Latin formula,
in which the former styled himself *Augustus Divi
Filius* or the son of his adoptive father Julius Cæsar,
who had now begun to be officially called *Divus* or
the god.   So Tincommios had inscribed on his money
the legend—*Tinc. Commi F.*, or even shorter abbreviations, meaning Tincommios, son of Commios; and
the grotesque traits derived from the stater soon disappeared in favour of classical designs of various kinds,
proving very distinctly that the influence of Roman
art was beginning to make itself felt in the south of
Britain.   With the sons of Commios the coinage of
the western portion of their territory seems to have
ceased, whereas in Kent it would appear to have
continued later.   This is supposed to be accounted

[1] That of Ancyra in Asia Minor; see the Berlin "Corpus
Inscr. Lat.," iii. pp. 784, 785, 798, 799.

for by the influence of the trade with Gaul, where everything was fast being Romanized under Augustus; but it would hardly explain why a native coinage should continue longer in Kent, which was after all the nearest part of Britain to Gaul. It is rather to be supposed that the western part of Eppillos's kingdom fell after his day under the power of the encroaching Catuvellauni, and that we have to look for the coins representing it later among those of that people.

Now most of the latter are found to have been issued by a prince, whose name occurs Latinized as Tasciovanus, Tasciovanius, and Tasciovans (genitive Tasciovantis), the Tenuantius of Geoffrey of Monmouth, and by his sons Cunobelinos and Epaticcos. The father's capital was Verlamion or Verulam, near St. Albans, and the name of the town appears on many of his coins, as does that of Camulodunon or Colchester, which was Cunobelinos's capital, on his. The great variety of Tasciovant's coins seems to show that he must have had a long reign, and some of them at any rate were struck as late as the year 13 B.C., as they are found to have been modelled after coins of Augustus, which were not current till that time;[1] but it has been supposed that he lived a good many years later, and died only after the beginning of our era. Others of his coins show that he reigned for some time during the life of Eppillos, but at what date he began we have no means of finding out, though it has been supposed to have been as early as the year 30, when Augustus was made emperor, and some of the coins would seem to point even

[1] Evans's " Coins of the Anc. Brit., " p. 223.

to an earlier date. This would bring Tasciovant sufficiently near Cassivellaunos in point of time for him to
have been his son or a brother's son ; but possibly
we should rather say a grandson. In either case, there
is no reason to suppose that there had in the meantime been a revolution or a change of dynasty, especially as we find Cunobelinos, the Cymbeline of
Shakspere, styling himself on some coins *rex* or king ;
and we seem to be at liberty to assume, in the absence
of evidence to the contrary, that the people of the
Catuvellauni had been guided by the more or less
uniform policy of one dynasty in their treatment of
neighbouring states. This appears on looking into
the scanty data at our disposal to have been one of
conquest and aggression. Thus Cæsar mentions how
the king of the Trinovantes had been slain by
Cassivellaunos, when his son Mandubratios fled to
him. How long the losses which Cassivellaunos and
his people suffered during Cæsar's campaign inclined
them to leave the Trinovantes alone cannot be made
out, but we learn from the coins that Cunobelinos
ruled there and had made Camulodunon in the heart
of their country his capital, which probably happened
during Tasciovant's life and with his help. Possibly
Mandubratios was left unassailed as long as he lived ;
but the coinage of the country of the Trinovantes
bears evidence to the rule for a time of a prince
whose name was Dubnovellaunos, and who is mentioned on the Augustan monument, already referred
to, as one of the two British princes who sought
the emperor's protection. His history is rendered
somewhat difficult by the fact that his coins are also

found in Kent (and those, so far as can be guessed,
his earlier ones), whence it would seem that he ruled
over a certain extent of territory on both sides of the
Thames. From his southern position he may have
been driven by Eppillos, with whom he appears to
have been contemporary, and from the northern one
some time later by Cunobelinos. It is not impossible
that the territory of the Trinovantes originally comprised a part of the southern coast of the estuary of
the Thames, and certain it is that both the Isle of
Thanet and that of Sheppey are placed opposite the
Trinovantes by Ptolemy, who may, perhaps, have
regarded them as belonging to that people.

Between the Catuvellauni and the North Sea there
were, besides the Trinovantes, the people of the
Eceni, occupying the country between them and the
Wash. When the former had been reduced by the
Catuvellauni, the turn of the latter, in case it had not
come before, could not be very far off: it may be
that we have them heading Cæsar's list of the states
which, after the example of the Trinovantes, deserted
Cassivellaunos in the hour of need. But that is by no
means certain, since the name appears in the manuscripts of Cæsar as Cenimagni, Cenomagni, and Ceno-
manni, which may possibly be considered mutilated
forms of some such longer title of the nation of
the Eceni as Ecenimagni or the like: it may be
that he meant a Belgic tribe from the south of the
Thames. The others mentioned were the Segontiaci,
Ancalites, Bibroci, and Cassi, all probably Belgic
tribes, living near the Thames or between its
basin and the Severn, and included as it may be

supposed under the more general name of Atrebates. Such the Bibroci appear to have been, whose name reminds one of the town of the Remi, called Bibrax, and of Cæsar's statement, that almost all the Belgic peoples of Britain bore the name of the Continental state they had come from ; but the exact locality either of the Bibroci or of the Ancalites cannot be said to be known, though nothing serious stands in the way of the guess which identifies the name of the former with the Berroc, whence the modern name of the county of Berks is derived.   The Segontiaci are connected with the neighbourhood of the Silchester Calleva by the finding there of a Roman inscription in honour of a divinity styled the Segontiac Hercules; and as some of Tasciovant's coins bear the name of this people, or of one of its towns, we may conclude that they had been forced into an alliance with the Catuvellauni.   This does not stand alone ; for the coins of Epaticcos seem to prove that he held sway south of the Thames, in what is now the county of Surrey.   The name of the Cassi would be lisped in Gaulish and then spelt CADDI or Caθθi, which less accurately written in Latin letters may be detected in the *Catti* of coins found in Gloucestershire and the neighbouring county of Monmouth.   They were either a branch of the Atrebates, or else, perhaps, of the people of the Dobunni, to whom they were near neighbours.   The latter occupied most of the tract between the two Avons and between the Severn and the states of the Atrebates and the Catuvellauni, while Dion Cassius, in speaking of the campaign of Aulus Plautius in that

district in the year 43, gives one to understand that
either the whole or a portion of the people of the
Dobunni was subject to the Catuvellauni at that time.
The inland tract between the Catuvellauni and the
Dobunni on the one hand, and the tribes grouping
themselves with the Brigantes of the north beyond
the Humber and the Mersey on the other, was
inhabited by two peop'es, that of the Coritani in the
district between the Wash and the Trent, which contained the towns of Lincoln and Leicester, and that
of the Cornavii to the west of the Coritani, which
reached from about the Worcestershire Avon to the
mouths of the Dee and the Mersey. Of these peoples
exceedingly little is known, and they play no appre-
ciable part in the resistance offered to the Roman arms
in the time of Claudius, so we may, perhaps, infer
that they were virtually conquered with the Catuvellauni, as having been for some time the allies or
subjects of that state. In that case the Catuvellauni
may be regarded as the Mercians of those days, a
supposition aptly illustrated by the fact that they
chose to call themselves by a name meaning battle-
rulers or war-kings, like that of the Caturiges of
Gaul; and it is in their aggressiveness that we have
probably to look in the first instance for the secret of
the influence of Commios in Britain, which Cæsar has
left unexplained. The Belgic tribes of the Thames
Valley were, we may take it, hard pressed by the
Catuvellauni; they sent to ask their kindred in Gaul
for help, and Commios came over to aid them with
his genius, and possibly with armed men; but whether
that was so or not—for there is no evidence—there

would be nothing very surprising in a man of his ability having organized such resistance as would stay for a time the advance of the Catuvellauni. It may, indeed, be that he was not the first to come over for that purpose, but that something of the kind had happened already in the time of Diviciacos, who, as Cæsar was informed, had been king of the Belgic people of the Suessiones within his time, and not only possessed more power than any other man in Gaul, but exercised it also in Britain.[1] However that may be, Commios may have seen that the advance of the Catuvellauni could not be long stayed, and that was his reason, or at least one of his reasons, for taking an active part in Cæsar's invasion. If so, it may be that the losses which Cæsar inflicted on the Cantii and the Catuvellauni resulted in relieving the Belgic states of all immediate fear of their neighbours, and in adding to the popularity of Commios. In that case he would have little or no trouble in making himself the head of a league directed against the Catuvellauni, when he was forced to leave Gaul, whence he brought with him also credit for an intense hatred of the Romans. All this would agree well enough with the fact that it was probably among the people of Kent that he was detained in bonds, when he landed as Cæsar's envoy ; and it has already been suggested that it was possibly by force of arms that his son Eppillos asserted his power there some time afterwards.

[1] "Bell. Gall.," ii. 4.

CHAPTER II.

BRITAIN DOWN TO THE CLAUDIAN CONQUEST.

FOR a good many years preceding the Claudian invasion in the year 43, Cunobelinos was the most con-
spicuous figure in Britain, and Suetonius, who wrote
his history of the Cæsars some seventy or eighty
years later, speaks of him as Rex Britannorum[1] or
King of the Britons. From this, together with other
indications, it would seem that his power reached to
the southern coast, though it is hardly probable that
he had removed all the princes of the states south of
the Thames. It is more likely that he was satisfied with
forcing them into an alliance with him, and allowing
some of them to rule in their own states subject
to some kind of supremacy on his part. Whether
the fugitives who sought the aid of Augustus were
able to induce him to assist them we are not told,
but historians state that Augustus once meditated
an expedition against Britain, and it may be that it
was the representations of the former that led him
thereto. This never came to anything, for the princes
of Britain hastened to send ambassadors to him to
prevent war, and some of them, we are told, gained
his friendship. We may take it that Cunobelinos, the

---

[1] Suetonius, " De Vita Cæsarum," Caligula, 44.

most wealthy and powerful of them, was the most successful in winning the emperor's good graces, and if
the exiles ever returned it was probably subject to certain conditions which he thought it right to indicate.
Strabo, who wrote not many years after the death of
Augustus, in 14 B.C., goes on to say that the British
princes who were on friendly terms with the emperor
dedicated their offerings in the Capitol at Rome,
and brought the island well-nigh to a state of close
connection with the Roman power. This is quite
in harmony with what we learn from Cunobelinos's
coins. His father's, which were much on a level
with those of Eppillos, show far less of the influence of Rome, while it is unmistakable on those of
Cunobelinos, with the exception of some few of his
early ones, which are purely British and belong to
the series derived from the Macedonian stater. The
workmanship improves, and a variety of classical
figures, such as Jupiter Ammon, Apollo playing on
the lyre, Hercules with his club or with the trophies
of some of his labours, Janus, Diana, Cybele on a
lion, Victory in various attitudes, and many other
mythical personages of the same class, together with
sphinxes, griffins, and other monsters of southern
mythology, take the place of the clumsier forms on
the more purely British money. The coinage of
Gaul was now becoming Roman, and the improve-
ment in that of Britain was no longer perhaps so
much a matter of taste as of commercial expediency,
on which some light is thrown by the fact that
Augustus thought proper to commute the year's

tribute for a light export and import duty on the
trade between it and Gaul. This, so far as it goes,
would indicate that the trade was not inconsider-
able.   In any case we are not to suppose the
emperor capable of despising any source of income
which could be made to bring money into his
coffers.

Augustus was succeeded by Tiberius, who died in
the year 37 without having troubled himself in any
way, so far as we know, with the affairs of Britain.
He was followed by Caligula, who was emperor until
his death in the year 41.   In his time Britain appears
again in history, as follows :—In the year 40 a son
of Cunobelinos, called Adminius by Suetonius who
gives the account, surrendered himself with a small
number of followers to Caligula in Gaul, when he had
for some reason or other been banished by his own
father. Thereupon the emperor sent a letter to Rome
describing in fine language how the island of Britain
had been added to the Roman power, the messengers
being charged to deliver his message to the senate
only in full assembly in the Temple of Mars. This
freak of imperial madness corroborates the view that
Cunobelinos was at that time, in the opinion of the
Romans, the only British king who was worth considering, and explains why Suetonius calls him king
of the Britons. But of his son, who made this cheap
surrender of his father's kingdom to Caligula, nothing
further is known, excepting that he was possibly the
same person whose name is written Amminus on some
coins of this time, the finding-place of which tends

to connect him with some part of Kent. Cunobelinos had other sons, but the only ones known to history were Togodumnos and Caratâcos, who ruled over their deceased father's kingdom when Claudius sent Aulus Plautius here. So he must have died between the years 40 and 43, at a very advanced age, and after having carried into effect with considerable success the family policy of bringing the neighbouring states under the rule of the Catuvellauni.

A variety of coins, of which neither the exact age or place of issue nor the sequence has been satisfactorily made out, are assigned to the country of the Dobunni ; but, on the whole, none of them are considered to date before the Christian era, while some appear to be as late as the time of Claudius, whose reign begins with the year 41. They tend to show that some of the Dobunni were so far independent of the Catuvellauni as to have had a coinage of their own. It may be, however, that the latest of them were struck after the death of Togodumnos in 43 and the conquest of his people by the Romans, that is, in the interval before the reduction of the country in the neighbourhood of the Bristol Avon by Ostorius Scapula in the year 50. They all belong to the series of imitations of the Macedonian stater, and show hardly a trace of the influence of Rome, excepting that two or three of the names are given in a Latin rather than in a Gaulish spelling. One group, that of the Catti, a word already mentioned as being probably the name of a people, the Cassi of Cæsar's

Commentaries, is remarkable as showing no trace of the name of any prince or king.

The next region distinctly indicated by the peculiarities of its coinage is the country of the Eceni, otherwise called Iceni, and inhabiting approximately the modern counties of Norfolk and Suffolk. Trade and the east wind travelled westwards, leaving the Eceni on their peninsula to defy a little longer the Roman influence to which Cunobelinos and his people had been giving way, and which now reached the land of the Dobunni on the banks of the Severn. The Eceni seem, from what we read of them afterwards, to have been a remarkably hardy and warlike race, but, just as they may have been among those who deserted Cassivellaunos in order to make their own terms with Cæsar, so their old jealousy and fear of the power of the Catuvellauni when Cunobelinos had succeeded in combining with it that of the Trinovantes were partly, no doubt, the cause which led them in 43 to make an alliance with the Romans, which they soon began to regret. The earliest group of coins which has been supposed to belong to them bears the name of Addedomaros; but it is by no means certain that the prince so named ruled over the Eceni rather than over some neighbouring tribe, among whom Cunobelinos found the means of supplanting or succeeding him. His coins would then be the only gold ones of the Eceni with any reading on them, and, had they really been theirs, it is hardly probable that they would have reverted to uninscribed ones, for such they certainly seem to have had after his time, both

in gold and silver.   But together with their uninscribed silver coins they used inscribed ones, some of
which are remarkable as showing the name of the
people in the abbreviated form of ECEN without a
trace of that of any prince or king accompanying it,
which calls to mind the coins of the Catti.   It would
thus seem that at this time the Eceni had no kings.
Their latest coins, however, show the name of one
Antedrigus, who may have been king or else chief
magistrate of a state which had no king : we cannot
say which, as there are no means of deciding.   But if
the following facts be put together, to wit, that Antedrigus, the name of this man, appears a little later,
sometimes in its Celtic spelling and sometimes Latinized, on coins in the land of the Dobunni ; that Dion
Cassius[1] mentions one Bericos, who, driven out of
Britain by an insurrection, went to persuade Claudius
to send out an expedition against it, which was
done in 43 ; and lastly that, when the Romans came,
the Eceni entered into an alliance with them without
fighting, though they were by no means a likely
people to have shrunk from the horrors of war,
their history may be guessed—that is all—and sum-
marised thus :—The Eceni had experienced a revolution, which put an end to the kingly power among
them ; the state became the prey of two factions,
headed by Bericos and Antedrigus respectively ;
their dispute may have been of the same nature as
that which Julius Cæsar was called upon to decide

---

[1] " Roman History,' lx. 19, 23.

among the Ædui,[1] that is, one between two nobles, each
of whom insisted that he was the duly elected king for
the year ; Antedrigus prevailed, and issued coins with
his name on them ; and Bericos fled to Claudius to
ask him to invade the island, promising him the aid
of his friends and of the state of the Eceni if he
placed him in the position occupied by his rival.
When the Roman forces arrived, Bericos and his friends
made a handle of the Eceni's jealousy of the power
of the Catuvellauni to induce the former to enter into
an alliance with the Roman power ; he obtained his
desire, and Antedrigus had to flee, but was hospitably
received by the Dobunni, among whom he organized
resistance to the Romans for some years afterwards,
much in the same way as Caratâcos did among the
Silures after having to leave his own people in the
power of the conqueror. All this, though only a
conjecture, would agree best with the view that the
Eceni never were reduced by Cunobelinos ; and he
certainly can have had no hand in regulating their
coinage, which betrays no trace of the influence of
Roman art or of the Latin language, except in so far
as the Gaulish orthography used in this country at
that time was a sort of mixture of Greek and Latin
letters.

Nothing can be said to be known as yet of the
coinage of the Cornavii and the Coritani, though it
is not improbable that both peoples may have had
for a short time coins of their own make. In fact, it
is thought that it was through the latter that acquaint-

[1] "Bell. Gall," vii. 32, 33.

ance with money was first made by the people on
the shores of the Humber, whose coinage is the
rudest of all, and the one most like that of the
Eceni, though it is impossible to trace it directly to
the latter.   This coinage, moreover, appears to have
been the latest, being apparently of the time of
Claudius or in part later ; it may be supposed to have
come to an end about the time when the Brigantes,
whose sway extended over much of the country from
the Humber and Mersey as far perhaps as the Caledonian Forest, submitted to the Roman yoke soon
after the year 69.   In vain, however, do we scan the
coins in question for any of the historical names of
that people, such as Cartismandua, Venutios, or Vello-
catus ; in fact, there is no reason for supposing them
to have belonged to the Brigantes so much as to a
people inhabiting the districts now known as Holderness and the Yorkshire Wolds—possibly the whole
coast from the Humber to the Tees.   In Ptolemy's
Geography, a great work published about the year
120, they are called Parîsi, which makes it probable
that they were a branch of the Parisii on the Seine,
who have left their name to the city of Paris.   Their
town, called Petuaria, has its name possibly perpetuated in that of *Patrington* in Holderness, and
Ptolemy places them also around what he calls the
Fair-havened Bay, referring probably to the once important harbour of Hornsea.   We find other towns of
theirs besides Petuaria in the Delgovicia of the ancients,
which was probably Market Weighton, and in Der-
ventio, somewhere on the Derwent, probably Kexby

or Elvington. Some of the barrows of this people, containing the remains of war-chariots and other things of the Iron Age, also connect them with Market Weighton, Beverley, Pocklington, and other localities in the East Riding. It is also very possible that they took possession of a large tract of country to the south of the Humber. But when did the Parisi arrive in this country? Was it before the Brigantes, so that the latter had to land on the coast north of their territory? or did they come after the Brigantes, and succeed in seizing a part of their territory by main force? and, if so, how late did they make their appearance in the Humber? These are questions one has at present no means of answering; but it is clear that at the time in question the Parisi were sufficiently independent of their powerful neighbours to have had a coinage of their own. Some of the pieces extant are interesting moreover as giving the title granted to the person in whose name they were issued. Thus one Volisios styles himself sometimes Domnocoveros and sometimes Domnoveros, which may possibly have meant the guardian of the state, or the man of the people. At any rate, it has been observed that the same term occurs on a coin of Dumnorix, the Æduan, whose great popularity[1] with the common people Cæsar dwells upon more than once. This, in fact, was one of the reasons why he was distrusted and ordered to be cut down when he refused to follow Cæsar on his second expedition to Britain. On another of these northern coins the

[1] "Bell. Gall.," i. 3, 9, 18, 20.

person who issued it gives himself a title, which, if correctly read Senotigirnios, would literally mean the old lord or old monarch, whatever the exact official signification of that may have been among the Parisi. Unfortunately, the relation of these two kinds of coins to one another in point of time is not known ; should they turn out to be of the same date, they might be taken to prove the state to have been divided into two parties, the one clinging to the representative of a dynasty, and the other rallying round one who gave himself out as the friend of the people. If we do not misunderstand their coins, the Parisi may briefly be said to have been in the condition of a people who were either struggling to cast away the kingly yoke, or who had succeeded in doing so, and were threatened with a tyranny of a different kind—that of the adventurer who seeks power by hoodwinking the crowd. A somewhat doubtful exception is to be made as to the language being Gaulish, in the case of a group of coins with the letters VEP CORF, which are possibly to be treated as Latin, standing for VEP. COR.F., meaning " Vepogenos son of Correos," or the like. In that case they might reasonably be regarded as the last native money coined in early Britain.

Pomponius Mela, a Spanish writer of the first century, states that the farther a British people was from the Continent, the less it knew of any other wealth than flocks and land ; but some of them probably made use of ingots of bronze, of bars of iron, such as Cæsar alludes to, and also, perhaps, of rings or pellets of gold, as a medium of exchange. Nor did

the coined money of the southern states fail to get
admission to others far away from them.   Thus there
is an instance on record of one of the coins of the
Dobunni being found as far north as Dumfries, while
several have been discovered in Monmouthshire—that
is to say, in the land of the Silures, who would seem
to have been the people meant by Solinus, when he
states that the inhabitants of what he calls the Island
of Silura would have nothing to do with money[1] at a
time not before the first century, and possibly a good
deal later.   A study of the early money of Britain
also throws some light on the paths of intercourse
between it and the Continent.   The shortest of these,
and probably the earliest in use for trade, was between
Kent and the neighbouring coast of Gaul : it always
continued, no doubt, to be the route along which
the trade with the south-east of Britain was carried
on.   According to Pliny[2] quoting from Timæus, who
wrote about the middle of the fourth century before
our era, and got his information probably from
Pytheas, Thanet may have been the island at high
tide to which the tin of the west was brought in
coracles by the natives for sale to the merchants who
came for it from Gaul.   The coasting voyage seems to
have taken the former six days to make.   But there
was another line of communication, the use of which
was probably never discontinued from the time when
Belgic tribes first settled in the island.   The Belgæ
advanced westwards into Gaul, being pressed forward

[1] "Solinus," edited by Mommsen, p. 114.
[2] "Hist. Nat.," iv. 16 (30).

probably by the Teutonic peoples in their rear. When
they got familiar enough with the sea to cross the
Channel, some of them continued the westward
course of their race, and may be supposed to have
landed in the harbours between Dungeness and the
mouth of the Dorsetshire Stour. There is no evidence
that either the Cantii on the one side, or the Durotriges
and the peninsular tribes behind them, on the other,
should be considered Belgic. From the intervening
line of coast the Belgæ spread to the Thames and
pressed westwards to the Severn Sea; while the territory of those who retained that name in Britain lay
between that of the Regni, the Atrebates, and the
Dobunni on the one hand, and the line on the other of
the Dorsetshire Stour and the Mendip Hills, beyond
which were the Durotriges and the Dumnonii. The
early coins on the Belgic seaboards of Britain and Gaul
are far from easy to distinguish, and they bear ample
evidence to the truth of the tradition reported by
Cæsar that Belgic tribes had made themselves a home
in the south of the island. How far their line of
communication became also the route for trade it is
hard to say : possibly some of the tin of Cornwall was
brought into their territory and then conveyed to
some place near the mouth of the Seine. There
is also numismatic evidence of a connection between
the British coast and the Channel Islands, whence
it probably extended to the opposite coast of Gaul :
the coins in question point to the time of Claudius,
but the intercourse they indicate may have begun
much earlier. No inscribed money seems to have

been coined by the tribes west of the Belgæ, but it
is possible that the Durotriges may have had an uninscribed coinage ; and they seem to have had the coins
of other tribes in circulation among them, both inscribed and uninscribed ones at the same time, so
that they were in that respect somewhat more backward than the Eceni. Whether the Durotriges were
Goidels or Brythons is not quite certain, but, on the
whole, they may be classified with their neighbours,
the Dumnonii, the remains of whose language in Devon
and Cornwall leave us in no doubt that they were of
the earlier Celts or Goidels, not of the Brythons. Nor
is it improbable that, in point of civilisation, they were
behind the inhabitants of the south-east of the island,
with the exception of the people of the tin districts,
which in ancient times were chiefly Dartmoor, with
the country around Tavistock, and that around St.
Austell, including several valleys looking towards
the southern coast of Cornwall   In most of the other
districts where tin existed it is supposed to have
lain too deep to have been worked in early times.
In the Scilly Isles, which have been sometimes
erroneously identified with the Cassiterides of
ancient authors neither is tin worked now, nor are the
old workings there either numerous or deep. The
information which we have about this part of the
country is scanty : some uninscribed coins which
were current among the Durotriges and on the
Belgic coast of Britain have been found in Cornwall, which would again suggest a trade in tin along
the southern coast in the direction of Thanet.   Then

we come to a contemporary of Cicero's, the Greek
geographer Posidonius, to whom we have already
alluded as having extended his travels to Cornwall,
which he called Belerion, a name given afterwards
by Ptolemy to the Land's End: his account of the
country he saw has been preserved to us by Diodorus,
who wrote a little later.   That author tells[1] us, among
other things, that the inhabitants of this promontory of Britain called Belerion were very fond of
strangers, and that from their intercourse with foreign
merchants they were civilised in their manner of life.
According to him, they prepared the tin by working
very skilfully the earth in which it was found: the
ground was rocky, but it contained earthy veins,
the produce of which was ground down, smelted, and
purified.   The metal, we are further told, was made
into slabs of the form of knuckle-bones, and carried
to a certain island lying off the coast of Britain, called
Ictis.   During the ebb of the tide the intervening
space was left dry, and to that place they carried over
abundance of tin in their waggons.   And, after a few
words about such islands at high water, he goes on to
say that in one of them the merchants bought the
tin from the natives and carried it over to Gaul ; and
that, after travelling overland for about thirty days,
they finally brought their loads on packhorses to the
outlet of the Rhone, that is to say, to the meeting of
the Rhone and the Sâone, where the wharfs for the
tin barges were erected.   Diodorus further states,[2]

[1] See " Bibl. Hist.," v. 22, and Elton, p. 36.
[2] See "Bibl. Hist.," v. 38.

after mentioning the tin brought from the Cassiterides, which he places off the coast of Spain, that much was also carried across from Britain to the opposite shore of Gaul, and was thence brought on horse-back through the midst of the Celtic country to Marseilles, and also to the city of Narbonne. This refers to the tin of the Dumnonian peninsula, and shows that quantities of it were then carried to an island lying to the east, whence the passage to Gaul was short. It has been argued that the island itself can hardly have been St. Michael's Mount, as some suppose, since that, it is said, does not seem to have been an island at all in old times ; nor was it the Isle of Wight, for that was never accessible on foot ; while some authors are strongly of opinion that it was no other than Thanet,[1] which must formerly have corresponded completely to the description already cited. This view would explain Cæsar's singular statement that British tin came from the inland parts of the country ;[2] but the question of the transit is too difficult for us to settle. In earlier times the tin seems to have been brought from the west in boats, if one may trust the somewhat obscure account given by Timæus. So one might infer that between his time and that of Posidonius and Cæsar some considerable improve-ment had been made in the matter of roads in the south of Britain.

Was there, then, any trade in tin carried on directly

[1] See this question discussed in Elton's book, i. pp. 34, &c.
[2] "Bell. Gall.," v. 12.

between Cornwall and the Continent, continued
from the time of the Carthaginians or Phœnicians?
The evidence as to the presence of Phœnicians in
Britain at one time is not very convincing; but we
have a sort of proof in the writings of Festus Avienus,
a somewhat confused poet of the fourth century, that
Himilco, in the flourishing times of Carthage, carried
his voyage of discovery as far as this country.   Recent
writers are inclined to accept this; and if there ever
was Carthaginian commerce with the tin districts of
Britain, it was probably continued by the Veneti, in
whose hands the trade with this country was in
Cæsar's time.   These last traded in tin, which they
landed at the mouths of the Garonne and the Loire,
whence it was carried across to Marseilles and Narbonne: at one time they probably landed British
tin at the mouth of the latter river, and they fetched
some of it, at any rate, from the south-east of Britain;
but whatever direct trade in tin there may have been
between the tin districts of Britain and the Loire
must have been utterly unknown to Cæsar.   It is
remarkable, also, that the Dumnonii neither had a
coinage of their own, nor appear to have made much
use of money at all.   This seems to suggest the inference that they lived practically much farther from
the commerce of the south of Europe than did the
British peoples to the east of them.   However fond
they may have been of strangers, they would seem to
have bartered their tin mainly for the trinkets of the
Mediterranean and other such ornamental rubbish as
a barbarous people is wont to delight in.   But this

must not be understood to prove that there was no
communication between the Dumnonii and the nearest
part of Gaul during the Venetic period : in fact,
Dumnonia was probably the part of Britain in which
the Gaulish students of druidism mentioned by Cæsar
usually landed : possibly, however, this communication
is not to be regarded as being then of very old standing.
The Carthaginians had extended their trade in tin from
Spain to Gaul, and some stream-works of the Bronze
Age are known to have been carried out in certain
localities, among others in the Morbihan[1] or the
country of the Veneti. It is to this contact with the Carthaginians that we are, no doubt, to trace the beginning
of the naval power of the Veneti, who, at the end of
the Second Punic War and the downfall of the Carthaginian power in Spain, succeeded so completely to
their trade in tin, that there is no record of any inter-
ruption in the supply to the markets of the Mediterranean. They landed the metal at the mouth of
the Loire and of the Garonne, bringing some of it
from the Cassiterides or tin-islands, now supposed to
have originally meant the British Isles. The trade
with the Cassiterides had been kept in such mystery
that no Roman could find out anything respecting it
until Publius Crassus[2] succeeded in personally ascertaining all about it; but that he was Cæsar's lieutenant
of that name, who was sent by him to subdue the
hostile tribes in Aquitania, is very doubtful. If the
Veneti were in the habit of importing the tin of

[1] Boyd Dawkins's "Early Man in Britain," p. 403.
[2] Strabo, iii., 11 (C. 176).

Britain directly from where it was found to the mouth of the Loire, the fact that Cæsar did not know of it, would go to prove how closely they kept their secret.

Cæsar's account[1] of the fleet of the Veneti shows that it had made a deep impression on his mind: their ships, he says, were of a large size and stood so high out of the water that the Romans could not well attack them with their missiles, and even when they raised turrets on their galleys they were not so high as the poops of the Venetian ships. They were made of solid oak, with decks a foot thick, fastened with bolts of iron as thick as a man's thumb, while the metal used in making the ships in which Cæsar passed into Britain is mentioned as being bronze. The former vessels had sails of hides, and their anchors were fastened by means of iron chains instead of ropes, while the beaks of the Roman galleys could do their hulls no harm. When, however, they had to manœuvre within a small area, they had the worst of it as soon as the Romans bethought themselves of sharp hooks with long handles to cut their ropes and render the sails, on which they depended, useless. Up to their unsuccessful contest with Cæsar in 56, the Veneti not only carried on most of the trade with Britain, or levied a tax on all others who took part in it, but they counted among their allies all the maritime tribes from the Loire to the country of the Morini and Menapii, and they obtained help also from Britain, whence it may be gathered, as they mainly relied on what they could do at sea, that the ships of

[1] "Bell. Gall." iii. 13.

all the members of this Armoric or maritime league
were much of the same make, whether in Gaul or
in Britain : some idea of their number may be
formed from the fact that the Veneti managed to get
together on their own coast south of Brittany about
220 vessels fully manned to oppose Cæsar's fleet, as
soon as it sailed out of the Loire. They were, as
already suggested, not fitted for war, but for trading
on a sea which Cæsar ever and anon dwells upon as
vast and exposed, where the difficulty of navigation
seemed to him, who never knew exactly what to
make of the ebb and flow of the tide, to be extreme,
and where the harbours were few and far between, or
hardly existed at all; in other words, he seems to have
regarded their vessels as eminently qualified for
long voyages. But how far those ancient sailors of the
Armoric league, who had not the mariner's compass,
ventured out on the open sea, where they had no
coast-line to guide them, we have no means of ascertaining, but, as a rule, they may be supposed to have
hugged the shore. The most important elements in
the Veneti's trade with Britain in Cæsar's time appear
to have been the exportation of tin and the
importation of various kinds of articles to be
worn as ornaments and amulets ; and, when
Strabo wrote some seventy or more years later,
he groups the imports contemptuously together as
ivory rings, necklaces, red amber, glass-ware, and
such-like trumpery.[1] Still more interesting is
Strabo's account of the things produced in the island,

[1] Strabo, iv. 5 (C. 199, 200).

namely, corn, cattle, gold, silver, and iron : these, he writes, were all exported to the Continent, together with skins, slaves, and dogs fitted for the chase and for war as carried on by the Gauls. The exportation of corn and cattle would seem to imply that the country had enjoyed a period of considerable prosperity after Cæsar's departure, and the mention of gold and silver is interesting, but not so much so as the fact that by this time iron, which was very scarce when Cæsar was here, was now found in sufficient quantities to become an article of export. Where the slaves chiefly came from is not indicated, but it was probably from the more remote parts of the island, and possibly also from Ireland ; a still more important question about them must likewise be left unanswered, and that is whether they were wholly or mostly captives taken in war.

By way of summarizing these remarks, one may say that there is no reason to think that the conquest of the Veneti and the Armoric league by Cæsar caused the art of ship-building, such as they had learnt it from the Carthaginians of Spain, to be lost on the shores of Gaul and Britain ; indeed, his breaking down their monopoly may have had quite the contrary effect, and it is not improbable that the ships of the Veneti became the pattern for all vessels used afterwards by the Romans in British waters, so that our marine of the present day may be regarded as, in a manner, deriving its descent through the shipping of the Veneti from that of the Carthaginians and the proud merchants of Tyre and Sidon.

In other respects, the connection with the Roman
world into which Cæsar brought Britain gave a
powerful impetus to the trade between them, and
opened a door for the Roman influence evidenced
here by the way some of the coins, to which attention
has been called, were got up, as well as by the
beginning, to which they testify, of the use of Latin
as the official language of this country. Looking,
then, at its inhabitants from this point of view,
and as they were before the Claudian invasion,
we may say that those of the south-east were the
most civilized, and that some of those of Brythonic
or Gaulish descent, occupying the tract from the
Severn Sea to the Isle of Thanet, and from the
Channel to the Tees, had progressed so far as to
have money of their own coining. Of the Goidelic
branch, it appears that the Durotriges may have had
a letterless coinage, that the Dumnonii, without
actually excluding coins from their country, showed
probably a marked preference for the nick-nacks of
Mediterranean workshops, while barter was the only
way of doing business understood by the Silures
and the other Goidelic tribes of the remoter parts
of the island.

Let us now leave the coins and commerce of the
early Britons, to take a somewhat more comprehen-
sive view of their habits. Cæsar, who penetrated
north of the Thames, had ample opportunities of
observing the appearance of the country, and of
learning much about the inhabitants, but there is no
reason to suppose that he saw any representatives

of the older Celtic settlers, or of the non-Celtic aborigines, excepting possibly as slaves. He considered the country very thickly inhabited, and the abundance of cattle to be deserving of notice. The buildings he saw resembled those of Gaul, and were very numerous, but according to him the British idea of a town or fortress was a place with a tangled wood round it, and fortified with a rampart and ditch ; inside this they would, as Strabo tells us, build their huts and collect their cattle, but not with a view of remaining there long. Cæsar regarded the people of Kent, whom he thought by far the most civilized, as only slightly differing from those of Gaul ; and Diodoru draws a contrast between the simple and frugal habits of the Britons and the luxurious way of living, consequent on riches, with which he was familiar. The thickness of the population in the south-east, and the habit of harvesting the corn in spacious barns, would naturally lead one to suppose that it was largely and successfully grown there even then ; but the population was probably more sparse and corn less extensively grown in the districts where the ears reaped were stowed away in holes underground until wanted to meet the needs of the day ; and when Cæsar goes on to say that most of those in the interior sowed no corn, but lived on flesh and milk, and wore skins for their clothing, we have, doubtless, to do with statements which were in the main true, though one has no means of fixing to a nicety on the tribes to which they applied. In making them, he had probably nothing to go upon but the vague hearsay reports which may have been current among the more civilized people of the south-eastern part of the island, with regard to the backward state of some of the inhabitants of the remoter regions of the west and the north. The same remark applies to Strabo, when he states that some knew nothing about gardening and other things relating to the farmer's life ; but when he mentions that, with abundance of milk at their disposal, there were some who were too ignorant to make cheese, his statement is at least illustrated by the negative evidence involved in the Welsh word for cheese, *caws*, which, like its English equivalent, is nothing but the Latin *caseus* bor-1owed. It is somewhat otherwise when Cæsar says that all the Britons painted themselves with woad : one could hardly have expected this to have been in vogue among the inhabitants of the south-east ; but he wrote probably from the evidence of his own eyes, so it must be accepted as true even of them. After all, it may have meant no more than painting the face for battle or certain religious rites, a habit not to be confounded with the much more serious one of tattooing, which prevailed in parts of the north of the island down to a comparatively late period. The poet Ovid, of a later date, sings of the painted Britons. The custom may be regarded as one which once prevailed very widely. Some authors allude to the Agathyrsi and Geloni as practising it, others in like manner to Sarmatians and Dacians, and Herodotus to the Thracians, while Sidonius, Bishop of Clermont in the fifth

century, graphically describes how some Saxons he
had seen daubed their faces with blue paint, and
pushed their hair back to the crown, to make the
forehead look larger.[1]   Cæsar further tells us that
the Britons shaved all except the upper lip; and the
hair of the head was allowed to grow long.   But
no statement of his has attracted more attention than
what he says about the morals of the people, to the
effect that ten or twelve men living together and consisting especially of brothers or of a father and his sons,
would have their wives in common, the children being
reckoned those of the man to whom the maid was
first given in marriage in each case.   So far from this
having been the custom of the Celts of Britain, it is
not certain that it can have been to any great extent
that of any Aryan people whatsoever.   If one could
be sure that this singular statement was not a passage
from some Greek book of imaginary travels among
imaginary barbarians, which Cæsar had in his mind,
it would be possible to point out the facts to which
it bore a kind of relation.   In the first place, one
might suppose that he had heard and misunderstood
some description of the families of the Britons to
the effect, that it was usual for ten or twelve men,
with their wives and children, to live together under
the *patria potestas* or power of one father and head,
a kind of undivided family well known to the student
of early institutions, and marking a particular stage

[1] See his letter to Lampridius in the 8th book of his
" Epistles."

in the social development of most Aryan nations. In the next place it is probable that the Britons of the south-east of the island, and some of the Gauls of the Continent, had heard of tribes in the remoter parts of Britain, whose view of matrimony was not the one usual among Aryan nations : this is probably the sounder conclusion.[1] A statement, similar to that made by Cæsar, is mentioned and doubted by Strabo,[2] but by his time this manner of living had to be sought in Ireland, and Dion Cassius,[3] who wrote at the beginning of the third century, repeats it of the people of Scotland. Later still, it entered into the picture drawn, but in a far less hideous form, of the pauper King of the Hebrides, by the interpolators of Solinus,[4] and it is repeated of the grass-eating community of Thule, where it might have been appropriately allowed to drop, but that St. Jerome and others thought they had reasons to associate it with the name of the Scotti and the Atecotti, which suggests that both Britain and Ireland contained down to a comparatively late date non-Celtic peoples, who

[1] Professor Zimmer on analysing Cæsar's statement has no doubt that it refers to the non-Aryan inhabitants of Britain, and he is probably right : see the "Zeitschrift für Rechtsgeschichte," xv., pp. 209, et seq.

[2] Strabo, 5, 4 (C. 201).

[3] See his Roman History (abridged by Xiphilinus), book lxxvi. 12 ; also lxxvi. 16 for Argentocoxos' wife's well-known reply to Julia Augusta, when the latter found fault with British morals.

[4] Mommsen's Edition, pp. 234-5.

were not Celtic or Aryan in their family arrangements.[1]

The political condition of the people of Brythonic
Britain towards the end of the early Iron Age and
the close of their independence, is best studied in
connection with that of Gaul as described by Cæsar.
The Celts, like all other Aryan nations, were once
under the rule of kings resembling those of early
Rome, or those of Greece in the Heroic Age, as
depicted in Homer's Iliad. This kind of personal
rule came to an end among various Aryan peoples
at different times, owing to the action of the chiefs
subordinate to the king seizing his power and making
it temporary and elective in their own class. This
step led the same man to govern and obey in turns,
and thereby formed no doubt, a very distinct step in
advance. In this way the kings had been superseded
in the 7th century before our era, throughout nearly
the whole of Greece and the Greek Colonies;
and in every instance it was an oligarchy or the
rule of a class that rose on the ruins of the
kingly power; so also at Rome when the Tarquins
were driven out, practically all power was seized by
the patricians. A similar revolution, though no
Gaulish Herodotus or Livy was found to commit it to
the pages of history, had taken place in Gaul before
Cæsar came there; but not very long before, since he
appears to have found almost everywhere the sulking
and plotting representatives of the fallen dynasties,
and to have readily turned them to use, either in

[1] See also Stokes's note in the " Revue Celtique," v. p. 232.

bringing him information about what was going on in
the senates of the peoples who had expelled their ancestors from the office of king, or in keeping their states
in subjection by appointing them kings in the room
of their fathers and under Roman protection.[1] This
was notoriously the policy of Rome at all times, and
it was exceedingly distasteful to most of the Gauls,
for their detestation of kings was, perhaps, not a whit
less intense than that of the Romans themselves;
thus we find[2] that the intriguing Æduan, Dumnorix,
knew of no readier way of filling the Æduan senate
with hatred for Cæsar, than by quietly suggesting
to them that he had been given the office of king
over them. The punishment fixed by law among
the Helvetii for trying to secure supreme power
was that of being burnt alive, and to escape it
Orgetorix was believed to have committed suicide
before his trial came on.[3] But, though the oligar-
chical form of government was an advance on the
old monarchy, it could not, as a rule last long, for
the very important reason, that it was wont to do
nothing for the bulk of the people. At Rome, the
difficulty was solved in a peculiar way, by unwilling
concessions on the part of the patricians, but in
Greece the immediate outcome was a plentiful crop
of despots, who prevailed for a time. The same
thing had begun to take place in Gaul, although it
had been foreseen, probably, in every state, and

[1] See, among other passages in point, " Bell. Gall.," i 3;
iv. 12 ; v. 25, 54.
[2] Ib., v. 6.   [3] Ib., i. 4.

stringently legislated against. The Ædui,[1] for instance, had enacted that neither of the chief magistrates, elected to discharge the office of king for the space of a year, could be of the same family as one who had previously held the office, in case the latter were still alive : they could not even be members of the senate at the same time. We said *neither* of them, because Cæsar's narrative, supported by the evidence of Gaulish coins, proves that the Ædui had not one chief magistrate whose office they called *vergobretos* or the administrator of justice, but two,[2] whose position may be supposed to have been analogous to that of the consuls at Rome. This dual office, which does not seem to have been confined to the Ædui, survived as the duumvirate for administering the law in the cities of conquered Gaul, and helped the Gauls, doubtless, to accommodate themselves to the municipal customs of Rome. But the common people in Cæsar's time continued individually to occupy a position which appeared to him to have been hardly better than that of slaves, and in order to

---

[1] "Bell. Gall.," vii. 33.

[2] Cæsar's words occur at i. 16, and read in the manuscripts : " Diuiciaco et Lisco qui summo magistratui præerant quem uergobretum appellant Ædui." The editors, however, always print *præerat*, as they find a difficulty, probably, in reconciling this passage with Cæsar's account of the quarrel mentioned by him in vii. 32, 33, where he must, we think, be supposed to have been speaking of the election to only one of the two offices — possibly the two were not filled at the same time of the year. The question is one originally suggested by M. Mowat in the " Revue Celtique," v. pp. 121-4.

protect themselves against the tyranny of the more powerful members of the community they had to become the clients of some influential nobleman, and to add themselves to the number of those who were tied to him hand and foot by the bonds of debt. The condition of these men reminds one of that of the bankrupt plebeians of Rome before the secession to the Mons Sacer, and in both cases it was probably one of the results of the subjugation of a non-Aryan population by Aryan invaders. The great man, however, lost his influence over his clients the moment he failed to protect them. This being so, one is prepared for Cæsar's further statement that every state was torn asunder by factions. Some of the leaders succeeded in making themselves masters of their states, and the designs of a good many more were cut short by the advance of the Roman arms. The despots, as we may call them, for the sake of distinguishing them from the old kings, appear to have belonged to somewhat different stages of political development, the lowest being those who adopted the simple plan of hiring troops[1] to overpower the senate of the oligarchy : there were others who were more wary and showed more outward regard for law : these thought it needful to enlist the populace on their side, which they proceeded to do by eloquence and bribes. In fact, there is every reason to suppose that the common people were collectively beginning to acquire influence, and already, here and there, to understand their own power, though they had not

[1] "Bell. Gall.," ii. 1.

as yet taken the initiative. Their temper was the
first thing to be considered by any adventurous nobleman who desired his own advancement; and Ambiorix,
one of the most powerful Gaulish leaders at the head
of a formidable alliance opposed to Cæsar, once excused himself by saying that the multitude had no
less power over him than he had over them.[1] Without
trying to define the capacity of the ancient Gauls for
political development, we may say that they are seen
only as it were for a moment, in one of the most critical
periods in a nation's history. Indeed, the flippant
generalities formulated about them, from the days of
Cæsar to our own, seldom do them more justice than
if the independence of Greece had closed with the rise
of the tyrants, and we based our estimate of the Greek
character on the little that happens to be known of
the struggles between the tyrants and the oligarchies.
Nor is it quite an accident that the nation, descended
partly from the Gauls, forms at the present moment
a great and prosperous community, consisting neither
of the grumbling tenantry of an aristocracy nor of the
unwillingly drilled liverymen of a Cæsarism.

The state of things, politically speaking, which
existed in Gaul, existed also most likely among the
Belgic tribes in Britain, when Commios (supposing
the Atrebat of that name to have been the same man
as the Commios of the British coins) was enabled to
procure sovereignty for himself in the island and to
transmit it to his sons. So much may also be
gathered from the excuse, which the ambassadors,

[1] "Bell. Gall.," v. 27.

who came to ask Cæsar for peace soon after his
first landing in Britain, made for having put Commios in bonds, namely, that it was the act of the
multitude that knew no better.   Now, whether it was
the real cause or not, it is clear that it was a possible
cause, which might be pleaded by those among whom
Commios had landed, but not with any show of
dignity, if we suppose them to have been under the
rule of a king of the old type, who brooked no med-
dling on the part of the common people.   Here we
have apparently to do with a people to the east of the
Belgic tribes, namely, the inhabitants of Cantion or
Kent, among whom Commios and the ambassadors
returning from Gaul had probably landed.   These,
according to Cæsar's account of his second expedition, had no less than four kings acting in obedience
to Cassivellaunos as commander of the organization
against the Romans : the probability is that not
one of the four in a country so near Gaul was a
king of the old description.   The same conclusion
is likewise indicated by the coins of the Parisi, which
have already been alluded to, and by those of the
Catti, which seem to show only the name of the state,
as do also some of those of the Eceni.   But as the
most advanced people of Britain were old-fashioned
enough to paint themselves and to rely so much in
war on their chariots, it is not surprising to find that
kings, and those probably of the old sort, were not
extinct by any means among them.   One of the most
powerful states was that of the Catuvellauni, who
may have been too much occupied in war with

their neighbours to have paid as much attention to
the form of government under which they lived as
they might otherwise have done.   The Trinovantes
also had been living under kings, until the last of
them before Cæsar's raids had been slain by Cassivellaunos.   The remaining Brythonic peoples of
Britain have left the historian no means of making
out anything definite about their form of government so far as we know ; but it is not improbable
that the kings and queens of the Brigantes were of
the old description.

As to the earlier Celtic inhabitants of the island
we have no evidence that any of them had got beyond
the rule of kings of the older kind.   The series of the
old kingships may be supposed to have been completely interrupted or profoundly modified in Britain
by the Roman occupation ; consequently little is to
be learned as to their nature from that of the kingships which rose after the Roman legions left for
good.   The earlier ones, however, may be presumed
to have been most likely of the same type as those of
Ireland, where the series were never broken by Roman
rule.   As among the Greeks the king of the ancient
Irish legends may be said to have reigned by divine
right and by divine favour, so he must not be dis-
figured by any blemish[1] or have lost a limb.   The
mythical Irish King (in reality, perhaps, the Celtic
sea-god) Nuada, said to have had his hand cut off
in battle, was, we are told, compelled to resign

[1] See the " Senchus Mór," i. 73

his office until a western Æsculapius provided
him with a wonderful hand of silver with motion in
every finger. Moreover as the man who criticised
the kings before Troy was found to be the ugly
Thersites, so the usurper of the power of the rightful
king in Irish legend is sometimes described as a
cat-headed monster with the displeasure of Heaven
attending on his footsteps: the land in his time
yields no corn, the trees no fruit, the rivers no fish,
the cows no milk. When, however, the rightful king
that is to say, the king of the right stock, recovers his
power, the seasons become tranquil, the cows give
milk in abundance, the earth is fruitful, the rivers
teem with fish, and the trees bend heavy-laden under
their crop of fruit.[1] The Goidels of Britain entertained
the same opinion: we catch a glimpse of it among
the descendants of the ancient Silures as late as the
12th century in the belief recorded by Giraldus, that
the birds of the lake of Savaddon, near Brecon,
would all begin to sing at the bidding of the rightful
prince of Wales: the story relates how Griffith son
of Rhys got them to warble and to beat the water
with their wings for sheer loyalty after refusing to
obey the Norman barons, who were then masters
both of Griffith's person and of his land.[2] A king
of the old sort was responsible to nobody, but he

[1] See "The Four Masters' Annals of the Kingdom of Ireland,"
A.M. 3303, 3310, 3311; A D. 14, 15, 76; also the "Senchus
Mór," iii. 24, 25.

[2] Giraldus's "Itinerarium Kambriæ," I. ii. (p. 34 of the Rolls
Edition).

usually consulted the chiefs beneath him (who, in
Gaul, survived the kingship to form the senate
under the oligarchy in their respective states), and
when he had discussed his views with them he
declared his plans to a larger assembly and published
his decrees by means of it. " In this government,"
says Mr. Grote,[1] speaking of the Greek king as described in epic poetry, " the authority, which pervades
the whole society, all resides in the king. But on
important occasions it is exercised through the forms
of publicity; he consults, and even discusses, with the
councils of chiefs or elders—he communicates after
such consultation with the assembled Agora,—who
hear and approve, perhaps hear and murmur, but are
not understood to exercise an option or to reject."
This would all apply to ancient Ireland if only for the
Greek Agora or the market place we substitute the
Irish Aenach or the fair ; and presumably also to the
Goidelic portions of Britain generally about the time
we are speaking of. The old idea of kings and gods
probably placed them on somewhat parallel lines,
and, as there were gods and goddesses, so there were
royal persons of both sexes. In the case of the
ancient Gauls this is indicated by the fact that the
Gaulish word *rix* entered into the composition of
names not only of men as Orgetorix and Dumnorix,
but also of women as Visurix and Biturix. It is
etymologically the same vocable as the Latin rex,
king, which may possibly have also once been epicene,

[1] " History of Greece " (the ed. of 1862), ii. 223 ; see also
i. 457, 461.

custom having in the long run ruled in favour of calling
a king's wife a *regina* or royal person of the female sex.
The old Irish *rí*, genitive *ríg*, king, and *rígan*, queen,
would be somewhat analogous, though the Welsh
rhian, the equivalent of the Irish *rígan*, differs in being
mostly a poetic term for a lady, who need not be royal.
Whether most of the king-ruled Belgo-Brythons of
Britain were so far rid of the patriarchal idea of
monarchy as to let a woman exercise the power of
king is not certain: the history of Boudicca, queen
of the Eceni and widow of a king given them probably
by the Romans, does not prove the point: still less
decisive is the case of Cartismandua, queen of the
Brigantes, who is described as married or re-marrying.
There is, however, no reason to think that among the
older Celtic peoples of Britain a woman could hold
supreme power either in the state or in the family.
But as the old kingly rule was above all things mainly
a large type edition of the power of a father over his
household, and as the wife probably occupied a place
of authority and respect by his side, so the queen
may be supposed to have been similarly placed with
regard to the king: the system would have been
regarded as incomplete without her, whether we
have in view Britain or the sister island. We have
an illustration of this in a very curious Irish tale
which relates how a king of ancient Erin was
compelled to marry because the magnates of his
realm with one accord flatly refused to hold the
great periodical feast of Tara under the presidency of
a king who had no wife; so he was obliged to

marry.[1] And as to personal rule altogether, nothing, perhaps, illustrates more compendiously and clearly the difference between the Brythons and the Goidels than the history of an early Celtic word meaning power or authority, which has yielded the Welsh their *gwlad* in the sense of the state or the country, while in Irish it has taken the form of *flaith*, which means a lord or prince: the signification had begun to set strongly in that direction as early at least as the tenth century.

Exceedingly little is said by ancient authors about the religion of the people of Britain. There is, however, no reason to suppose that, in so far as they were Celts, they had not the same sort of religion as the Gauls and the Italians, or the Greeks, and other Aryan nations. Cæsar found the Gauls given to the worship of gods, whom he roughly identified with those of Rome, namely, Jove and Minerva, Apollo and Mars, and, above all, Mercury, whom they honoured more than the others. Much the same gods were probably worshipped by the Celts in Britain; and among them was the sea-god Nodens (in Irish *Nuada*), who was of sufficient importance, during the Roman occupation, to have a temple built for him at Lydney on the western side of the Severn, while the Irish formerly called the goddess of the Boyne Nuada Necht's wife.[2] Every locality had its divinity, and the rivers were identified

---

[1] See Windisch's "Irische Texte," pp. 118, &c.

[2] See O'Curry's "Manners and Cust. of the Anc. Irish," iii. p. 156, and a remarkable passage in the Book of Leinster, fol. 186*b*.

with certain divine beings : witness the streams that
still bear the name of Dee and kindred ones.   The
Dee or *Deva* of North Wales had another name,
which appears in Welsh literature as Aerven or the
genius of war ; and so late as the time of Giraldus it
retained some of its ancient prestige : it was still
supposed to indicate beforehand the event of the
frequent wars between the Welsh and the English by
eating away its bank on the Welsh or on the English
side, as the case might be.   The name of another
river marks it out as one that was formerly considered
divine, the Belisama, probably our Mersey : the name
occurs in inscriptions found in Gaul as that of a goddess equated with the Minerva of Italy.[1]   And, like
the Greeks and the Romans, the Britons personified
diseases, as may be gathered from the fact that in a
part of Mid-Wales the ague is still known by the name
of *Y Wrach* or *Yr hen Wrach*, that is, the Hag, or
the old Hag, and from the tradition that Maelgwn, of
whom we shall have occasion to speak again, died of
the *Fad Felen*, or Yellow Death, which is described
as a strange figure with teeth, eyes, and hair all
golden, coming from a neighbouring marsh and
fixing her baleful gaze on him in a church he had
entered.[2]   This was an elastic system of polytheism,

---

[1] See Orelli, Nos. 1431, 1969, and de Belloguet's " Ethnogénie Gauloise," i. p. 375 : she is detected also at Carleon on
the Usk : see Lee's " Isca Silurum," p. 19.

[2] See " the Myvyr'an A ch. of Wales," i. 27 ; Pennant's " Tours
in Wales,' iii p. 138; and the " Cymmrodor," v. p. 167.

or perhaps, more strictly speaking, not a system at all ; and possibly the priesthood it implied did not form a class distinctly marked off from other men ; but we have no data, so we must pass on to the non-Celtic natives, who had another religion, namely, druidism, which may be surmised to have had its origin among them.   Druidism possessed certain characteristics which enabled it to make terms with the Celtic conqueror, both in Gaul and in the British Islands.   A somewhat analogous case was that of the Magi in the East, and that of the non-Aryan peoples of Scandinavia, where the word for a Finn or Lapp is synonymous in Old Norse with that for a sorcerer.[1] Whatever else druidism as a system may have been, magic doubtless constituted one of its most important elements in this country, and the chief means of enabling it to hold its own ; for the well-known tendency of higher races to ascribe magical powers to lower ones serves, so far as it goes, to make the position of the latter more tolerable than it would otherwise have been in respect of the treatment dealt to them by their more powerful neighbours.[2]   The Goidelic Celts appear to have accepted druidism, but there is no evidence that it ever was the religion of any Brythonic people.

[1] See Vigfusson's "Icelandic Dict." s. v. *Finnar ;* also Milton's " Par. Lost," ii. 665.

[2] The whole question has been treated at length by Dr. Tylor in his work on " Primitive Culture," i. pp. 112-117, where a variety of instances are brought together from different parts of the world.

Thus the men of Britain might perhaps be classified, so far as regards religion, into three groups: the Brythonic Celts, who were polytheists of the Aryan type; the non-Celtic natives under the sway of druidism; and the Goidelic Celts, devotees of a religion which combined Aryan polytheism with druidism: here again data are wanting, and one is at a loss to know what people Pliny[1] had in view when he wrote that the wives and daughters-in-law of the Britons attended certain religious rites without their clothing, and with their bodies painted black as if in imitation of Ethiopians. Nor have ancient authors told us much about their most influential order of men, the druids, excepting those of Mona, who witnessed the landing in their island of Suetonius and his troops: these, Tacitus gives one to understand,[2] stained their altars with the blood of human beings, sought auguries in the entrails of their victims, and practised some, at least, of their cruel rites in groves which the Romans proceeded to cut down. Something is also to be learnt from the use made of the words for druid in the Celtic literatures of later times. Among the oldest instances in Welsh poetry[3] of the use of the word *derwyddon*, druids, is one where it is applied to the Magi or Wise Men, who came with presents to the infant Jesus, and its Irish cognate *drui* was not only used in

[1] "Hist. Nat.," xxii. 1 (2).

[2] "Ann.," xiv. 29, 30.

[3] See an obscure poem in the Book of Taliessin in Skene's "Four Ancient Books of Wales," vol. ii. p. 174.

the same manner, but was usually rendered into Latin by *magus*, a magician. Now and then also, point is given to this term by giving the druid the name of Simon Magus, whose appearance on Celtic ground is otherwise inexplicable. The Goidelic druids accordingly appear at times under the name of the School of Simon Druid : [1] they were soothsayers, priests, and medicine men, but their principal character was, perhaps, that of magicians. Thus the lives of St. Patrick describe the druids of the king of Ireland striving to surpass that saint in working miracles : among other things, one of them causes snow to fall so thickly that men quickly find themselves neck-deep in it : at another time he brings over the plain darkness that might be felt, so that all trembled with fear. But, like Moses with Pharaoh's magicians, Patrick always has the best of it. Indeed, so completely did the Irish recognise the similarity between their magicians and those of the Nile, that a writer of glosses on a ninth century manuscript of St. Paul's Epistles explains to the Irish reader that Jannes and Jambres were the names of two Egyptian druids.[2] The same was probably the character of the druids of Britain : it certainly was that of those at the non-Celtic court of the Pictish king in the sixth century. A life of St. Columba, written in the seventh century, mentions

[1] A curious passage about *Simon drui* and his School, kindly pointed out to the writer by Dr. Stokes, occurs in O'Mulconrys' Glossary in MS. H. 2, 16 (col. 116) in Trin. Coll. Library, Dublin. See also Reeves's " Adamnan," p. xlvii.

[2] " Glossæ Hibernicæ," ed. Zimmer, p. 183.

the saint's contests with one of those wizards of the
North, who is described as bringing on thick darkness and a great fury of the elements just at the
time when he found the saint setting sail on Loch
Ness.[1] Nor is it quite certain that the notion of a
druid as magician was not the one uppermost in the
mind of the fervent writer of an ancient hymn
ascribed to St. Columba, who is therein made to say :
Christ the son of God is my druid.[2] Such being the
character of the druids in the north of the island in the
sixth century, we may suppose that among the Goidels
of the more southern parts they were much the same
about the time of Cæsar's invasions, namely, a powerful class of men monopolising the influence of soothsayers, magicians, and priests. In Gaul, under the
faint rays of the civilization of Marseilles and other
Mediterranean centres, they seem to have added to
their other characters that of philosophers discoursing
to the youths whose education was entrusted to
them, on the stars and their movements, on the
world and its countries, on the nature of things and
the power of the gods. The same influence had also
probably been operating to soften and moderate the
pristine grimness of their practices, and this may be
supposed to have been the reason why Gaulish
students came to this country to perfect themselves in
the druidic system. Here in the western parts of the
island it still retained, perhaps, its most rugged and
horrible features unmodified by the Aryan ideas which

[1] Reeves's ' Adamnan's Life of St. Columba," p: 149.
[2] *Ibid.*, p. 74.

may have been telling more forcibly on it in Gaul.
It is hard, however, to accept the belief, recorded by
Cæsar, that druidism originated here, and was only
imported into Gaul : the probability rather is that the
Celts found it both there and here the common
religion of some of the aboriginal inhabitants of the
west of Europe.

Some of the customs of the pagans of these islands
may be detected in the observances of their Christian
descendants : thus among many nations a mild form
of mutilation is found to have been the symbol of
slavery, and the minimum consisted not unfrequently
in cutting off some of the hair of the head.   Among
the Brythons we find in the Welsh romances called
the Mabinogion a youth, who wished to become one
of Arthur's knights, having his hair cut[1] off by the
king with his own hand, but this practice is now best
known in the Roman church, where the priest, literally
regarded as a *servus dei* or God's slave, has his crown
shaven.   The Celtic languages bear ample evidence
to the same idea among the Celts : thus, the Welsh
word for a hermit, which is *meudwy*, means God's
slave, and such an Irish name as *Maelpadraic*
signifies the bald or tonsured slave of Patrick, and
is found Latinized into *Calvus Patricii*[2] in the ninth
century.   The tonsure usual in Britain and Ireland
was the same, and was merely a druidic survival, so,
when the Church of Rome insisted on the Christians of these islands conforming more completely to

[1] Guest's " Mabinogion," ii. 204 : it is mistranslated at p. 258.
[2] Nigra's " Reliquie Celtiche," p. 19.

its practices, the druidic tonsure was one of the differences which it wished to be rid of. The Irish Church began to conform in this matter of hair-cutting in the year 630, while the British Church held out till 768. There is an exceedingly curious, though somewhat confused, passage in the Second Epistle of Gildas, possibly not a part of the original, but written, at any rate, before the druidic tonsure had disappeared : it is to the following effect[1] :—" The Britons, contrary to all the world, and hostile to Roman customs not only in the mass but also in the tonsure, are, with the Jews, slaves to the shadow of things to come rather than to the truth. The Romans say that the tonsure of the Britons is reported to have originated with Simon Magus, whose tonsure embraced merely the whole front part of the head from ear to ear, in order to exclude the genuine tonsure of the Magi, whereby the front part alone was wont to be covered. But the originator of this tonsure in Ireland is proved by Patrick's discourse to have been the swineherd of king Loigaire MacNéill, from whom nearly all the Irish adopted it." The man meant by Loigaire's swineherd (a mis-translation of *mocu*) was Dubthach mocu Lugir, who was chief poet of Ireland, at the head of a large number of pupils : the legend relating how Patrick sought the "materials of a bishop" among his pupils, throws some light on the meaning

[1] Haddan and Stubbs' "Councils and Eccl. Doc.," i. pp. 112-3 : see Mommsen's "Chronica Minora Saec., IV., V., VI., VII. (in the *Monumenta Germaniæ Historica*), iii. p. 88, and Bede's "Hist. Eccl.," v. 21.

of the tonsure among the Celts :—" Find for me," said Patrick, "a man of rank, of good family, and good morals, one who has one wife and only one son."—"Why," said Dubthach, "askest thou that, for a man of that sort ? "—" To put orders on him," said Patrick.—" Fiacc is the man," said Dubthach : "he is gone on a circuit in Connaught." Just while this conversation is going on Fiacc returns from his circuit, and Dubthach says, " Here is he of whom we spoke."—" Be it so," said Patrick ; " but suppose that what we said were not pleasing to him."—" Let preparation be made," said Dubthach, " for tonsuring me, while Fiacc is looking on." Now, as soon as Fiacc saw that, he asked what they were preparing to do. " To tonsure Dubthach," said they.—" That is idle," said Fiacc, "for there is no poet equal to him in Erin."—" Thou wouldst be accepted in his stead ? " said Patrick—" The loss of me to Erin," said Fiacc, " is less than that of Dubthach." So Patrick shore his beard then from Fiacc, and great grace came upon him thereafter . . . so that a bishop's rank was conferred on him, and so that he is archbishop of Leinster thenceforward, and his successor after him."[1] A great deal more might be said on this subject of early Celtic religion ; but, as it is a matter of inference rather than of history, it would take up too much of our space to speak of it at length ; some points, however, connected with it will again come under the reader's notice as we go on.

[1] The original, of which this is a free rendering, will be found in Stokes's " Goidelica," p. 126, and a shorter version at p. 86.

CHAPTER III.

THE ROMANS IN BRITAIN, AND HOW THEY LEFT IT.

THE first part of this chapter will be devoted to the successive steps taken by the Romans to bring the island into subjection, as well as to the principal events of the Roman occupation ; but only so far as it tends to throw light on the position of the peoples living here and their relations to one another, since the Roman administration of the government of Britain is to be treated at length in another volume of this series.

For nearly a century after Cæsar's last invasion no attempt was made to bring Britain under real subjection to Rome, but his expeditions had the effect of bringing it into a sort of connection with the Roman world, the influence of which we have already pointed out. In the year 43 Claudius Cæsar resolved to send Aulus Plautius with an army to conquer the island. The same political changes seem to have been then going on here, which Julius Cæsar found at work in Gaul years before, and it is hinted that the nominal connection between Britain and Rome was in danger, owing to exiles from the island being sheltered and protected by Claudius Cæsar. To these we may suppose Bericos, mentioned in

the previous chapter, to have belonged. He used
his influence to induce Claudius to invade the island,
a course which seems to have readily recommended
itself to the emperor, who happened to be anxious
to find an excuse for enjoying a triumph at Rome.
The Roman general is supposed to have landed without opposition, but where it is hard to say. One of
the last views published on the subject is that of Dr.
Hübner,[1] who would bring him along the path of the
Belgæ to the neighbourhood of Southampton, and
make him then march northwards to Winchester and
Silchester in quest of the enemy. The first mention
of an engagement is that of one in which Dion Cassius[2]
tells us that Plautius defeated Caratacos and Togodumnos, the sons of Cunobelinos, who had died not
long before. Togodumnos was probably king in the
place of his father, with Caratacos ruling over the
western portion of the territory over which the Catuvellauni held sway : it was in this district probably that
they were defeated; and their flight resulted in bringing
the Dobunni who were subject to the Catuvellauni
into submission; and a Roman force was left among
them. Then we read of a series of engagements
extending over two days, in which the Britons offered
stout resistance to the advance of the Romans, but
owing greatly to the skill and bravery of Vespasian,
who had been sent over to be the general's lieutenant,
the invaders ultimately proved victorious, though the

[1] See his elaborate article entitled " Das Römische Heer in
Britannien," *Hermes*, xvi. p. 527.

[2] " Roman Hist.," lx. 20, 21.

British charioteers had selected positions of great
strength near a deep river, which the Gaulish auxiliaries
were the first to cross : they succeeded in wounding
the chariot horses of the enemy and in otherwise
giving much trouble. Whether that river was the
Thames or not, we next read of the native army
being south of the tidal portion of the latter, and escap-
ing from the Roman legions by crossing it. The
Gauls swam across as readily as their insular kinsmen had done, while the Romans crossed higher
up the stream by means of a bridge. They gained
some advantages over the native forces, but pressing
forward too rashly they lost many of their men,
while the fall of Togodumnos had the effect of combining his people to avenge his death. Plautius
now takes steps to secure the part of the country
he has conquered, and advances no farther, but
sends word to the emperor in accordance with the
instructions he has received. The latter accordingly comes in person, and finds the Roman legions
awaiting him near the Thames. He crossed the
river and took Camulodunòn, which had been the
capital of Cunobelinos. Then followed the submission of several tribes, and Claudius, after spending sixteen days in the island, hastened to Rome
to enjoy his triumph, and to amuse the Romans
with spectacles in which Britain was represented.
The operations here up to the time of the emperor's departure resulted in bringing the Catuvellauni and the States dependent on them under
Roman rule, together with the district between the

Thames and the coast, from the mouth of that river to the neighbourhood of the Isle of Wight. Within this area Rome soon found a princely tool called king Cogidumnos, who had certain cities given him, and who, Tacitus[1] tells us, continued faithful to his imperial masters for many years afterwards. It is not merely an accidental coincidence, perhaps, that an inscription[2] has been found at Chichester, mentioning a king of that name. He may have been the man or a descendant of his, and his subjects may have been the Regni, who inhabited what is now Sussex. Plautius was left in Britain with orders to carry on the work of conquest, but he appears at Rome in the year 47, to receive an ovation for having managed the war with ability. Several historians dwell also on the deeds of Vespasian, who, as they assert, engaged the enemy no less than thirty times both under Plautius and the emperor. He also reduced the two most powerful peoples of Britain, together with more than twenty towns and the Isle of Wight.[3] His son Titus likewise served here, and is mentioned as having once rescued his father when hemmed in by the enemy on all sides. Who the two most powerful peoples of Britain subdued by Vespasian may have been we are not told, but they were most likely the Belgæ and the Dumnonii, who occupied nearly the whole of the south-west of the island, including the

[1] "Agricola," 14.
[2] The Berlin "Corpus Insc. Lat.," vol. vii. no. 11.
[3] Suetonius, "Vespasian," chap. 4.

tin districts, which cannot have escaped the attention of the Romans, whose operations are spoken of as having, by the time of the departure of Plautius, made Britain emphatically a part of the Roman empire.

According to Tacitus, the principal authority on the later Roman conquests in Britain, the command of the legions here was given to Ostorius in the year 50. He at once adopted active measures against the tribes who were openly defiant, disarmed those whom he suspected of being disaffected, and prepared to keep in check all those who dwelt on his side of the Severn and the Trent,[1] which rivers may be taken as marking the boundary of the province at the time. Possibly the building of Vriconion or Wroxeter, near Shrewsbury, is to be traced to Ostorius's policy, and perhaps we may assume that it marked on the Severn the farthest corner of the tract of country which had then been conquered by Roman arms. Among other consequences of his policy may be reckoned the revolt of the powerful people of the Eceni, who had hitherto accepted the alliance of the Romans and escaped the bitter consequences of war. They now succeeded in persuading the neighbouring states to join them, and chose a strong position, which they fortified in a skilful fashion and afterwards defended

[1] This is the meaning of a passage in the " Annals," xii. 31, where Dr. Henry Bradley happily conjectured (the *Academy*, April 28, 1883, p. 296) that we should read, *cunctosque cis Trisantonam et Sabrinam fluvios cohibere parat.* He seems to be also right in regarding *Trisantona* as the early form of the name which became Tre(h)anta, Trenta, now Trent.

with great valour, but in vain. After humbling the
Eceni, Ostorius led his men across the island until
they reached a point not far from the sea which looks
towards Ireland, in the territory of a people called,
according to the best conjecture, the Deceangli,[1] who
may have inhabited Cheshire, or more probably the
part of North Wales between the Dee and the Clwyd.
The Deceangli did not face the legions in the open
field, but they harassed their plundering parties, and
were at length rid of them, for news of discord among
the Brigantes induced the general to lead his men
away in that direction. The relation in which the
Brigantes stood to the Romans at this time is a matter
of uncertainty, but they were possibly allies of some
kind. With a view both to overawing the conquered
tribes in the east of the island, and to having a
reserve to fall back upon, Ostorius established a
strong colony of veterans at Camulodunon.

The Silures now come to the front as a people whom
neither severity nor clemency could induce to put up
with Roman rule. They occupied the eastern half of
the country between the lower course of the Severn
and Cardigan Bay, the rest of that tract being the land
of the Demetæ. The middle of Wales, north of these
peoples, was occupied by the powerful state of the
Ordovices, who probably belonged to the later Celtic
settlers of Brythonic origin, while the Silures and
Demetæ were presumably of the earlier Celts, and
also represented by assimilation and absorption
whatever non-Celtic tribes had managed to remain in

[1] Tacitus, " Ann.," xii. 32.

that part of the country. The Silures were less
civilised than the Brythons to the east of them, but
they were also more intrepid and indomitable ; their
territory probably bordered on a portion of the
country which had been under the rule of Cunobelinos's
son, Caratacos : we find him, after resisting the
Roman arms for nearly nine years with various results,
which gave him pre-eminence over all other native
leaders, actively engaged among the Silures, to whom
he may be supposed to have brought superior skill in
the operations of war, and in whom he found braver
warriors than in his own land. The sequel is so well
known that we need not give Tacitus' account[1] in detail
as to how he led his forces into the country of the
Ordovices, how he chose an advantageous position and
fought bravely but unsuccessfully against Ostorius, how
he escaped to the Brigantes and was given up to the
Romans by their queen Cartismandua, and how his
manly bearing struck the Romans and obtained for
him and his family the emperor's pardon, guilty as he
was of the crime of fighting for his own. It is hard to
say at what point in Caratacos's career the coin reading
CARAT or CARA[2] was struck, but it was probably
his.

While the idlers of Rome crowded to behold the
man who had defied the legions for so many years, and
the senators compared Ostorius's victory to the most
remarkable successes of Roman generals in previous
ages, Ostorius found that he had by no means

[1] Tacitus, " Ann.," xii. 33–7.
[2] Evans's " Coins of the Anc. Britons," p. 552, pl. xx. 8.

done with the Silures; for we read of them very soon afterwards inflicting severe losses on the forces left in their country. So persistent did they prove in their opposition to Roman rule, that there was a talk for a time that they were all to be cut off; but in the meanwhile Ostorius died, and his enemies boasted that, though he was not slain in battle, it was the worry of the war that killed him. His successor, Aulus Didius, personally took no very active part in the operations; but he had to deal not only with the Silures, but also with the Brigantes, whose king, Venutios, was the most able native leader since Caratacos had been taken. The former had been faithful to the Romans for some time, but a disagreement with the queen, Cartismandua, who was his wife,[1] but preferred his armourbearer, brought him into collision with the Romans, who interfered successfully to save the queen from Venutios; nevertheless, their victory led to nothing further. Didius was followed in command by Veranius in 57, but he died the next year without having effected anything except ravaging the land of the Silures.

Nothing had been done since Ostorius's death to extend the Roman conquests, until Suetonius Paulinus, whom Nero sent here in 58, led the legions into Mona or Anglesey, which is described as being a receptacle for fugitives. He ordered flat-bottomed boats to be got ready, in which the foot soldiers were carried across the Menai, and the following is

[1] " Ann ," xii. 36, 40; " Hist.," iii. 45.

the account which Tacitus[1] gives of the scene :—" On the shore stood the forces of the enemy, a dense array of arms and men, with women dashing through the ranks like the furies; their dress was funereal, their hair dishevelled, and they carried torches in their hands. The Druids round the host, pouring forth dire imprecations, with their hands uplifted towards the heavens, struck terror into the soldiers by the strangeness of the sight; insomuch that, as if their limbs were paralysed, they exposed their bodies to the weapons of the enemy without attempting to move. Afterwards, at the earnest exhortations of the general, and from the effect of their own mutual importunities that they would not be scared by a rabble of women and fanatics, they bore down upon them, smote all that opposed them to the earth, and wrapped them in the flames they had themselves kindled. A garrison was then established to overawe the vanquished, and the groves dedicated to sanguinary superstitions destroyed; for they deemed t a duty to their deities to cover their altars with the blood of captives, and to seek the will of the gods in the entrails of men."

While Suetonius was thus occupied in Mona,[2] news reached him that the rest of the province, left denuded of troops, was in revolt. It was headed by Boudicca, the widow-queen of the Eceni, whose husband, Prasutagos, had probably been set over that people after their unsuccessful rebellion some eight years previously. Prasutagos, who was known for his opulence,

---

[1] " Annales," xiv. 29, 30.   [2] Ann. xiv. 30, &c.

had thought it prudent for the safety of his family to make the emperor joint heir with his own daughters to his wealth. The Roman officials, however, regarded this as an excuse to treat his goods as the spoils of war : the queen was flogged, her daughters were ravished, and the chief Ecenians were treated as slaves. Boudicca, who would not quietly suffer, organized a revolt, which was joined by other tribes, and especially by the Trinovantes, who were robbed of their land by the colony established at Camulodunon. The result is well known : some 70,000 Romans were killed by the enraged Britons, and Suetonius is supposed to have retaliated by killing 80,000 of the natives, when he returned.

There is not much to record about Britain till Vespasian, who was well acquainted with it, seized on the Roman empire in the year 69 ; he successively sent here at least three great generals, the first being Petilius Cerealis, who effected the reduction of the Brigantes in the years 69 and 70 : they were reputed, Tacitus[1] tells us, to have formed the most populous state in the island (or the province, as the Romans were now in the habit of calling it), and their subjection was brought about only after many battles had been fought, some of which were attended with great bloodshed. His successor was Julius Frontinus, who undertook the task of subduing the Silures : this, in spite of the bravery of that people, and the difficult nature of their country, he accomplished not long probably before the advent

[1] "Agricola," ch. 17, &c.

in 78 of Vespasian's third great general, Julius
Agricola. It is, however, very remarkable that
this people should have been able to resist the
Roman arms with more or less success for so many
years, and it may be regarded as certain that a very
considerable force was left to occupy their country;
for afterwards the second Augustan legion is found
permanently posted at *Isca Silurum*, called later
Caerleon (or the Camp of the Legion) on the Usk,
a little above the present town of Newport, a site
well known on account of its Roman remains, and
among them a good number of inscriptions. It was
the middle of the summer of 78 when Agricola
arrived, and the soldiers were already thinking of
their winter quarters, although a considerable body of
Roman cavalry had not long before been cut off by
the Ordovices, on whose frontiers they were stationed,
and a great many of the natives were halting between
peace and war. Agricola quickly set out into the
territory of the Ordovices, and inflicted on them such
losses in this short war, that according to Tacitus[1] it
resulted almost in the total extirpation of that people;
but the statement is proved to have been an exaggera-
tion, both by their subsequent history and the extent
of the wild country they occupied. This included
the district north of the Silures and the Demetæ, a
portion of the adjacent counties of England, together with North Wales, except, roughly speaking,
the north-west corner within the basins of the
Clwyd and the Mawddach, which, with Mona, still

[1] "Agricola," ch. 18, &c.

belonged, it may be supposed, to the earlier Celtic settlers of the Goidelic branch, for there are reasons to think that the Ordovices who had thus reached the sea on the west formed the vanguard of the Brythonic invasion. As regards the Romans, the Ordovices and the Goidels in their rear usually acted together against them, and when the legions attacked the Ordovices they seem to have considered Mona as their goal, and so they did in this case. For Agricola, after crushing the Ordovices, pushed on until he came to the shore of the Menai; but the islanders, seeing that he had no vessels, thought they were safe. They were, however, soon convinced of their mistake; for the auxiliary troops, who were probably Gauls or natives of the low country near the mouth of the Rhine, suddenly plunged into the channel and safely swam across. The surrender of the island followed, and Agricola turned his attention to suppressing the abuses which made Roman rule so unbearable to the Britons, a policy attended with such success that the natives began to adopt Roman habits and customs and eventually set themselves to learn Latin.[1]

The army had been employed in the summer of 79 in harassing the natives who still held out, and it was not till the summer of the year 80 that Agricola undertook to extend the province towards the north. The lands of some of the Brigantian tribes were then overrun and fortresses erected in their midst, where the Roman troops, having been provided with

[1] Tacitus, "Agricola," c. 21.

a year's provisions, passed the winter. That, or the
year after, was probably the time when a legion
was first settled at Eburacon, or York.[1] Agricola's
fourth summer in command, that of 81, was spent
in securing the possession of these northern acquisi-
tions, which were now to be bounded by the Forth
and the Clyde, the neck of land between the estuaries
of those rivers being defended by a chain of forts.   In
his fifth campaign Agricola directed his attention to
the districts opposite Ireland, by which Galloway was
possibly meant.   This he did, not because he had any
fear from that quarter, but because he had a wish to
conquer Ireland, for which a single legion with a few
auxiliaries would have, he thought, sufficed.   With
that view he kept in readiness an Irish king who
had been obliged to flee his own country.   His sixth
campaign, the year following, was directed against
the tribes beyond the Forth, and the fleet sent out to
explore the harbours of the north, acting in concert with the army, is said to have struck fear into
the northern populations, that they should now
be cut off from the last refuge of the vanquished,
the secret retreats of their seas.   This was learned
from captives, and it shows that even then the natives
of the north knew how to turn their numerous lochs
and creeks to use.   They gathered courage enough
to act on the offensive, but in the general engagement which ensued they were worsted, and the
Roman soldiers now wanted to advance into the
heart of the country which Tacitus calls Caledonia.

[1] See Hübner, " Hermes," xvi. p. 543.

The Caledonians, however, far from being cowed, determined, by sinking their mutual jealousies, to oppose a united front to the invader the summer following—that is, in 85. Agricola sent his fleet to create fear and alarm along the coast, and marched his army as far as the Tay, at the meeting of which with the Isla, he is supposed to have found the Caledonians encamped to the number of 30,000 men. Their leader was one Calgacos, whom Tacitus describes as haranguing his countrymen in the most eloquent terms: Agricola is made to do the same with the legions, and then a terrible battle began, in which the historian asserts that the Caledonians lost one-third of their number. Among other things, he tells us that the natives were provided with short targets and long, pointless swords, which were useless in the thick of the fight, and that the chariots helped to increase the confusion into which they fell. This battle, in 86, is known as that of *Mons Granpius* or *Graupius;* and when it had been won Agricola led his troops into the country of the Boresti, situated somewhere between the Firths of Tay and Forth. He took hostages from the Boresti, and proceeded to winter quarters, probably south of the estuaries of the Forth and the Clyde, while the fleet was ordered to coast round the north of the island, which it did after passing the winter at a port which Tacitus terms *Trucculensis* or *Trutulensis*.[1] The Caledonians were molested no further, for the Roman general was now

---

[1] "Agricola," ch. 38.

recalled by Domitian, who had been emperor since 81, and was getting jealous of Agricola's reputation.

Under Agricola's successor the northern part of the province became independent again, and when Hadrian came here, in the year 120, to quell an incipient insurrection, he thought it best to draw a line from the Solway Firth to the mouth of the Tyne, and to defend it with a ditch, a stone wall, and an earthen rampart, together with castles and watch-towers. Antoninus, who succeeded Hadrian, found it necessary to send here Lollius Urbicus in the year 139 to subdue the Brigantes between Hadrian's Wall and the Firth of Forth : he then restored to the province the boundary fixed by Agricola, and made an earthen rampart between the Forth and the Clyde. Most of the country of the Brigantes and kindred tribes had now been brought under Roman rule, but not the whole ; for there were peoples of this group beyond the two great rivers, though they usually appear under other names, leaving that of *Brigantes* to be identified chiefly with their kinsmen between the Forth and the Tees, where in a later age they yielded to an Anglian kingdom its name of Bernicia. Our authority on this war is Pausanias,[1] a Greek author who flourished about this time, but his words have seldom been fully understood. He states that the Romans attacked the Brigantes because they had invaded a people tributary to Rome, and called by him ἡ Γενουνία μοῖρα, the Genunian Division or Cohort. This word Genunia seems to betray itself as of Pictish

[1] Didot's Pausanias's " Description of Greece," viii. 43.

origin, and identical possibly with the name of a
people of the Western Highlands opposite Skye,
termed by a writer of the 7th century Geona Cohors,[1]
or the Geonian Cohort. Such a singular use of μοῖρα
and *cohors* is only to be explained by the Goidelic
word it was meant to render, and the latter can have
been no other than *dál*, a division or part, which was
frequently used in forming ethnic names, like Dál-
Riada, Dál-Cairbre, and Dál-Cais. The Genunians,
then, cannot have been Brythons, but Picts of the
mainland opposite Skye, unless we ought rather to
treat them as the Pictish dwellers between the Solway
Esk and Loch Ryan. The latter, however, seem to
have been the same people who appeared later as
Atecotti,[2] and later still as the Picts of Galloway.
They were a highly indomitable race, and seldom on
good terms with their Brythonic neighbours ; so it is
by no means probable that they had as yet fought it
out with the Romans. Their tributary condition,
which may have lasted until the time when the
Atecotti appear among the fiercest enemies of the
province, would most likely be of the nature of an
alliance. This surmise would agree well enough with
the fact that their country lay beyond the southern
wall, and with the usual policy of Rome, which offered
the Genunians ready means of checkmating their

---

[1] See Reeves's " Adamnan's Life of St. Columba," p. 62. It
is by no means impossible that *Gcona* is a defective spelling of
Genona, and that in *Genona Cohors* we should have the
descendants of the Γενουνία μοῖρα of Pausanias.

[2] Ammian. Marcell., xxvi. 4 ; xxvii. 8.

hereditary foes, the encroaching Brigantes of Brythonic stock.

Irruptions into the province by the independent tribes beyond the two Firths are recorded as taking place in 162 and 182. Not long afterwards they appear again in a threatening attitude, though they had been bribed to be quiet for some years. This time, in 201, they are spoken of as Caledonii and Mæatæ,[1] the latter being in all probability the peoples that lived between the Ochils and the sea coast, and from Dion Cassius's account they would seem to have been in possession of a district adjoining the Northern Wall : possibly they had even gained a footing on the southern coast of the Firth of Forth. These were the two names under which the independent tribes of the north now made their appearance in history, and the state of things which they had produced was considered serious enough by Severus to demand his presence in the province. He undertook an expedition against them in 208 at the head of a larger force than had ever before threatened their home. The northern confederates sent to sue for peace, which they did not get as they had been hitherto accustomed, since the emperor had resolved to open up the North and make it passable for troops. Severus set to work making roads, throwing up bridges, and clearing the country of jungles. He appears to have advanced as far as the Moray Firth, and to have returned through the heart of the Highlands, without having to fight a

[1] Dion Cassius, lxxv. 5 ; lxxvi. 12, 13.

battle, though the continuous skirmishing carried on by the natives cost him the lives of a very large number of his men. When he came back he re-reconstructed the wall between the Clyde and the Forth, but he had not long been at York when the Mæatæ were again in arms, with the Caledonii aiding them.[1] Severus died in 211, and his son Antoninus patched up a peace with the northern enemy.[2]

Little is known of Britain from that time to the usurpation of power by Carausius in 287, when he severed the island for a while from the Roman empire. He had risen to be the head of a fleet intended to repress the Saxons and other German tribes who now ravaged the coasts of Britain and Gaul. He was at length suspected of conniving at their doings; and when Maximus, one of the emperors, resolved to be rid of him, he revolted with his fleet and got possession of Britain, which enjoyed considerable prosperity till his death in 294 at the hand of Allectus, one of his followers. Allectus enjoyed power for three years, until he was slain in 296 in a battle with the army of Constantius Chlorus, who joined Britain again to the Roman empire after ten years of independence. In 306 he seems to have marched an army beyond the wall into the country of the Caledonians and the other Picts, supposed to be the Mæatæ of previous historians. For it is to be remarked here that the habit of tattocing the body was so uncommon in southern Britain that the term *Pictus* appears mostly as

[1] Dion Cassius, lxxvi. 15.
[2] Zonaras, xii. 12 (612).

synonymous with a native from beyond the Wall of
Severus. In the year 360 the Picts were joined in
their ravages by the Scotti from Ireland, who set
out most probably from the north-east of the island.
There is reason to believe that they were also Picts,
and that this was not their first appearance in Roman
Britain. When the Romans had left the northern
part of the province these invaders had their bands
swelled in 364 by the Atecotti, a people inhabiting a
part of the country between the walls. At the same
time the coast was ravaged by the Saxons, whose
piratical descents were directed mostly to various
points between the Wash and the Isle of Wight.
Theodosius was sent against them in 369, when the
Saxons retreated to the Orkneys, the Scots to Ireland,
and the Picts to the country north of the Wall of
Severus, which was then repaired, while the territory
up to it was garrisoned and made into a province
called Valentia or Valentiniana, in honour of Valen-
tinian, who was then emperor. As regards the
Atecotti, who had been more ferocious in their
inroads than the others, they were enrolled in the
Roman army, to be stationed on the Continent, so
that some of them were seen by St. Jerome, who has
left on record the report that they were a British
people of cannibals. The Picts, or the independent
natives of the north of the island, are again mentioned[1] as two distinct nations, called respectively
Dicalydones and Verturiones. Under the former
name, which seems to mean the twin tribe of the

[1] Ammianus Marcellinus, xxvii. 8.

Caledones, we appear to have to do with the Caledonians proper, while the word Verturiones yielded in the Goidelic of later times the well-known name of the Brythons of the kingdom of *Fortrenn*, and practically it may have applied for a time to those Brythons as acting at the head of the Mæatæ or Boresti[1] as their subjects.

We have now come to the time when Maximus, having served under Theodosius, and afterwards obtained the command of the Roman army in Britain, got himself proclaimed emperor here in 383. He had repressed the Picts and Scots in 384, but soon afterwards, in the year 387, he led the army away, and drained the country of its able-bodied men, in order to contend on the Continent for the imperial power, a struggle which cost him his life in 388. Britain was now exposed to the inroads of the Picts and the Scots, until Stilicho sent hither in 396 a legion which drove them back, and once more garrisoned the Northern Wall. In 402 the Roman troops were again withdrawn, and then followed another access

---

[1] Mr. Skene speaks of the latter as Horestii, and connects ("Celtic Scotland," i. pp. 52, 89) with them two inscriptions at Niederbieber, on the Rhine, in which he recognises *HOR* and *H* as abbreviations of their name; but the late Dr. Hübner assured the author of this little book that the one is a part of the word *horrci*, and the other of *honorem*, while neither has anything to do with Britain, the *Brittones* mentioned in one of these being, as he thinks, a Continental people; this is a question we shall have occasion to return to later, but for the inscriptions the reader should turn to Brambach's "Corpus Inscr. Rhenanarum," Nos. 692, 694.

of devastation. In answer to the application of the
Brythons for aid, an army is found to have been present here in 406. In 407, however, it was led away by
Constantine, never to return : he was the third emperor
made by the army after the time when the invasion
of the Roman empire (by the Vandals, the Alans, and
other German peoples in the year 406) had inspired
the soldiers with fear lest the barbarians might cut
them off in an isolated province. This fear was
dispelled by Constantine gaining a great victory,
which soon made him master of Gaul and Spain, so
that the emperor Honorius reluctantly gave him,
usurper as he was, a share in the imperial authority.
One of Constantine's ablest generals was a Brython
called Gerontios, who after a time, thinking himself
slighted by Constantine and his son, set himself to
work to overthrow both : among other expedients
he had recourse to the Germans, whom he
invited to invade Gaul and Britain, which they did
in 409. Britain had, it is true, enjoyed little quiet
from the time the Saxons and other pirates first
made their appearance on her coasts. Most of
Constantine's troops were in Spain, and Honorius,
unable to render any aid, wrote letters to the cities
of Britain urging them to defend themselves. They
did so, and with such vigour that in the following
year, 410, they not only rid themselves of the invaders, but also packed away the few Roman officials,
who were still here to carry on the government.
Honorius, holding Constantine responsible for the
loss of Britain, and the death of certain of his rela-

tives, sent an army against him. Constantine shut himself up in the town of Arles, where he was killed. This happened in 411, and was followed shortly after by the death of Gerontios. When the latter invited the Germans to invade the provinces, he probably intended thereby to secure Britain for himself; but, while the Roman force which had disposed of Constantine was in quest of Gerontios, his own men conspired against him and set fire to his dwelling. He defended himself for a while, aided by a servant, who was a German of the nation of the Alans, but at length he found himself forced to slay his servant and his wife at their own request, and then to put an end to his own life : his son fled for refuge to the Alans. Such is a summary of his history given by the contemporary writers, Olympiodorus and Zosimus. By Gerontios we are reminded of some of the features of the Vortigern of the well-known Hengist story, which we read first in the pages of Bede and Nennius, while only a few of its elements can be detected in the writings of Gildas in the latter part of the sixth century.

In order to form an idea of what happened in Britain after the Roman officials were driven away, we must briefly relate how it was ruled as a part of the Roman empire. From the time of Severus the province was divided into Upper and Lower Britain : Dion Cassius[1] gives us to understand that the legions stationed at Caerleon on the Usk and Chester on the Dee were in Upper Britain, while that located

[1] lv. 23.

at York was in Lower Britain. This statement has been construed as proving that the Romans were guided in their division of the island by the parallels of latitude rather than by the natural features of the country, which suggest a boundary marked by the Bristol Channel, the Severn, the Avon, the hills beginning between the Dove and the Derwent, and extending as far as the Tees : all east and south of such a line would be Lower Britain, consisting of the area covered by the province which Ostorius left bounded by the line of the Severn and the Trent, with the plain in which York stands added to it, and possibly also the coast from the Tees to the Tyne. The country beyond it stretching from the Bristol Channel to the Solway Firth, and embracing two mountainous tracts with the level ground of Cheshire and South Lancashire lying between them, would form Upper Britain. It has, however, occurred to an Italian authority[1] on Roman administration, that it was the custom of the Romans to call the portion of a country nearest to Rome upper, and that farther off lower ; but this conclusion, drawn from the geographical accident that few of the rivers of Europe could be said to flow in the direction of Rome, only shows, when the facts are examined, that the Romans, like other people, allowed the ready test of running water to decide what was upper and what lower. Thus they

[1] See Borghese, "Opera Omnia," iv. p. 458 : his view has been accepted by Dr. Hübner in the "Corpus Inscr. Lat.," vii. p. 4.

spoke of a lower Germany at the mouth of the
Rhine, and of an Upper Germany higher up that
river; similarly, on the Danube, they had an Upper
Pannonia and an Upper Mœsia, situated in the same
relation to Lower Pannonia and Lower Mœsia:
they do not seem to have proceeded differently when
at one time they spoke of Dalmatia as Upper
Illyricum; not to mention that Lower Egypt seems
to have always been nearer to Rome than Upper Egypt.
So it is natural to suppose that Upper Britain was
mainly that part of Roman Britain which the legions
had to approach by marching in the direction of the
sources of the Thames, and of the streams that meet
to form the Humber. In an arrangement made by
Diocletian, and perfected by Constantine the Great,
the two Britains were subdivided, Upper Britain into
prima and *secunda*, or first Britain and second Britain,
and Lower Britain into Maxima Cæsariensis and
Flavia Cæsariensis. In the case of these last pairs of
adjectives, the word Britannia was dispensed with, so
that it came to be more closely associated with Upper
Britain. Subsequently to the formation of Valentia into
a separate province in 369, a survey of the great offices
of the empire, or, as it is usually called, the Table of
Dignities, gives us the names of the British provinces
in the following order: Maxima Cæsariensis, Valentia,
Britannia Prima, Britannia Secunda, Flavia Cæsariensis.[1] Here as elsewhere in the Western Empire
the sequence was not intended to be that of locality,

[1] "Notitia Dignitatum," ed. Otto Seeck, pp. 105, 107, 111,
172.

but of the dignity[1] of the governors of the respective
provinces, and we learn from the same Table that the
men in charge of Maxima Cæsariensis and Valentia
were of consular rank, while those at the head of the
other three, being of lower rank, were called *præsides*
or presidents. No less than three other lists exist of
the provinces of Roman Britain, and at least two of
them are older than the one we have mentioned.[2]
The order varies in all, but always so as to keep the two
Britannias together. Roman Britain was sometimes
spoken of as a province, but technically it was a
diocese, consisting of five provinces under the rule of
a vice-prefect or vicar, as he was called. The vicar of
Britain was responsible to the pretorian prefect of the
Gauls, who had under his authority the vicars also
of Gaul and Spain, so that his power reached from
the Firth of Forth to North Africa. He had to
do with finance and the administration of justice,
while the military command was divided between
three generals, called the Count of Britain, the
Count of the Saxon Shore in Britain, and the Duke
of the Britains. This last was so called because probably he had to do mainly with the two Britannias or
provinces of Upper Britain, but towards the close
of the Roman occupation the forces under his
command were located in places which were mostly,
if not all, in the northern part of the territory intrusted to him for its defence, especially the stations

---

[1] See Mcmmsen in the " Abhandl. d. Ak. d. Wissenschaften
zu Berlin," 1862, pp. 510, 511.

[2] See Mommsen's paper just referred to.

on the Southern Wall; and it is probable that for military purposes the part of Lower Britain north of the Humber had sooner or later to be treated as a part of Upper Britain. The Count of the Saxon Shore had under his command the troops stationed at various points between the Wash and the Isle of Wight, the coast which was most exposed to invasion from Saxons and kindred Germans. The Count of Britain had the entire diocese under his control, and his command does not appear to have been localised like that of the other two. On the whole, his position seems to have been analogous to that of the Count of Italy in the Neighbourhood of the Alps, and of the Count of the Territory around Strassburg : both of these had districts in their charge, which were subject, like Britain, to the inroads of the Germans.[1]

In the course of the Roman occupation, which lasted more than three centuries and a half, most of the Celts of the province had both become Christians, and grown familiar, to some extent, with the working of municipal institutions, which here and there probably survived the hurried departure of the officials of the empire, who were, doubtless, highly unpopular wherever they settled. It may further be supposed that Latin was beginning to make rapid conquests : not only was it the official language of the province but, in all probability, it was the ordinary means of communication over a considerable area of the south and east of the island, where, more than elsewhere perhaps, the descendants of the motley popu-

[1] "Not. Dig.," pp. 180, 182, 209, 173, 179.

lation that had followed the Roman standards hither formed the nucleus of a Latinizing party. Among its strongholds may safely be reckoned York, Lincoln, Colchester, and London, which was even then so ancient a town that the Roman attempt to change its name for ever into Augusta has so far failed that it is now known to few. But, whatever Roman refinement and institutions survived in this country, the study of Roman inscriptions found in the province cannot fail to show that, as compared with most of the other portions of the empire, Britain was remarkable for its military character and the little consideration, relatively speaking, it allowed the civil element. This probably arose in the first instance from the warlike temper of the people, together with the time and trouble it took to subdue them, and later, from the necessity of being constantly prepared to ward off the outer barbarians, who granted the province no repose. At all events, it is from the military point cf view that we set out with most hope of being able to pick up the thread of transition that should guide us through the mazes of the dark period of history extending to the latter part of the 6th century.

It would be a mistake to take for granted that the people of Roman Britain, as soon as they were rid of the officials of the empire, resolved themselves into small communities or tribal states independent of each other—a stage which the Britons had pretty well left behind them before the Roman Conquest, and it is not to be believed that the prolonged lesson of imperial centralisation had been altogether lost on

them.   Did they proceed, then, to choose an emperor
or a sole king ?   There is no satisfactory proof
that anything of the kind occurred to them, and they
seem rather to have simply persisted on the lines of
the military leaderships which the Romans had made
a reality among them.   What became of the office
of the Count of Britain we know not, but there
are reasons to think that those of the Duke of
the Britannias and the Count of the Saxon Shore
continued, doubtless in a modified form, to exist
long afterwards.   How that should have come to pass
is by no means hard to see.   Even when Maximus
took away the army in 387, it is not improbable that
he placed a small native force to defend the north
of the province against the Picts and Scots, and
another to watch the south-eastern coast.   It is very
probable that the commander of the legion that came
here afterwards and left in 402 did the same thing on
a larger scale.   And when the legions finally de-
parted for Gaul under Constantine in 409, we are
told by Gildas that the Romans, when on the point
of going away, not only urged the Britons to defend
themselves, but that, in order to help them in so doing,
they had a wall built for them in the north, and gave
them the fortifications to garrison, while on the south-
eastern shore, which had been guarded by a Roman
fleet, they built towers at intervals within sight of
the sea, which were also to help the inhabitants in
their defence of the country.   This implies that the
Britons were to have an army in the north
and another in the south-east : that these armies

were a reality is proved by their successfully repel-
ling the Germans in 410, and by the comparatively
small extent to which the Picts from beyond the
Friths were able to settle, in the long run, in
the country between the Walls.   Those armies
took possession, doubtless, of the quarters left by
the Roman troops, and it is highly probable that
their leaders were regarded as the successors of the
Dux Britanniarum or *Britanniæ* and the *Comes Litoris
Saxonici*, and as having a right to those titles.   The
difference between a *comes* or count, and a *dux* or
leader, was only an unimportant one of imperial
etiquette in favour of the former ; the office of both
was called a *ducatus*, and both *comes* and *dux* appear
to have been rendered into Welsh by the term
gwledig, a ruler or prince, which is the title always
given in Welsh literature to Maximus, who was probably Duke of the Britannias before he made himself
emperor.   It is a significant fact that, with the
exception of Arthur, those who seem to have succeeded to supreme power here when the Romans
left are always styled in Welsh literature *gwledig*,
instead of being described by a title signifying
emperor or the familiar office of king.

The man to whom Gildas and Nennius, together
with Welsh tradition generally, point as the one who
succeeded to the command of the Count of the
Saxon Shore, or, as we may put it, the one who became the Gwledig of Lower Britain, appears under
the name of Ambrosius Aurelianus or Aurelius
Ambrosius : in Welsh the latter vocable becomes

Emrys. According to Gildas, who wrote not more than one hundred and fifty years after the time of Ambrosius, and who loudly sings his praises, he was descended from a Roman family which had enjoyed the purple of office, but his relations had been killed in the contests with the Saxons, or some of the other Germans who harassed the coast: possibly Nectarides, Count of the Saxon Shore, who was slain by them in 364, was of his family. So far as his history can be made out, Ambrosius was a very fit man for his work, and one calculated to enlist on his side the lively sympathies of the Latinizing party. But Nennius darkly hints that there was opposition to him, and that he had a quarrel with a certain Guitolin, who was possibly the head of a faction opposed to the Latinizing element. It would seem to have been overcome, for we find the title of Gwledig confined to Ambrosius, who, according to Gildas, was the leader of the Britons in their successful effort to drive away the Germans. The latter, however, must have soon returned, as we find them gradually seizing on one portion after another of Lower Britain. How much of this Ambrosius lived to see cannot be ascertained: the following are the names of the English states which rose south of the Humber, together with their traditional dates, which will do well enough for our purpose :—

In 449 the Jutes had established themselves in Kent, the country of the ancient Cantii: they also possessed themselves of the Isle of Wight, together with the nearest portion of the mainland.

The setting up of the kingdom of the South Saxons, now represented by the County of Sussex, and surrounded then by the great forest of Anderida, is ascribed to the year 477 : this was the country of the ancient Regni.   In 495 another and greater Saxon power, that of the West Saxons or Wessex, is represented as springing up in what is now Hampshire, and rapidly enlarging itself at the expense of the old inhabitants of the Belgic districts.   Some time in the sixth century there arose also an East Saxon kingdom, the name of which survives in that of the County of Essex, once the land of the Trinovantes, and of the Roman colony of Camulodunon : it is this colony, probably, that has yielded the English town its name of Colchester.   The district between Essex and the Wash, where the Eceni formerly dwelt, was taken by the Angles, who formed a South Folk and a North Folk.   Other Angles seized on the coast between the Wash and the Humber, which formerly belonged to the Coritani. In time these Anglian settlers came to be included in the great kingdom which rose last into prominence and power, that of the men who went up the Trent into the heart of the country and fixed, against the Welsh, the frontier or march, from which the whole has come to be known to historians by the would-be Latin name of Mercia.   Besides this it took in the West Saxon conquests north of the Thames, and most of the region covered by the Midland Counties of modern England.   From the early contact with the West Saxons into which the Celtic inhabitants were forced, they learned to call them by their national name of Saxons, which, slightly modified into Saeson, has come to be the Welsh word for Englishmen generally.

Welsh legend associates the name of Ambrosius mostly with the southern portion of Lower Britain, especially with Ambresburh or Amesbury in Wiltshire, a part of the country where the contest with the West Saxons was probably very severe. About the middle of the sixth century Gildas, a Welsh monk, to whom we have already alluded, denounced in the bitterest style of the Hebrew prophets the princes of his race in his time; but of the five at whom he preaches only two seem to have belonged to Lower Britain,[1] Constantine, king of Dumnonia, in modern terms, Devon and Cornwall, and Aurelius Conan,[2] as to whose territory Gildas gives no hint, though we may guess that it was the country which happened to be still in the possession of the Brythons between the Severn Sea and Poole Harbour. Gildas appears to have been well acquainted with the descendants of Ambrosius Aurelianus: he gives us to understand that they were still in power; and perhaps Aurelius Conan was their head, a view to which his name lends some support. Welsh tradition calls him Kynan, and gives him the title of Gwledig, but the charge Gildas brings against him, of thirsting for civil war, would

[1] Haddan and Stubbs's "Councils," &c., i. pp. 49-51.

[2] Mommsen *loc. cit.*, p. 43, prints in the vocative *Aureli Caninc*, but gives as other readings of the second vocable *Chunine* and *Conane*.

seem to imply that he was unable to maintain his
supremacy without using force. What portion of the
original power of the Gwledig still belonged in reality
or in theory to his family, we have no means of
making out ; but it was probably under its head
that the great battle of *Mons Badonicus*, of uncertain site, was fought, according to Bede, in the
year 493,[1] when the Welsh gained an important
victory, which is sometimes attributed to Arthur.
After this the West Saxons seem to have remained
quiet most of the time till the reign of Ceawlin, who
became king in 556, and fought against the Welsh,
both along the Thames and the Severn, winning a
great victory over them at a place called Deorham
in 577. This battle, in which fell three Welsh kings
(called in the Saxon Chronicle Conmægl, Condidan
and Farinmægl), was followed by the taking by
Ceawlin of the important towns of Bath, Gloucester
and Cirencester, whereby the West Welsh, as those
of the peninsula south of the Severn Sea came to be
called, were completely severed from their kinsmen.
After the death of Condidan, in whom one recognises[2]
the Kynddylan of Welsh literature which connects
him with what is now Shropshire, his country was
fearfully ravaged by Ceawlin, and his court at Pengwern
or Shrewsbury given to the flames.[3] These northern
conquests were lost by Ceawlin, owing to a serious

[1] This date will be found discussed and established by M. de
la Borderie in the " Revue Celtique," vi. pp. 1-13.
[2] Green's " Making of England," pp. 128, 206.
[3] Skene's " Anc. Books of Wales," ii. pp. 279, &c.

defeat at Fethanleag, supposed to be Faddiley, on the borders of Cheshire, in the year 584 ; but it is to him that we have to ascribe the advancing of the Saxon boundary on the south to the Axe, while what still remained in the possession of the Welsh of the country east of the Axe and the Parret appears to have been conquered by the Saxons under Cénwalh, who died in 672. In the eighth century Ine of Wessex seems to have succeeded in advancing the Saxon boundary to Taunton, though he had to fight with a very able prince of the Brythons of those parts, whose name appears in Welsh literature as Geraint ; and we read of Devon being under English rule in the time of Ecgbyrht, who ravaged Cornwall in 815. Still the Welshmen of that peninsula do not seem to have been wholly subjected to English rule until the time of Æthelstán, who fixed on the Tamar as their eastern boundary. It is needless to add that they continued to be Celtic for a long time afterwards, and that their language finally died out not much more than a hundred years ago. This was in West Cornwall : among the intermediate stages we may mention, after William of Malmesbury, the division of Exeter between the Welsh and the English in Æthelstán's time, and the fact that the Welshman Asser, King Alfred's friend, was familiar with a number of Welsh names in Dorset such as *Durngueir* for *Durnovaria*, the old name of Dorchester, *Cairuuisc* for Exeter, and *Frauu* for an earlier *Frāma* for the river Frome ; not to mention from Wiltshire the name *Guilou* for the Wiley that joins the Avon at Salisbury.[1]

[1] See Stevenson's e lition of Asser's Life of King Alfred (Ox'ord, 1904), pp. 241, 249-51, and p. lxxv , and seq.

The survival of Welsh in that region is suggested also by the Brythonic names of persons, on the few inscribed stones[1] in point, at the Devonshire church of Lustleigh, for instance, and at St. Mary's Church, Wareham, where there is a remarkable little group which the church "restoring" vandals of the last century have not wholly succeeded in destroying. The spelling of the names and the form of the letters seem to point to the ninth or the tenth century.

Now that we have very briefly shown how the English mastered Lower Britain, the question arises, how far the old inhabitants were allowed to remain. It has sometimes been supposed, that, as long as the conquerors continued to be pagans, they gave the former no quarter; but a more humane treatment may be expected to have prevailed with them after their adoption of Christianity : some of the principal events implied are the following :—the conversion of Edwin, King of Northumbria, in 627; the baptism of Cynegils, King of Wessex, in 635, and of his son in the following year. Mercia was pagan until Penda's death in 655, but under his sons it became Christian. The conquests by those states after the above dates need, therefore, not imply a complete displacement of the previous population, and there are not wanting indications that there were even as late as the time of Æthelstán in the tenth century patches of country, especially in Wessex, which were under English rule,

[1] For Lustleigh see the Ar. Cam. 1880, pp. 161-3, 1882, p. 50, and for Wareham the Proceedings of "The Dorset Nat. Hist. and Antiq. Field Club," 1892, p. xxiv., plate.

but still inhabited by the Welsh, who only ceased to
be such by being gradually assimilated to the Saxons
around them.　The subject, which is a difficult one,
will be found discussed in another volume of this
series ; but, on the whole, one may consider that it
still remains to be proved that the ancient inhabitants
were not to a certain extent allowed to remain as
slaves and tillers of the ground, even in the south
and the east, and in districts where they did not
succeed in maintaining themselves in their towns
until the conquerors became Christians.　On the
other hand, those who are inclined to think that the
Celts and Latinizing populations were cut clean
off the ground must not make too much of the
negative argument, that English in its earliest stages
contains hardly any words borrowed from Celtic ; for
the language of a considerable portion of the south
and east of the island may be supposed to have
become Latin by the time of the English conquest.
Indeed it has been argued with great probability that
the inhabitants of Britain, whom the English first
called Wealas, or Welshmen, were not the Brythons,
or Brettas, as they termed them, but the provincial
Romans, or the Latinizing part of the population,[1]
though the name came eventually to include the
Brythonic Celts of the west of the island.　In that
case what should rather be asked is, how many Latin
words there are to be found in the earliest known
specimens of English.　Much the same remarks
apply, of course, to Upper Britain, with which we
have next to deal.

See Coote's " Romans of Britain," pp. 176-180.

CHAPTER IV.

THE KYMRY.

LET us now see what became of the people of Upper
Britain when the Romans went away. Before that
event the Picts and Scots had more than once been
able to carry their plundering expeditions into
the heart of the province ; but the comparative
efficiency of the native army, which undertook
the defence of the north, is proved by the fact
that the only settlement worth mentioning which the
northern tribes were able permanently to make within
what had been Roman Britain was that effected by
the Picts on the Southern side of the Firth of Forth.
It is called in Welsh Manaw of the Gododin, to distinguish it from another Manaw beyond the Forth, as
well as from the Isle of Man, which appears in the
same language as the Island of Manaw. This Pictish
settlement included the part of Lothian in which
Edinburgh is situated, and a portion of the Pentland Hills, a name which is, nevertheless, not derived from Pehtland, the land of the Peht or Pict.
These, however, were not the only Picts south
of the Northern Wall : the district on the Solway,
between the Nith and Loch Ryan, was inhabited
in Bede's time by a people whom he terms Picts,

while he adds that they were also known as *Niduari*
or men of the Nith.[1] They are more usually called the
Picts of Galloway : they had probably been there from
of old, and consisted of a remnant of the Atecotti,
which signifies that they agreed with the other Picts
in tattooing themselves, and in being always ready to
help against the Brythons. There is no reason to
think that any very considerable portion of Upper
Britain was seized immediately after the departure
of the Romans by German invaders, though it is
possible that small German settlements had been
made on certain points of the coast between the
Tyne and the Forth at a comparatively early date.
The time usually fixed on as that of the rise of a
regular state on that sea-board is 547, when Ida is
said to have commenced his reign, in the course of
which he fortified Bamborough to be his capital.
Some think that there were Jutes or Frisians in the
neighbourhood 'of the Firth of Forth ; but, even if
that be true, the state as a whole, and as known to
history, was an Anglian one, and strangely enough
the people were known in Bede's time by a name
derived from that of the ancient Celtic Brigantes.
For he speaks of them in Latin as Bernicii, a word
made from the Anglo-Saxon Bærnicas, which appears
to have been the English pronunciation of the
Welsh equivalent *Brëennych* or *Brenneich* : this in
its turn is to be traced to the same origin as the

[1] See Bede's " Life of St. Cuthbert," chap. xi. : the passage
is quoted with interesting remarks in Skene's " Celtic Scotland,"
p. 133.

name of the Brigantes : thus the term Bernicii seems
to have meant the people of the Brigantic land, which,
in this case, was mostly that of the ancient Otadini,
better *Votadini*, the Gododin of Welsh literature,
together with a part possibly of that of another
people, the Dumnonii.   Another Anglian people had
seized on the country of the ancient Parisi between
the Humber and the Tees.   Like the northern
Angles, but unlike the other Angles and the Saxons,
they also got to be known by a name of Celtic origin.
In Latin they have been called from Bede's time,
Deiri, and their country Deira, both suggested by the
English pronunciation of one or more forms derived
from the same source as the Welsh name of the
district or of its old inhabitants : this was Deivr, which
has probably come down from early times, though it
is not read in any ancient author.   It is not known at
what date Bernicia extended itself southwards to the
Tees, so as to have a common boundary with Deira ;
nor is much known at all about the latter, till the time
of Æthelfrith, a king of the Bernicians whom we shall
have to mention again as we go on.   He had taken
possession of Deira and made himself king of both
states, and thenceforth Deira and Bernicia were sometimes separate and sometimes united.   In the latter
case the whole is known as Northumberland, or else
in quasi-Latin as Northumbria, which may serve to
prevent the thoughtless from confounding the whole
with the part that forms the county now bearing the
former name.

But even after the encroachments, briefly described

as ultimately embracing the whole seaboard from the
Humber to the Firth of Forth, the tract of country
still in the possession of the Celts of Upper Britain
was very considerable, comprising all the west of the
island from the Severn Sea to the Solway Firth and
thence to the Clyde. Was it anything more than
a tract of the island in the meagre geographical
sense, and did it contain any of the political essen-
tials of a state? This would seem at first sight to
admit of no other than a negative answer, and its
length of indefensible frontier would have led one to
expect that it would be divided in a short time into
two or more pieces. But, as a matter of fact, we find
that it kept together for more than two hundred
years; that when it was permanently cut in two, in
consequence of the defeat of the Welsh at the great
battle of Chester and the events that followed, it
roused them to a fierce struggle; and that, when this
ended unfavourably to themselves, it was regarded as
the destruction of all their aspirations, and the rudest
shock ever given their traditions. Neither had Upper
Britain the advantage of being the patrimony of
a single and homogeneous race: not only were
there Picts in Galloway, but the north-west of the
Principality of Wales, and a great portion of the
south of it, had always been in the possession of
a Goidelic people, whose nearest kinsmen were the
Goidels of Ireland. The other Celts of Upper
Britain, that is to say, the Britons proper or Brythons,
were no doubt in the ascendant, but there were
also Brythonic communities elsewhere, some north of

the Forth, about whom little is known, some south of the Severn Sea, and some in a Britain of their own in Gaul. Yet the ties of union between those of Upper Britain proved so strong and close, that the word Kymry, which merely meant fellow-countrymen, acquired the force and charm of a national name, which it still exercises over the natives of the Principality. This name is better known to Englishmen in connection with Cumberland or its Latinized form Cumbria, and the still more distorted one of Cambria. Nor was a common name the only or most important outcome of this feeling of unity ; for the Kymry developed a literature of their own, differing from that of the other Brythonic communities : above all the destruction of their state in the seventh century is the burning theme of many a Welsh poem, sung in a language now but imperfectly understood. Since the union of the Kymry seems to have been neither dictated by reasons of geography and frontier, nor clearly defined for them by considerations of race, we have to look for the historical accidents which served to determine it in the first instance, and to invest it afterwards with an intelligible form. This takes us back again to the last years of the Roman occupation.

The Romans were in the habit of forcing the natives of Britain, like those of their other provinces, to enrol themselves in the imperial army, and at first it was, doubtless, the rule for them to serve on the Continent, far away from their kith and kin : as danger ceased at length to be apprehended from the

provincials themselves, and came to be expected from
without, some of the native troops were allowed to
serve in Britain. Inscriptions and other documents
give us the locality and official names of a few such
regiments posted in the northern part of the province. Both during the absence of the Roman troops
previous to 410, and after the final departure of the
officials of the empire in that year, the work of
defence devolved on the inhabitants, and it is by no
means probable that any corner of the country wont
to be under the charge of the Dux Britanniarum
could be excused from supplying the native army
with its quota of men who were to fill the place of
his soldiers : any reluctance which may have here and
there shown itself must have been promptly borne
down by the pressing necessity of acting in concert
for the defence of the country against the barbarians,
who were pushing their way southwards. It may be
gathered that it was the fact of being under the
charge of a single general, the Dux Britanniarum,
which had the effect of marking off from the other
Brythons those who afterwards gave themselves the
name of Kymry, and of first teaching them, perhaps,
in some measure to act together : it was probably
the violence of the invader from without that supplied the force which was to weld them more closely
together. The area of the country to which this
applies was most likely coextensive with the military
authority of the Dux Britanniarum, but unfortunately
the boundaries of the latter can only be guessed, partly
as already hinted, and partly from the indications we

have as to the territory which the Kymry called their own after Britain was severed from the empire.

The earliest of their native rulers, so far as we know, was called Cunedag or Cunedda, about whom Welsh literature has a good deal to say, though not enough to give us a complete view of his history. His name is Celtic, and tradition, which makes him a son of a daughter of Coel, speaks of him as a man from Coeln.[1] This would connect him with the North, where Coel's country seems to have been the district since called Kyle, in the present county of Ayr. It is from the North also, from Manaw of the Gododin, that Nennius describes him and his sons as coming into Wales, and, for anything we know, he may have been the head of one of the noble families of the Brigantes : it is not improbable that he had also Roman blood in his veins, for we find that the names of his father and grandfather were Æternus and Paternus, whose father was named Tacitus. Further, some of his ancestors had very probably worn the official purple under the Roman administration, which derives support from the fact that the Welsh pedigrees[2] always give Paternus or Padarn the epithet of Peisrudd or him of the red tunic. All this would, no doubt, greatly help Cunedda into a position of influence and authority : the following things are in

___

[1] See the elegy on Cunedda in the Book of Taliessin in Skene's "Ancient Books of Wales," ii. pp. 200-2 ; also the "Iolo MSS.," pp. 120, 121, 126.

[2] See the Harleian MS., 3859, fol. 193*b*, at the British Museum.

point, and more or less clearly asserted by Welsh
tradition :—That Wales was under his sway and that
of his sons ; that his power was supreme from Carlisle
to Caer Weir, supposed to be Wearmouth on the
eastern coast, where the territory of the Angles was
not destined to become suddenly continuous ; that
he had his court at Carlisle ;[1] that his retinue on
the wall consisted of 900 horse ;[2] that he wore the
badge of office of the Dux Britanniarum, which, as in
the case of other *duces* under the Empire, consisted
of a gold belt,[3] to which an obscure passage in a
Welsh poem [4] seems to allude as Cunedda's girdle ;
and that he was the ancestor from whom a great
number of the more remarkable saints of Wales
traced their descent.   The account which Nennius [5]
gives of Cunedda states that he and his sons came
to Wales from Manaw of the Gododin 146 years
before the reign of Maelgwn, the most powerful of his
descendants.   This would seem to allude to the time

[1] "Iolo MSS.," p. 147, where Cunedda the Gwledig is styled
king of the Island of Britain.

[2] This is alluded to in the elegy already mentioned.

[3] Gibbon's "Roman Empire" (Smith's ed.), ii. p. 320 (chap.
xvii.).

[4] It is the elegy already mentioned, and the word used is *crys*,
which now only means a shirt ; but it seems to have meant a
girdle in another old poem given in Skene's "Anc. Bks. of
Wales," ii. p. 267, &c., and the cognate Irish *criss* always
meant a girdle, while the intermediate meaning of the Welsh
word as that of an upper dress is attested by passages in "The
Mabinogion" (Guest's ed.), ii. p. 13 ; iii. p. 266.

[5] Mommsen's "Chronica Minora," iii. c. 62 (p. 205).

when the Picts succeeded in possessing themselves
of a part of Manaw, and it settles the date as falling
somewhere very near the departure of the Romans
from Britain.

Nennius, in speaking of Cunedda's sons, says that
they were eight,[1] but later versions of the legend add
to their number and trace to their names those of
various districts in Wales. Among other things we
are told that the eldest son died before leaving the
North, that his son inherited among his uncles, and
that his name, which was Meirion, clung to the
district still called Meirion or Merioneth : another
story, preserved by Geoffrey of Monmouth, makes
Meirion, whom he calls Margan, brother to Cunedda,
who slays him in battle in the land bearing his
name. Keredig, another son of Cunedda, left his
name to Keredigion, our Cardiganshire ; and similarly
in the case of others of his sons, who are said to
have left their names to districts lying more towards
the north-west of Wales. With the exception of a
part of Merioneth, this probably represents the encroachments of the Brythons on the territory which
belonged to peoples of the Goidelic branch, the
Scotti of Nennius. He mentions them as driven
out of the country with terrible slaughter by
Cunedda and his sons, the limits of whose territory
in Wales are afterwards variously stated to have
been the Dee and the Teivi,[2] the southern boundary
of Cardiganshire, or the Dee and a stream called the

[1] Mommsen's "Chronica Minora," *ibid*.
[2] Harleian MS., 3859, fol. 195*a*.

Gwaun,[1] which reaches the sea at Abergwaun or Fishguard in Pembrokeshire. The centre of gravity, so to speak, of the power of Cunedda in Wales was in the country of the Ordovices, a Brythonic people that does not seem to have resisted his rule. Nor do we find a clue to any complication with the Silures of the south-east of Wales ; so it may be presumed that they also acquiesced in the supremacy of Cunedda. How, then, was his power established here in the first instance ? The only answer we can suggest is that his rule was recognized as that of the Gwledig, or per-petuator of the command of the Dux Britanniarum ; that the office gave him the means of making his sons kings of various districts in Wales ; and that, the Goidels of the south and the north-west being opposed to his rule, his sons gratified the Brythons by giving them their land. Probably Cunedda, while enjoying the power of the Gwledig as far as the Severn Sea, identified himself more closely with the part of his charge north and east of the Dee ; nay, it is even possible that he never visited Wales in person at all. In any case, he found the means of bequeathing to his descendants power of two kinds, that is to say, power over the special districts which they then treated as their own, and the power of the Gwledig, which they seem to have jealously kept among them-selves for centuries afterwards. Some light is thrown on the Scotti of Nennius by the Irish story[2] of the

---

[1] "Lives of the Cam.-Brit. SS.," p. 101.
[2] This will be found in the Book of the Dun, fol. 53a-54b ; also in the Bodley Manuscripts, Laud Misc. 610, fol. 99b, 2 ; and Rawlinson, B. 502, fol. 72a 2.

banishment from Meath of a people called the Déisi,
who are said to have sailed to Dyved and to have
made a settlement there.

We have, however, no knowledge who were the
Gwledigs of the Kymry for more than a hundred
years after Cunedda's time; but about the middle
of the sixth century we have the help of the
writings of Gildas, in which he denounces five princes
of his time :[1] three of these appear to have had
their homes in Wales. Their names were Vortiporios,
which in the Welsh predigrees becomes Guortepir ;[2]
Cuneglasos, later Cinglas and Cynlas; and Maglocunos,
a name better known in Wales in its later form
of Maelgwn. Now Gildas, while bringing against
Maelgwn very grievous charges, of the grounds of
which we have no means of forming an opinion, gives
us to understand that he had for a time been a monk
and had for instructor one of the most accomplished
men in Britain, who, it may be inferred from a life
of St. Cadoc, was no other than that philosophizing
saint himself.[3] Gildas not only represents Maelgwn
as a great warrior, and superior in stature to the
other princes he names, but he alludes more than
once to the fact of his standing far above them also

[1] Haddan and Stubbs's "Councils," &c., i. pp. 50-56, and
Mommsen's "Chronica," loc. cit. pp. 41-5. Gildas calls two of
them lion's whelps, the next is "pardo similis moribus," the fourth
addressed as a bear, and the fifth is a dragon. This last refers
probably to his standard (p. 136 below), and a similar remark
applies possibly to the other four.

[2] Harleian MS. 3859, fol. 193 b.

[3] See the "Lives of the Cam.-Brit. SS.," p. 52.

in point of authority and power. Cuneglasos or
Cynlas is not described in such a way that we can
be sure where he ruled, but the name was borne by a
grandson of Cunedda's son Einion, of whom Maelgwn
was also grandson, while a story recorded in the "Iolo
MSS." (p. 171) mentions Cynlas as lord of Glamorgan
and father of St. Cadoc. But this differs from the
usual account, and it would not be safe to rely upon
it, as the history of St. Cadoc is a most difficult one
to disentangle. Provisionally, one may regard the
prince in question as being Maelgwn's relative, acting
as a sort of lieutenant to him and having as his head-
quarters the ancient place known as Dineirth, in the
neighbourhood of the town of Llandudno.[1] Lastly
Vortiporios, whom Gildas terms tyrant of the Demetæ
or the people of Dyved, was probably king of the
portion of Dyved which had not been included in
Keredig's territory. Vortiporios was the direct representative of the leader of the exiles from Ireland who

---

[1] The text of the beginning of the paragraph devoted to
Cuneglasus offers difficulties : among other things, he is ad-
dressed as "urse multorum sessor aurigaque currus receptaculi
Ursi," where *receptaculum Ursi* is probably a translation of a
place-name ; and I conjecture the latter to have been Dinerth
(or Dineirth) for an early *Dūnos* or *Dūnon Arti* " Bear's fortress " :
compare *Din-cat* interpreted as *Receptaculum Pugnæ* in the
Life of St Paul de Léon (Revue Celtique v. 418). In that case
Auriga receptaculi Ursi might be rendered "the driver of the
Chariot of Dinerth." A different interpretation has been given
by Mr. Nicholson in "The Academy," Oct. 12, 1895, p. 297 ;
and, lastly, one wonders whether Gildas had not the Constella-
tions in his mind as he wrote the passage.

settled in Dyved, and he had doubtless to submit to the power of the Cunedda family, which is corroborated by the fact that Keredig's grandson, St. David, was about this time establishing himself as bishop in the latter region. Now the head of that family at this time was undoubtedly Maelgwn, whose authority reached to every corner of Wales. His own kingdom, however, was that of Venedot, Gwyndod or Gwynedd, the last of which is a name that now means all North Wales : it appears at one time to have denoted, more strictly speaking, that portion of it, approximately, which is covered by the Vale of Clwyd and the district west of it and north of the Mawddach. Gildas gives us no clue to the history of the Kymry from the Dee to the Clyde, and most other sources of information on the point have long since been closed by the disappearance of Welsh and Welsh traditions in Cumbria. What Gildas tells us about the many princes Maelgwn had overthrown, as well as the obscure allusions in Welsh poetry to Maelgwn and his hosts in the North, together with the later history of the Kymry, would tend to show that whoever the princes were who reigned over them north and east of the Dee, they must have done so subject to Maelgwn as Gwledig or whatever the leader had begun to be called by his time.

Brave and intrepid in war as Maelgwn undoubtedly was, his authority was certainly not altogether the direct result of his success in the field : it was in part at least due to the standing rule of the princes of the house of Cunedda, whereby one of them obtained the office of Gwledig, or, as it might now be termed, that of over-king. This is very clearly seen, as far as regards Wales, in a story invented afterwards to account for Maelgwn's supremacy : it occurs in some of the manuscripts of the Welsh Laws,[1] and is to the following effect :—The nation of the Kymry, after losing the crown and sceptre of London and being driven out of England, assembled by agreement to decide who should be chief king over them. The place of meeting was Maelgwn's Strand, near the mouth of the River Dovey, whither came the leading men from all parts of Wales : there Maeldav the Elder (lord of Moel Esgidion in Merioneth, according to one version, but of Pennardd in Arvon according to another) placed Maelgwn in a chair cunningly made of birds' wings. When the tide rose, it drove all away except Maelgwn, whom his chair enabled to stay, and thereby he became chief king, and his word and law paramount over the other princes, without being himself bound by theirs, while Maeldav for his services on the occasion obtained certain privileges for his own lordship. This legend, whatever else it teaches, clearly shows that Maelgwn's supremacy was in some way or other the result of the suffrages of the other princes of the Kymry. We have no means of ascertaining how the selection was usually made : as a rule the most shrewd and powerful member of the family of Cunedda managed to get himself declared head or over-king, and this may be

[1] See the 8vo. edition of 1841, vol. ii. pp. 49–51 ; also the "Iolo MSS.," pp. 73–74.

supposed to have not unfrequently been the cause of quarrels and civil wars.

Not only was Maelgwn beyond doubt the greatest prince of the Kymry from the time of Cunedda, but he succeeded in so strengthening the position of his family that the over-kingship remained afterwards with his descendants. This will appear from a brief outline of their history. Maelgwn's son Rhun, who inherited his father's power, had only a portion of his ability, and the manuscripts of the Welsh Laws [1] speak of Gwynedd being devastated in Rhun's time by the Men of the North, and of his successfully carrying the war into that region, where the men of Arvon distinguished themselves in the van of his hosts in crossing the Forth. Rhun had a son Beli, of whom nothing is known : he may have died before his father, but he left a son Iago, who died about the time of the battle of Chester in 616,[2] in which several Welsh princes fell, including Selyv, son of Cynan, whom the Irish annalist, Tigernach, calls *Rex Bretanorum* (Revue Celtique, xvii. 171). For anything known to

[1] Vol. i. p. 104.

[2] Mr. Plummer, in his edition of Bede's works, ii. p. 77, shows that the true date was not 613 as given in the Welsh Chronicle, otherwise called *Annales Cambriæ*, but 616, and that the death of Æthelfrith occurred soon after, in 616 or 617. The "Annales" date Iago's death in the year of the battle, but their use of the word *dormitat* (or *dormitatio*) negatives a violent death, and contradicts the Triad that ascribes Iago's death to Cadavael. In the Red Book dialogue put into the mouths of Myrdin and his sister Gwendyd, the succession is the following : --Maelgwn, Rhun, Beli, Iago, Cadfan. No Selyf is mentioned : see Skene, ii. 220-21.

the contrary, he may for a short time have enjoyed the
position of over-king of the Kymry and acted as their
general in that war : a superficial reading of the
oldest allusion to the battle, namely, in Bede's Ecclesiastical History, has sometimes led to the supposition
that the man who acted in that capacity was Brochvael,
the only Welsh prince whose name he gives. What
Bede says, however, is, that very many priests, belonging mostly to the monastery of Bangor Iscoed, had
come after a three days' fast to pray for success to their
nation in the contest which was about to take place ;
that the priests had soldiers to defend them a little
apart in a secure place under the command of Brochvael ; that Æthelfrith, on hearing of this, resolved to
begin by making an onslaught on the priests; and
that Brochvael and his men took to flight, when about
1,200 of the monks were slain, and only fifty escaped.
This slaughter was afterwards regarded by the English
as a judgment on the Kymry for having refused to join
Augustine in Christianizing their nation ; he had some
years before had a meeting on the borders of Wales
with the bishops and learned men of the Kymry
under the lead of Dunawd, or Dinoot as Bede calls
him. The pride and arrogance of the priest filled
with anger the men whose assistance he had come to
seek. To return to Bede, he tells us little about the
battle which followed the massacre of the monks
and Brochvael's flight ; nor do we know whether
the latter took any part in it. The historian,
however, says that the Anglian king did not gain
his victory without great losses to his own army ;

and the reason Brochvael was told off to guard the
priests is not far to seek : he appears to have been
lord of the country around Bangor as well as
nearly connected with its abbot Dunawd ; and if,
perchance, he was the Brochvael who died in the
year 662, he cannot be supposed to have been old
and tried enough to have had the command of the
whole army intrusted him in the presence of not
a few princes, who probably were more experienced
than he could well have been. We have supposed
Iago to have been the chief of these, a view not discountenanced by the likelihood that his son Cadvan,
who must have followed him as king of Gwynedd,
about the time of the Battle of Chester,
was also for a short time over-king of the Kymry.
Even this, favoured though it be by Welsh tradition, is not certain. It seems, however, to be the
key to the flattering language of Cadvan's epitaph,
which happens to be still existing at the Anglesey
church of Llangadwaladr close to Aberffraw, where
the kings of Gwynedd lived, probably from the time
of Maelgwn. Llangadwaladr is thought to be so
called from Cadvan's grandson Cadwaladr, who
appears to have died in 664. The church was built
by him, or in his honour, and the inscription cut, in
the so-called Hiberno-Saxon character, on a stone,
has the appearance of being of the seventh century :
the words are—*Catamanus rex sapientisimus opina-
tisimus omnium regum*—King Cadvan, the most wise
and renowned of all kings. We now come to Cadvan's
son and successor Cadwallon : there is no room for

doubt concerning the union of all the Kymry under his leadership in the closing struggle with the Angles of Northumbria; but we must revert to the battle of Chester.

Æthelfrith was at first king only of Bernicia; but, at the death of his kinsman Ælle of Deira, he succeeded in adding that to his own kingdom; and thus he became the first king of all Northumbria, while Ælle's young son Eadwine or Edwin, with his friends, sought refuge in other lands, among which may be mentioned Gwynedd, where Welsh tradition speaks of him as being brought up for a time at the court of Cadvan in Mona.[1] There is probably some truth in this, and it is possible that it was the cause of Æthelfrith's expedition to Chester. At any rate, it is quite in keeping with his later conduct as described by Bede; for Edwin, according to this author, found refuge soon after the battle of Chester at the court of Rædwald, king of the East Angles, and Æthelfrith, hearing of it, offered gifts to Rædwald to compass Edwin's death: he sent a second and a third time, adding the threat of war in case he persisted in turning a deaf ear to his wish. As Rædwald did not comply, Æthelfrith set out with an army to execute his threat. Rædwald and Edwin met him and fought a battle in which the Northumbrian king fell, so that Edwin succeeded him as king both of Deira and Bernicia: this took place in the year 616 or 617, or at any rate soon after the battle of Chester. But, for some reason or other, Æthelfrith's advantages

[1] See the "Myv. Arch." (ii. p. 17) triad 81.

were not vigorously followed up, although Bede gives him the credit of being a most brave and ambitious prince, who harassed the Welsh more than any other English king, and seized on more of their country than any one before him : possibly the Kymry offered him some kind of submission, and promised no longer to harbour Edwin. It was partly due, perhaps, to the losses suffered by the Anglian army, which were so serious that Bede mentions them as great, and that Welsh tradition has construed them into a victory for the Kymry. Above all it must have been due to the death of Æthelfrith himself, the originator of the war. The battle of Chester left the city desolate, never to be afterwards haunted by its Kymric dwellers, and it was probably the first time that the Kymry found the whole force of the Angles north of the Humber arrayed against them ; and, on the whole, the battle seems to have had the decisive character which it has been the fashion to ascribe to it of late. Something much more decisive, however, was shortly to follow : it was the succession of Edwin to Æthelfrith's place as king of Northumbria   He is said to have subdued all the English princes to his rule except his father-in-law, the king of Kent ; the Kymry suffered likewise from his power. Among the first of them were probably those of the small kingdoms of Loidis and Elmet, the former of which has left its name to the town of Leeds, and the latter to Barwick-in-Elmet and Sherburn-in-Elmet in the West Riding of Yorkshire. Their land was annexed to that of Deira, on the

confines of which they lay; but Edwin did not
stop here, as we read in Bede's history of his
having conquered the islands of Man and Mona,
the latter of which is known in Welsh as Môn and
in English as Anglesey. Bede's statement is significant, for Anglesey was, as it were, the home and
stronghold of the kings of Gwynedd: in fact, both
this conquest and the utterances of Welsh tradition
would lead one to suppose that the Kymry were
for some time wholly at the mercy of the Northumbrian king,[1] while Cadwallon, who appears to
have succeeded his father, Cadvan, about the same
time that Edwin attained to power, had at one
period of his life to seek refuge in Ireland: unfortunately, we have no sure indication of the dates we
want. The Northumbrian king became Christian in
627, and was baptized by Paulinus, a bishop who
followed northwards the former's Christian queen, who
was daughter to the King of Kent; and that prelate
is usually given the whole credit of converting the
Northumbrians. On the other hand, Nennius claims it
for a Welshman named Rhun[2] son of Urien, and the
Welsh Chronicle assigns his efforts to the preceding
year. So it may be supposed that during those years
the Kymry were under the Northumbrian king's

[1] Tigernach, in his entry of Edwin's triumph over Cadwallon,
describes the former as a man "qui totam Britaniam regnavit"
("Rev. Celtique," xvii. 181).

[2] It has been suggested that Rhun son of Urien was the
pre-ordination name of Paulinus: see Nicholson's paper on
Filius Urbagen in Meyer & Stern's "Zeitschrift für celtische
Philologie," iii. 105, 109.

yoke, and that they joined in the work of converting
his subjects to Christianity.   Next, the Chronicle
above mentioned speaks laconically of King Cadwallon as being besieged or blockaded in the year 629
in the island of Glannog, now better known as
Priestholm or Puffin Island, opposite Beaumaris on
the coast of Anglesey.   This was probably done by
Edwin's fleet, and it may be taken as possibly marking
the close of the drama which ended with Cadwallon's
escape to Dublin.   Again Welsh tradition speaks of
several battles fought by Edwin, which we cannot date,
one near the Conwy and one also on Digoll or the
Long Mountain in Shropshire, a spot with which the
Triads connect a fierce struggle known as one of the
Three Discolourings of the Severn : [1] these engagements possibly took place before Cadwallon's flight.
Cadwallon returns [2] after a time to recover his
power, and is introduced by Bede as rebelling against
Edwin in conjunction with Penda, the pagan king of
Mercia : a battle followed, in which Edwin fell and
his army was cut to pieces, in the year 633, at a place
called Hethfeld and Meiceren in the Saxon and Welsh
chronicles respectively : this spot is supposed to be
Hatfield, in the neighbourhood of Doncaster.   The
year after, 634, Edwin's son, Osric, then king of
Deira, tried to besiege Cadwallon in the city of York,
and was slain with his men in a sally made by the
Kymry.   All Northumbria was then for a whole year

[1] Skene's " Anc. Bks of Wales," ii p. 206.
[2] See the " Myv. Arch.," Triads i. 75, ii 41, 60 (vol. ii. pp. 16,
22) ; see also Skene's " Anc. Bks. of Wales," ii. pp. 277–9, 442.

under Cadwallon, who now killed Eanfrith, Æthel-frith's son, that had been in exile during Edwin's reign, and had come back after his death to be king of Bernicia. This was followed by Eanfrith's brother, Oswald, collecting a force and giving Cadwallon battle, in which the Angle won a great victory at a place called Hefenfelth and Catscaul by Bede and Nennius respectively. It was fought near the Roman Wall and the present town of Hexham in 635, and both those writers and the Welsh Chronicle assert that Cadwallon there met with his death, though the more legendary traditions of the Welsh speak of him as living many years afterwards. Under his son and successor, Cadwaladr, the Kymry seem to have continued to act with Penda of Mercia against Northumbria, of which both kingdoms were now ruled by Oswald. This contest resulted in 642 in a battle, which proved Oswald's last, at a place called Maserfelth by Bede, but Cocboy by Nennius and the Welsh Chronicle. Bernicia and Deira became again separate kingdoms, the former under Oswiu, a brother of Oswald, and the latter under Oswine, a cousin of Edwin ; but Oswiu got rid of Oswine by foul means and possessed himself of both kingdoms. He could, however, get no peace from Penda, who is said to have been bent on extirpating the Northumbrians : according to Bede, he was offered royal ornaments and gifts innumerable by Oswiu, if he would go home and leave off harassing his people, while Nennius, in a somewhat confused account of this transac-

tion, goes further, and would lead one to the following
conclusions—that Penda and the kings of the Brythons
had led a large army to the neighbourhood of the
Firth of Forth against Oswiu, who seems to have had
the Picts of that region then subject to him; that Oswiu
found himself forced to withdraw into a place which
Nennius calls Iudeu (whereby he may have meant
either Carr-iden or Edin-burgh[1]), and eventually to give
up to Penda, as the price of peace, all the treasure and
booty which he had there with him.   This was distri-
buted by the Mercian king among the kings of the
Brythons, and Nennius gives us to understand that it
was known in Welsh as Atbret Iudeu, or the restitution
of Iudeu.   But soon afterwards came the end, in the year
655, at the great battle of Winwæd, or, according to
Nennius, the slaughter of Gai's Field, which would seem
from its name to have been in the Pictish part of
Manaw.   There Penda is stated by Bede to have had
thirty legions under the command of most noted
leaders : nevertheless, the result was that they were
defeated, and that Penda was slain then or soon after,
for Oswiu is represented as now ending the war
in the region of Loidis, after most of the princes
helping Penda had fallen.   According, however, to
Nennius, the king of Gwynedd, whom he calls Cadavael, had escaped with his army by night, which may
have been the cause of Penda's defeat, and which
certainly gained for the Welsh prince the nickname of

[1] Nennius's " *Urbem quæ vocatur Iudeu*" may have been
in the original, say, *Caer* or *Dūn Iudenn* : see " The Welsh
People," pp. 115, 116.

Cadavael Cadommedd, or the battle-seizer who battle declines. Who he was is not known, but it may be guessed that he represented a Goidelic element hostile to Cadwaladr ; for the name Cadavael, which is not a common one, is found borne by a man said in one of the Triads[1] to have killed Iago, Cadwaladr's great-grandfather. He is not heard of after the war with Oswiu ; and all that is known with tolerable certainty about Cadwaladr is that he died during a plague which raged in Britain in the year 664; still some of the Welsh legends represent him as not dying till the 20th day of April, 689, at Rome, a date taken from what appears to be the true account of Ceadwalla, king of Wessex. After his victory, Oswiu grew in power and became ruler of the Mercians for three years after Penda's death, as he also did of other English peoples towards the south of the island ; not to mention that Bede speaks of his subjecting the greater part of the nation of the Picts to the sway of the Angles. As regards the Kymry, their state in its older and wider sense had now practically come to an end after a history extending over more than two centuries.

In the struggle between the Kymry and the Angles after the battle of Chester, the kings of Gwynedd, doubtless, considered that both their dignity and their power were at stake. These are spoken of in Welsh literature as the Crown of Britain ; for the Dux Britanniarum had not only passed into the Gwledig of Britain, but the latter had come to be spoken

1 See the "Myvyrian Arch.," Triads iii. 48 (vol. ii., p. 405) ; also Triads i. 76, iii. 26 (vol. ii., pp. 393, 403).

of as king or monarch of Britain.   This last title would
seem to have begun to come into use before the middle
of the sixth century, when Gildas described Maelgwn
as *insularis draco* or the island dragon, the island
being probably British, and not Mona, as is
sometimes supposed : here we have an early
instance of the habit so common in Welsh poetry
of calling a king or great leader a dragon, as
when a mythical Gwledig of Lower Britain is always
called Uthr Bendragon, or Uthr Head-dragon, the
reputed father of King Arthur.   The Welsh words
are *draig* and *dragon*, which, like the English
dragon, take us back to the Latin *draco, draconis*, a
dragon, and these in their turn to the Augustan era
of the Roman empire, when dragons[1] began to
figure in purple on the standards of some of the
legions and to be borne before military leaders : the
custom then extended itself to the emperors in
time of peace ; and the Welsh words make it highly
probable that the practice was among the Roman
traditions cherished by the Kymric gwledigs or over-
kings, whom the bards sometimes styled *Kessar-
ogion*[2] or Cæsarians, and men of Roman descent ;
we need not look elsewhere for the explanation of
the fact that the Red Dragon, which figures in the
story of Vortigern and Merlin, has always been the
favourite flag of Wales.   From the Maelgwn of Gildas
we now come to Bede's Cadwallon, whom that his-

[1] See the elaborate article and the copious references, s. v.
draco, in Ducange's Dic. (Paris, 1842).

[2] Skene's " Ancient Books of Wales," ii. p. 212.

torian usually styles *rex Brettonum*, or king of the
Brythons, though he once approaches the old technical
title of the *ducatus* or leadership by speaking of him as
Brettonum dux.[1] According to the legends put together
by Geoffrey of Monmouth, this title was an important
point in the dispute between Cadwallon and Edwin :
the latter is represented as demanding the former's
permission to wear a diadem in the east of the island
as Cadwallon was wont to do in the west, and to cele-
brate the great festivals as he did. These words contain
an allusion to the fixed meetings at which the feudal
lord received the homage of his men. There is probably
some truth in Geoffrey's account, and it is in harmony
with the fact that Edwin solved the difficulty by
driving Cadwallon out of Britain, and the latter in his
turn by taking the government of Northumbria into his
own hands for a while after Edwin's death. It is also
in a measure corroborated by Bede's words about the
seven English kings who exercised a sort of leadership
beyond the limits of their own kingdoms. He draws
no formal distinction between them, while an eighth is
added to their number (in the person of Ecgbyrht, the
first king of all England) in the Saxon Chronicle, the
manuscripts of which give them all the same title,
whether it be Bretenanwealda or Brytenwealda, that
is to say, Britain-wielder or ruler of Britain, or else
Bretwalda,[2] which meant Britain-wielder, ruler of the

---

[1] Bede's " Hist. Ecc.," iii. chap. 1.

[2] *Bretwalda* is the form in the oldest MS., and its meaning
is clearly seen in the longer *Bretcnanwealda :* the latter part of
this is *anwealda*, a lord, which is accordingly found applied

Brythons, or *Brettonum Dux* as Bede has called
Cadwallon. The leadership, already mentioned, of
the first four kings in Bede's list was exercised in
Lower Britain as a continuation, probably, of the
office of the Gwledig who succeeded the Count of the
Saxon Shore, and there is no reason to think that it
was actually known as that of Bretwalda or Brytenwealda : it survives possibly in the functionary called
the Warden of the Cinque Ports. The title of Bretwalda was most likely an exclusively Northumbrian
title assumed first by Edwin after conquering the over-
king of the Kymry in the person of Cadwallon, and
then by the other Northumbrian kings, Oswald and
Oswiu. Here it may be remarked that in *walda*,
wealda, *anwealda*, we have early English words which
happen to be of the same meaning and etymology as
the Welsh *gwledig*, or *uletic* as it would probably be
treated in the seventh century : this makes it hard to
avoid thinking that the English were in some measure

to the Almighty; it was otherwise written *anwalda*,
onwcalda, &c. Nor is it to be severed from *anweald* or
onweald, dominion, authority, power : see Sweet's "Anglo-
Saxon Reader," pp. 4, 27, 120. But it does not follow that
the scribes of the later MSS. were merely guessing the signification of the *Bretwalda* of the earlier MS., for they were not
wholly without other sources—witness their *Conmægl* and
Farinmægl, as compared with the much later forms in the
oldest existing MS. and with Bede's *Brocmailus*. The old-
fashioned explanations that aimed at dissociating *Breten*,
Bryten, and *Bret*, from *Britain* and *Britons*, were forced, and
dictated by the wish to keep clear of what was thought a
historical difficulty ; see the New English Dictionary, s.v.
Bretwalda.

guided in their choice of these terms by that which
was in use among the Welsh.   It is further worthy of
note that Edwin was the first English prince described
as wont to have, according to Bede's[1] account, a
standard borne before him wherever he rode, as was
the habit of the Cæsars of Rome, and probably also
of the Cæsarians of the Kymry after them and
their example : what device Edwin had on his,
whether it was, like theirs, a red dragon or not,
we have no means of knowing ; nor can we stay to
inquire whether the tuft carried before him when he
was pleased to walk consisted of a triad of plumes
used in the same way by the Gwledig, and to be
regarded as forming a middle term between the
insignia of office of the Dux Britanniarum and the
Prince of Wales's Feathers.

The disgrace the Kymry felt at losing the Crown
of Britain, whatever that somewhat indefinite expression implied, was probably nothing in comparison with
their bitterness at being robbed of one piece after another of their country.   We have already alluded to
Edwin annexing Loidis and Elmet to his own
kingdom of Deira ; but far more fatal to Kymric independence was the appropriation by the Angles of the
district of Teyrnllwg, described by Welsh tradition[2] as
reaching from the Dee to the forests of Cumberland
and the neighbourhood of the Derwent, which was
once the boundary of the diocese of Chester : the tract
consisting of the level part of Cheshire and South
Lancashire must have been taken from the Kymry

[1] "Hist. Eccl.," ii. 16.   [2] Iolo MSS., p. 86.

soon after, possibly before, the battle of Chester. Their loss of the plains of Teyrnllwg cut their state in two, and everything was calculated to rouse them to the highest pitch of fury and to the utmost exertion to rid themselves of their encroaching neighbours, to both of which Welsh poetry abundantly testifies. The struggle, of which the bards continued to sing [1] long afterwards, was no longer a struggle for mere glory ; it had become an effort on the part of their race to expel the Angles from the country and to drive the *Ellmyn* or Allemans, as they were sometimes termed, bag and baggage into their ships in quest of another home. It is in the heated atmosphere of this period that one can realise how closely the parts of the Kymric state clung together, and what a cruel wrench it was felt to be when it was torn in two ; and it is only in the lurid light of this all but forgotten context that one can read what the Brython meant, who first found that name too vague and began to call himself a Kymro, that is to say, *Cym-bro* (Combrox) or compatriot, the native of the country, the rightful owner of the soil, which he thought it his duty to hold against the *All-fro* (Allobrox), as he called the invader who came from another land, the devastating foreigner with whose head the fierce muse of his time and race loved to behold him playing football. Neither was this fire of hostility towards the intruder confined to the Kymry, for it seems more than once to have been spread by them to the other Celts,[1] from whom the

[1] See for instance Skene's "Ancient Bks. of Wales," ii. pp. 123-9.

bards represent them as drawing active assistance—
from the Brythons of Dumnonia and Armorica, from
the Goidels of Dublin and Scotland; nor does it by
any means appear improbable that all these peoples,
excepting perhaps those of Armorica, were represented in the motley host led by Penda of Mercia
to the North, when the curtain fell on the closing
scene of Oswiu's victory and Cadavael's inglorious
flight in 655.

From that time, or rather from the occupation by
the English of the plain of the Dee and the Mersey,
the Kymry dwelt in two lands, known in late Latin
as Cambria, in Welsh *Cymru*, which denotes the
Principality of Wales, and Cumbria or the kingdom of Cumberland; but for a considerable time
previously their territory must have been dangerously
narrowed in the direction of those rivers, for even
Ceawlin of Wessex had carried his conquests along the
eastern bank of the Severn into the heart of what
is now Shropshire, leaving on his right a peninsula of
Kymric country, reaching probably to the Avon : this
was afterwards acquired by the English tribes of Mercia
as the result of many a minor struggle lost to history,
though a careful study of place-names in that district
might still perhaps enable one to form an idea of the
spots where the old inhabitants were able to hold their
ground. As to the country west of the Severn, the kings
of Wessex appear to have made incursions into South
Wales from time to time, and possibly gained a per-

[1] See among others the poems in Skene's "Anc. Bks. of
Wales," ii. pp. 205-13.

manent footing on the west bank of that river ; but
it was not till the time of Offa that the English
frontier was materially advanced towards the west.
He reigned over Mercia from 755 to 794, and made
it the first power in Britain ; besides his conflicts with
the other English states, he had many wars with the
Kymry west of the Severn, especially during the last
twenty years of his reign. He encroached on them,
and they retaliated by ravaging his country ; so he had
an earthen rampart built from the mouth of the Wye
to the estuary of the Dee, to divide Mercia from
Wales : thus he severed from the latter a very considerable tract of country, including a large part of
Powys, with the important town of Pengwern, which
became English with its name translated into Shrewsbury. Thus the southern Cambria shrank into the
Wales of our day, in which we include the county of
Monmouth, and, roughly speaking, Offa's Dyke is
still regarded as the boundary between England and
Wales, though few remains of it are now to be seen.

We have thus rapidly followed the southern Kymry
into Wales, and we should now leave them, but that
a word or two touching their history there may serve
to give its full meaning to what we have already said
about the nature of their state before Oswiu's victory. From that time very little is known of them
for nearly a century, and it has therefore been supposed that for a considerable portion of that interval
they were under the domination of the English.
But, when at length we read a little more about them,
we find them still ruled by kings of the race of

Maelgwn ; and the Welsh Chronicle in recording, in the year 754, the death of Rhodri, grandson of Cadwaladr, styles him Rex Brittonum, or king of the Brythons. His son, Kynan, left a daughter only, who was married to Mervyn, said to have come, like Cunedda, from Manaw in the North. Mervyn became king of all Wales, and was followed by his son, Rhodri the Great, who was also king of all Wales, till his death in 877. Rhodri divided Wales between his three sons and made arrangements for the eldest to be over-king : that dignity may possibly, even in the period of confusion which followed the death, in the year 948, of Rhodri's grandson, Howel the Good, have had charm enough to make "confusion worse confounded." What with the wars of the Welsh princes with the English, with the Danes, and with one another, the web of Kymric history after the Norman Conquest is not easy to disentangle ; but the kingdom of the Welsh is sometimes spoken of as having finally fallen in 1091, when Rhys ab Tewdwr was slain in battle by the Normans, who seized on most of South Wales. In time it ceased to be the custom to speak of a Welsh leader who rose above his peers, as king of the Brythons, or even king of all Wales, a title which made way for that of Prince of Wales. That was the case, for instance, when the death of Llewelyn, the last Prince of Wales in any sense descended from Maelgwn and Cunedda, opened the way for the King of England to juggle the title into his son's lap. To go back to an earlier and more interesting fact, not only did the

bards continue for ages to sing the praises of the
Welsh princes who protected them, in such terms
as had ceased to be applicable from the time of Cadwaladr, but we meet with a curious relic of the same
past state of things in the tenth century edition of the
Welsh Laws, where they specify certain occasions on
which the Household bard of the King of Gwynedd
was to sing before his hosts a lay of which the subject
only is given : it was the significant one of the
Monarchy of Britain,[1] the last indistinct echo of the
long-forgotten office of the Dux Britanniarum.

We must now say a few words about the other
Cambria or Cumbria, for in point of origin we have
but one and the same word in both forms. *Kambria*
was regularly used for Wales by such writers as
Giraldus in the twelfth century, and Geoffrey somewhat
earlier had found an eponymous hero called Kamber
to account for it, just as he likewise had ready to
his hand a Locrinus[2] to explain Lloegr, the Welsh
word for England south of the Humber, and
Albanactus to be the ancestor of the Albanach,
the Gaels of Alban or Celtic Scotland. The
fashion was not yet established of distinguishing
between Cambria and Cumbria as we do. Thus
St. Petroc, who was probably a native of Wales, is in
one ancient life[3] called a Cumber, according to another version, a Cimber. On the other hand Joceline,

---

[1] Vol. i. p. 34.

[2] This is the *Locrine* of Milton's " Comus," which see.

[3] See Capgrave's " Legenda Angliæ," p. 266; and the
" Acta Sanct.," June 4, i. p. 400.

who wrote his life of St. Kentigern in the twelfth
century, speaks of the land of the Northern Kymry or
Cumbria, as Cambria, and uses the adjectives Cambrensis and Cambrinus accordingly; and Æthelweard
in his chronicle, written in Latin about the end of the
tenth century, mentions the Northern Kymry under
the name of Cumbri. So it may be supposed that
both countries of the Kymry were for some time
called Cambria and Cumbria indifferently, the Welsh
word on which they are based being, as now written
Cymrn, which denotes exclusively the Principality,
and is there pronounced nearly as an Englishman
would treat it if spelled Kumry. It is needless,
therefore, to say that Cambria is a less correct form
of the word than Cumbria, and that, in the language
of the Saxon Chronicle, it became *Cumerland* or
Cumberland, and also *Cumbraland*—the land, as it
were, of the *Cumbras*, the Cumbri or Kymry. The
latter consisted in the North of a considerable number
of small tribes, many of the princes of which claimed
descent from Coel or from a Roman ancestor, and
among them some from the Maximus who succeeded
for a time in possessing himself of the imperial throne
of Rome. The relations in which the former usually
stood to one another and to the Gwledig cannot
clearly be made out, but their wars were mostly
directed against the Angles of Bernicia, while Urien,
Rhydderch, and others who warred with Hussa,
king of Bernicia from 567 to 574, figure very con-
spicuously in old Welsh poetry : later Urien and his
sons are represented as also fighting with valour

and varying success against Theodric, who reigned
over Bernicia from 580 to 587. He was probably
the devastator known in Welsh literature as the
Flame-bringer.[1]

Hitherto Carlisle had no doubt been far the most
important town of these Northern Cumbrians ; but, in
consequence of a great battle fought by their princes
with one another in the year 573, that city found
much of its importance shifted to a more northern
point. The conflict took place at Arderydd,
identified by some with the Knows of Arthuret,
on the banks of the Esk, about nine miles from
Carlisle, and by others with Airdrie, in Lanark.
The cause of the war is not evident, but the
prince who issued victorious, with the aid probably
of the Gwledig, was Rhydderch : he thereupon
fixed his headquarters on a rock in the Clyde,
called in Welsh Alclud, whence it was known to
the English for a time as Alclyde, but the Goidels
called it Dúnbrettan or the fortress of the Brythons,
which has prevailed in the slightly modified form of
Dumbarton. The fact that Rhydderch, after firmly
establishing himself there, prevailed on Kentigern
to return from Wales to take the primacy of that
district as bishop of Glasgow, also contributed eventually in some measure to the importance of that
part of Cumbria. For a long time after Oswiu's
victory the Cumbrians, like the other Kymry,
remained under English domination; but at length,
in the year 685 Oswiu's son, Ecgfrith, the king of

[1] See Skene's "Anc. Books of Wales," ii. pp. 189, 199.

Northumbria, was defeated and slain at Dún Nechtain, supposed to be Dunnichen in Forfarshire.   The
Angles only retained their power over the Picts of
Galloway and the Cumbrians south of the Solway,
together with the city of Carlisle, which Ecgfrith
shortly before his death had given to St. Cuthberht,
with some of the land around it.   The Cumbrians
north of the Solway became independent, and had
kings of their own again, of whom one is recorded as
dying in 694, and another in 722.   But, the Picts
of Galloway continuing under the yoke of the
Northumbrians, the king of the latter managed in
750 to annex to Galloway the district adjoining it
on the north and west, which was then a part of the
land of the Cumbrians, though it may have long
before belonged to the Picts.   In the same year a
war took place between the former and the Picts of
Lothian, who suffered a defeat and lost their leader,
Talargan, brother to the King of Alban, in a battle
at a place called Mocetauc in the Welsh Chronicle,
and supposed to be in the parish of Strathblane in
the county of Stirling ; but in 756 we read of the
Picts and the Northumbrians joining, and pressing the
Cumbrians sorely.   Afterwards little is known of them
(except that Alclyde was more than once destroyed
by the Norsemen) until we come down to the end
of the ninth century, as to which we meet with a
Welsh tradition that the Cumbrians who refused
to submit to the English were received by the
King of Gwynedd into the part of North Wales lying
between the Dee and the Clwyd, from which they

are represented as driving out some English settlers who had established themselves there. How much truth there may be in this story is not evident, but it is open to the suspicion of being based to some extent on the false etymology which identifies the name of the Clwyd with that of the Clyde. It is needless to say that the latter, being Clôta in Roman times, and Clût in old Welsh, could only yield Clûd in later Welsh. Harassed and weakened on all sides, the Cumbrians ceased to have kings of their own race in the early part of the tenth century, when a Scottish line of princes established itself at Alclyde ; and in 946 the kingdom was conquered by the English king Edmund, who bestowed the whole of it from the neighbourhood of the Derwent to the Clyde on the Scottish king Maelcoluim or Malcolm, on condition that he should assist him by land and sea, the help anticipated being intended against the Danes. So Cumbria became what historians are pleased to call an appanage of the Scottish crown, which led to various complications between the English and Scots for a considerable time afterwards. Into these we cannot enter, and it will suffice to say that William the Red made the southern part of Cumbria, including the city of Carlisle, an earldom for one of his barons. Thus it came to pass that the name of Cumberland has ever since had its home on the English side of the border, while the northern portion, of which the basin of the Clyde formed such an important part, is spoken of in the Saxon Chronicle as that of the Strathclyde Welshmen. It may here be added that this last was still more closely joined to the Scottish crown when David became king in 1124; but its people, who formed a distinct battalion of Cumbrians and Teviotdale men in the Scottish army at the battle of the Standard in 1130, preserved their Kymric characteristics long afterwards. How late the Welsh language lingered between the Mersey and the Clyde we have, however, no means of discovering, but, to judge from a passage in the Welsh Triads, it may be surmised to have been spoken as late as the fourteenth century in the district of Carnoban,[1] wherever between Leeds and Dumbarton that may turn out to have been.

[1] See the " Myvyrian Archaiology," Triad iii. 7 (ii. p. 58).

CHAPTER V.

THE PICTS AND THE SCOTS.

To the remarks made in the last chapter on the Picts of Galloway, we may add, that we read of the Brython, whom Bede calls Nynias, labouring to convert them to Christianity about 412, and building a church dedicated to St. Martin, at a place called in the Saxon Chronicle Hwiterne, now Whitehorne, Whithern, or Whithorn, in the south-eastern part of Wigtonshire. They were, as a rule, little disposed to be friendly towards their Brythonic neighbours, but they appear, nevertheless, to have taken part with them in the war against Oswiu, when, as the result of his triumph, they became subject to the Northumbrians, who proceeded to incorporate their country with their own kingdom. Nor did the defeat and death of Ecgfrith in 685 enable them to free themselves; for the Northumbrians are found to have set up a bishopric at Whithorn in 727, and Bede speaks of a man, whose name was Pecthelm, acting as their bishop there in 731 ;[1] the bishopric, however, seems to have ended with another, whose name was Beadwolf, in the year 796 or thereabouts. This marks the beginning of a time when the hold of the Angles on Galloway grew feeble, and Northumbria itself fell into a state of con-

[1] "Hist. Eccl.," v. 23.

siderable disorder and confusion. But Galloway and Northumbria remained connected, after a fashion, a long time afterwards—probably until the former was bestowed with Cumbria on the king of the Scots by the English king Edmund. Not only did these Picts so far retain the individuality of their race as to be known by that name as late as the twelfth century, and to form a division of King David's army at the battle of the Standard, where they claimed the right of leading the van of his numerous hosts ; but there is no lack of evidence that they still clung, some four centuries later, to their Goidelic speech, which Scottish authors used to call Ersch or Irische, as they rightly identified it with the Celtic language of Ireland and the Highlands.

Allusion has also been made to the Picts on the south coast of the Firth of Forth, but a few words more must be devoted to them before we pass beyond the bounds of what was once Roman Britain. The whole seaboard from the Southern Wall to the Lammermoor Hills fell, as already mentioned, into the possession of the Angles, but the tract looking seaward from that range to where the Avon empties itself into the Forth or thereabouts, and commonly known as the Lothians, was occupied by a considerable mixture of races, as may be gathered from the place-names there. Thus the district north of the Lammermoors, forming the peninsula over against the county of Fife, would seem to have been Celtic, though it is not easy to say whether the Goidel or the Brython prevailed there ; apparently it was the former. But on the upper course

of the northern Tyne, which drains this region parallel
to the Lammermoor range, one comes to a place
called Pencaitland, a name which is, in part at any
rate, Brythonic. A little higher, however, the head-
stream of the same Tyne is called Keith Water, not to
mention the parish there called Keith-Humbie, which,
together with Dalkeith, between the two Esks, shows
that we have to do with a district not peopled by
Brythons ; but by whom ? This is a difficult question,
as will be seen from the following facts which have to
be taken together :—The vocable Keith cannot well
be severed from other place-names into which it
enters at various points in the east of Scotland from
Keith Water to Caithness ; among these are Inch
Keith in the Firth of Forth, and Keith Inch at Peterhead, the most eastern point of Scotland ; in the
former, Keith inevitably reminds one of the stronghold
in the middle of the Firth of Forth, called by Bede
Urbs Giudi ; and it is, moreover, on record that the
Irish formerly called the Firth of Forth, the sea of
Giudan[1] or of the Giuds, to which may be added that
the legendary son of the eponymous Cruithne or Pict
representing Caithness is variously called Cait, Gatt,
and Got, and that a Welsh form of another Pictish
name here in point is given by Nennius as *Iudeu*,
already mentioned at page 134 above. We are not
forced, however, to identify *Urbs Iudeu* with Bede's
Urbs Giudi, but phonologically they and *Giudan* seem
to go together, and not with *Keith* or *Caith*. One
may add to the former a kindred form from the Welsh

[1] Reeves's "Culdees," p. 124.

Chronicle, namely, where it calls Menevia or St. David's *Moni Iudeorum*. We need not here be troubled by the lost Ten Tribes of Israel, but it might be argued that under these names we have to do with Jutes, and it would be hard to prove the contrary; but on the whole it is probable at all events that we have here again to do with a small non-Celtic settlement of some kind. To return to the North, the Pictish country reached at least from the upper course of the Tyne to the range of mountains called after the village of Pentland, a name, however, which is probably a cor-ruption of a Brythonic *Pen-llan*. Following their direction towards the sea we reach what was once the stronghold of the Picts, namely, Edinburgh, which, owing to its conquest by Edwin, had its name some-times made into Edwinesburg. The inland boundary of this Pictish district is indicated by the Brythonic name, Penicuik, borne by a place on the upper course of the more northern of the two Esks. How far the Picts occupied the country beyond the Pentlands is not evident, but probably up to the river Almond at least. Beyond that we seem to reach a district which was in part Brythonic and in part Goidelic. Thus we have the former in *Carriden* (for *Caer Eden*, "Fort of Eden") near Abercorn; and we detect the latter in connection with the place where the northern wall ended on the Firth of Forth, which, according to Bede, was called *Peanuahel* or *Peanfahel* by the Picts, and *Penneltun* by the Angles. The former points back to a Latin term *penna(e)* or *pinna(e) valli*[1] "wing of the

[1] See Nicholson's "Keltic Researches" (London, 1904), p. 24.

vallum," that is, the pinnacle or turret at the end of
the wall.   The syllable *uahel* or *fahel* represents what
would be written later in Goidelic *fáil*, the genitive of
fál, 'a wall " (in Welsh *gwawl*).   But the position of
the *u* or *f* would force it to be elided sooner or later
in Goidelic pronunciation, as was done in the Anglian
Penel (of *Peneltun*) derived from the Goidelic
name.   In modern Irish spelling the latter would
have been represented as *Pean(n)fháil*, had the name
not undergone a further change, that of *p* into *c*,
making it into *Ceannfháil*, and causing it to be
interpreted henceforth as the "Wall's End."   This is
given in certain of the manuscripts of Nennius as
Cenail, now written Kinneil.   The non-Celtic Picts,
when we find them coming southwards, seem to have
been fast adopting the idioms of their Celtic neighbours ; so the contest of languages in the maritime
district south of the Forth came in time to be mainly
between Goidelic and English, which no doubt had a
footing there in the time of Edwin.   Nay, after what
has been already hinted, it is needless to say, that
some believe English to have been firmly established
on that coast as early as in Kent, namely, by a
branch of the same Jutish people.   We are, however,
by no means sure that this has been satisfactorily
made out.

When Edwin became master of the stronghold
of Edinburgh he probably did so only after reducing
the whole country between the Lammermoors and
the Avon, a conquest which may be supposed to have
made his dominions continuous from the latter river

to the Humber ; but when Penda and his Celtic allies
appeared in the north most of the non-Anglian inhabitants of Lothian were probably induced to join them,
so that Oswiu when he proved victorious not only
reduced them under his power, but extended his
conquests to the country beyond the Forth, as the
Picts there may have taken part with their kinsmen against him.   The yoke of the Angles must have
been thrown off at the defeat of Ecgfrith in 685.
After his time we read of battles between them and
the Angles, and, among others, of one fought in the
plain of Manaw in the year 710 or 711 : another battle
is mentioned as having been fought in 729 between
the Picts from the north of the Forth and the Picts
of Manaw : afterwards, little is known about the latter
till the year 844, when the Goidelic element became
supreme in the North.   Now the battle on the plain
of Manaw is specified as having been fought at a place
between the rivers Avon and Carron : it serves in
some measure to fix the position of the region called
by the Welsh the land of Manaw, and by the Goidels
Manann, a name which survives in Sla*mannan* Moor,
in which the river Avon rises, in the county of
Linlithgow, and also in Clack*mannan*, which suggests
that another piece of Manaw lay north of the Forth,
both having possibly been included in the territory
of the people whom Ptolemy calls Dumnonii.   Their
country touched two salt waters, the Firth of Forth
and the Firth of Clyde or the Irish Sea.   Adjoining
them, close to the former, was another piece of the
ancient Manaw, called by the Welsh the Manaw of

the Gododin : these were the people known in
Ptolemy's time as Votadini, and placed on the coast
from the Firth of Forth to the confines of the land
which he considered the Brigantes to have inhabited
as their own. Before leaving this district south of
the Forth, it may be mentioned that next to nothing
is known of the relation in which the Picts of Lothian
and of Galloway stood to their kinsmen in the north :
an unidentified son of the eponymous Cruithne
is called Fidach, a name doubtlessly representative of
the people or region called in Welsh poetry Goddeu :
it was possibly Lothian but more likely Galloway ;
for we seem to detect a cognate of Fidach or Goddeu
in the latter part of the name of Galloway as Latinized
into Galwadia[1]. This has usually been derived by
main force from Gall-Gaedhel, the name which the
Irish in later times gave the Picts of Galloway,
whereby they meant to describe them as Goidels or
Gaels who adhered or submitted to the *Gall* or the
stranger who came on his piratic visits from Denmark
or the fiords of Norway, rather than with any allusion,
as it is supposed, to the Anglian stranger who ruled
that district as a province of his own for a long time.

We must now go beyond the limits of what was
once Roman Britain, and say something of the Picts
who remained outside the Northern Wall : it will
lead to somewhat less complication if we speak first
very briefly of the Scots who settled in Britain. They
took up their abode in Cantyre and the island of
Islay, the part of Ireland from which they came being

[1] Mommsen's " Chronica Minora," iii. p. 19.

the nearest district to Cantyre and known as that of
Dál-Riada. The migration began during the last
years of the fifth century, under a prince called
Fergus mac Ercæ; and it was not long before the
new comers spread themselves over much of what is
now known as Argyle. They were then separated
from the Picts north of the Forth by the great
mountain chain which forms a part of the boundary
of the west of Perthshire, and used to be termed
Dorsum Britanniæ or Drumalban, which means
the ridge of Britain or Alban. The king of
the Picts, whose name was Brude Mac Maelchon,
drove them back about the year 560 to Cantyre,
and slew their king. The Scots were Christians,
while the Picts ruled over by Brude were still
pagans; and it is supposed that the mission of
St. Columba to Brude's court had as one of its
objects the bettering of the position of the Scots as
against their powerful neighbours. Columba, who was
connected with the royal family of the Dalriad Scots,
came over from Ireland in the year 563, and made
the islet of Iona, near the coast of the island of Mull,
the home of himself and his followers shortly afterwards: he succeeded in converting Brude and his
Pictish subjects to Christianity; but it does not
seem to have prevented their further pressing the
Scots, whom we read of as losing their king and
many of his followers in a battle fought in Cantyre
in 574. St. Columba at this point interfered in
the succession, and chose as king of the Scots a
great-grandson of Fergus mac Ercæ, whose name was

Aedan, and then he took him to Ireland to a meeting
known as the Council of Drumcett, where he obtained
the concession that the Dalriad Scots of Britain
should no longer have to pay taxes or tribute to the
mother state in Ireland, though they were to continue
bound to take part in her hostings and expeditions.
So Aedan became the first independent king of the
Scots, and he appears to have strengthened his
position by bringing a fresh colony back with him
from Ireland, and we read of him and Baetan mac
Cairill, king of the Dál-Fiatach[1] and over-king of
Ulster, driving the English out of Manaw, the
over-kingship of which is said by Irish tradition
to have belonged to Baetan. He died in 581, and
two years later Manaw was left by the Goidels,
which seems to mean that the forces from Ireland
left Aedan to carry on the contest alone with the
English, that is to say, the Angles of Bernicia; so we
read of him fighting a battle about this time in
Manaw, though nothing is known about it, excepting
that it ended in his favour. Next we learn from
Adamnan, who wrote the biography of St. Columba
in the seventh century, that Aedan fought a great battle
in which several of his sons fell, in what Adamnan
calls the war of the Miati or Miathi;[2] this battle, in
which he ascribes a dearly-bought victory to Aedan,
is otherwise known as that of Circinn, which took
place in 596: this can hardly have been the Circinn

---

[1] Another warlike tribe of the north-eastern corner of Ireland,
located in what is now the county of Down.

[2] Reeve's "Adamnan's Life of Columba," pp. 33, 36.

of Magh-Girginn, "plain of Circinn," the name of which was reduced to Moerne, and Mernis or Mearns in broad Scotch. That seems too far from the people of the Mæatæ: the Mearns are now, roughly speaking, represented by Kincardineshire. Later we find Aedan again helped by soldiers from Ireland under Maelumi, the son of Baetan, namely, at the great battle which was fought in 603, at a place called by Bede[1] Degsastan, supposed by some to have been Dawstone near Jedburgh, and by others Dalston near Carlisle, if not Dawstone Rigg in Liddesdale. Aedan had a very large army, consisting of his Scots, the Picts of Manaw, and his allies from Ireland, and it is not improbable that the Brythons of Cumbria had readily joined him in a great struggle against the Angles whose king was the aggressive Æthelfrith, of whom we have already spoken; but he obtained a complete victory over Aedan and his combined forces. Aedan died in 606; he was a Dalriad Scot, but something more, for he is traditionally said to have been the son of a daughter of Brychan, the ancestor of one of the three holy families of Welsh hagiology, who is supposed to have left his name to Brycheiniog or Brecknock. It is by no means clear what the object of all Aedan's wars may have been, but it would, perhaps, be not far wrong to assume that they were mainly directed against the Angles and the Picts beyond the Forth and Clyde. Aedan's sons took a more or less active part in the affairs of Ireland, and so did his grandson Domnall Brecc or the Freckled: the latter also

_____
[1] "Hist. Eccl.," i. chap. 34.

fought several battles in Britain. One of these obscure
conflicts took place in 634 at a place called Calitros,
or Calathros, Latinised Calabria, and supposed to
have been somewhere between the Carron and the
Avon.   In 638 we read of Etan (either Edinburgh or Carriden) as undergoing siege and of
another attempt made by Domnall, who was again
defeated.   On what terms he had hitherto been with
the Brythons of Cumbria we do not know, but at that
time a war took place between him and them, in
which they were victorious, and he was slain in the
upper part of the vale of the Carron.   The kingdom
of the Dalriad Scots of Argyle seems to have never
flourished much after this time.

As to the Picts or Picti, their name, referring as it
would seem to do, to the habit of colouring the body
which prevailed among them after it had disappeared
in most of the country under the Romans, was never,
perhaps, distinctive of race, as Brythons and Goidels
seem to have been sometimes included under it as well
as the non-Celtic natives to whom the term probably
applied most strictly at all times.   So historians
speak geographically of these peoples as northern and
southern Picts, meaning by the latter the dwellers of
the districts stretching from the Forth to the neighbourhood of Aberdeen and drained by the Forth, the
Tay, and the two northern Esks. Its inland boundary
may be described as a sort of semi-circle of mountains,
comprising the Mounth or that portion of the
Grampians which runs across the country and ends
near Stonehaven, on the north, and Drumalban on the

west, beyond which dwelt those whom it has been customary to call the northern Picts, excepting that the Dalriad Scots had taken possession of a part of Argyle from the end of the fifth century : it is more accurate to speak of them as the Picts on this side of the mountains and those beyond them. Now, the former, in the loose sense here suggested, were partly Celtic and partly non-Celtic, while the Celtic element was of two kinds, Brythonic and Goidelic ; for, when the earlier Celtic invaders, the Goidels, had presumably seized on the best portions of the island, their northern territory on the eastern sea-board may even have included most of the Lowland district drained by the Tay and the rivers that join it. A long time afterwards the other Celts—those of the Brythonic branch—came and drove the Goidels before them, as the latter had done with the aborigines. There is no evidence, however, that they had coasted beyond the Firth of Forth, though there is that they got possession of a good deal of country north-east of the river. The outlying tribes of the Dumnonii had pushed them-selves as far as the skirts of the great Caledonian forest, and laid claim to most of the tract probably between the Forth and the Perthshire Almond, in-cluding the northern slope of the Ochils. Ptolemy assigns to them three towns, Alauna, which may haveb een at Ardoch near the Allan ; Lindon, sup-posed to have been at Delginross, near Comrie, on the Earn ; and Victoria, possibly situated at Stra-geath on the same river. These tribes were probably the Verturiones of ancient authors, and their name yielded that of the Men of Fortrenn of Pictish history, which gives them Menteith, Strathearn, and Fothreve, or the western portion of Fife. They were probably a mixture of Dumnonian Brythons and Picts, and had around them on the north and east a zone of Goidelic territory comprising, perhaps, a portion of Athol in the Perthshire highlands, and Gowrie on the north of the Tay. The north-east corner of this Cismontane Pictland, the region of the twin Esks, belonged to those of the aboriginal Picts, whom Ptolemy calls Vernicomes; and in later times there is no certain evidence for extending the territory of the Mæatæ, Adamnan's Miati, to cover any part of that country. It is mostly known in history as the Mearns, to which may be added probably most of the province of Angus. The two correspond pretty nearly to the counties of Forfar and Kincardine respectively. This land, from Stonehaven to Stirling, and from Drumalban to the North Sea, with its three contending races of Brythons, Goidels, and non-Celtic Picts, is the theatre where most of the known history of the Pictish kingdom was acted.

The Pictish kingdom, we said, for historians are wont to speak of it in the singular; and, on the whole, the facts of the case warrant it, especially if the head of it be looked at as an Ard-rí or high-king, holding a position somewhat like the Gwledig among the Kymry. Moreover, the kingdom is rightly called Pictish, and not Goidelic or Brythonic : this leads us to the question as to its probable origin, and as to what became of the Caledonians, who were the most powerful people that Agricola and his legions met with in the north. Agricola found and fought the Caledonians on the banks of the Tay. But it may be doubted that any part of that district below Dunkeld belonged to them; and, for some reason or other, they seem not long afterwards to disappear lost in the background. This may have begun with the tremendous defeat the Roman general was able to inflict on them in the year 86, for it probably gave a rival people that had not taken part in the war with the legions, or taken only a subordinate part, the start it wanted in the race for the foremost place in independent Britain. From Tacitus we gather that those who benefited by the disaster to the Caledonians were not the Boresti, or any people between the Tay and Forth, for their country had most likely been overrun; and Agricola took hostages from them on his return from the banks of the Tay; but it was the people called the Vacomagi, who ranged from the land occupied by the Goidels of the Tay basin to the Moray Firth. And on this point something may be learnt from Ptolemy's Geography, which was published about thirty-four years after the great defeat of the Caledonians in 86. Beyond the Dumnonii, whose outposts reached the neighbourhood of the Perthshire Almond, and between the former and the Moray Firth he locates only three peoples, and of these far the most widely spread was that of the Vacomagi. Their country, as far as can be made out from the data he supplies, extended from the river Ness to the upper course of the Dee

and the Don, and from the Moray Firth into the
heart of Perthshire. He gives them four towns :
the first, called the Winged Camp, is supposed to
have been on the promontory of Burghead on the
south side of the Moray Firth; the second, called
Tuessis, near Boharm, on the Spey; the third, called
Tamea, on an island in the Tay called Inchtuthill;
and the fourth, called Banatia, at Buchanty, on the
Almond. The most eastern point of Scotland is
called by Ptolemy Tæxalon, and the people of that
district were the Tæxali, the bulk of whose territory
is represented by the modern county of Aberdeen :
they had a town called Devana, which has been
supposed to have stood in the strath of the Dee, near
the Pass of Ballater, and close to Loch Daven. The
rest of the eastern coast Ptolemy leaves to the people
whom he calls Vernicomes or Venicones, and who
thus overlap with the Mæatæ of later authors: the
former's country, at that time, would seem to have
comprised Mearn, Angus, and the east of Fife; while
their town, called Orrea, appears to have been on the
Fifeshire Eden, unless it was still more south, somewhere near the confluence of the Orr with the Leven,
not very far from the Firth of Forth. In the main
we take all those peoples to have been non-Celtic,
and their territory would seem to have surrounded
that of the Goidels of old standing in the Tay valley,
whence the influence of the latter people spread at
length as far as Athol. Ptolemy makes the
Caledonians extend across the island from the
neighbourhood of Loch Fyne to the Beauly Firth.

with the territory of the Vacomagi stretching parallel
to theirs from the river Almond to where Burghead
looks across the sea towards the Ord of Caithness.
The extension of the power of the Vacomagi across the
Tay, as far as Buchanty on the Almond, together with
that of the Vernicomes into Fife, was possibly of
recent date; in any case it only meant that the
Goidels and the Picto-Brythons had come under the
power of the more purely non-Celtic tribes beyond
them, and not that they had been displaced by them,
at least to any considerable extent; for the later
history of the Pictish kingdom compels us to regard
the central region, especially that exposed to Highland
raids on the lower banks of the Tay, as always
occupied by the most Goidelic race in the North.
Among the strategic points of prime importance
which the Vacomagi would seem to have won from
the latter, may be mentioned Dunkeld, rightly
termed the gate of the Highlands.   The ecclesiastical history of Dunkeld began comparatively
late, but the fact by no means proves that it had
not been considered a point of great importance
from the earliest times.   If could hardly, however,
have got its present name if it had not once been
in the possession of the Caledonʼans, since in its
Gaelic form of Dúncelden or Dúnchallann it means the
town or stronghold of the Caledones or Caledonians :
a similar remark applies to the well-known mountain
called Schiehallion (Sith-Chaillinn[1]).

[1] For the hint as to Schiehallion we are indebted to a letter
contributed some years ago to the columns of "The

This circumstance marking the impossibility of drawing an intelligible boundary between the Caledonians and the Vacomagi, and our deriving the latter vocable from Ptolemy alone, incline us to conclude that the Vacomagi were after all only Caledonians under another name, or at any rate a grouping of those of their tribes that occupied the portion of the Caledonian territory lying nearest to the lowland country. Hence we have ventured to treat the Caledonii and Vacomagi as forming a sort of twin people of Dicalydones : see page 94 above.

The Caledonians occupied the leading position in the league against Agricola, but by the year 201 we find them occupying the second place, when the Mæatæ take the lead in threatening hostilities against the Roman province, with the Caledonians preparing to assist them, contrary to promises the latter had made to keep the peace. When the governor of the province, in consequence of failing to get the necessary reinforcements from the Continent, was obliged to buy peace from the intrepid northerners at a great price, it was with the Mæatæ he seems to have had to negotiate. This clearly suggests that the Mæatæ were then the leading power, and that they had ready access to the frontier of the province. The original strength of the independent aborigines no doubt lay in the country of the Mæatæ, of the Vernicomes and Tæxali, and the part of the land of the Vacomagi consisting of the district near the Moray Firth, which is still remarkable

Northern Chronicle" by Mr Macbain on the question " Who were the Picts ? "

as being one of the most fertile regions of Scotland. So
we see several reasons why Severus, when he arrived in
208, bent on crushing the northern enemies of Rome,
does not appear to have stayed his march until he had
made his way through the Vernicomes and Tæxali to
the shoies of the Moray Firth, and why he then seems
to have thought it necessary to return through the
Vacomagi's territory and take possession of some of
the Mæatæ's land.[1]   And when Constantius Chlorus
marched beyond the Northern Wall, he is described
by a Roman panegyrist as reaching the forests and
swamps of the Caledonians and the other Picts ; for,
though he may not have penetrated beyond the land
of the Verturiones, these words were probably in a
manner warranted by the Verturiones being then more
or less a mixture of Picts and Celts.   Ammianus
however, writing of the irruption of the northern
populations in 364, says that they were at that time
divided into two peoples, the Verturiones and the
Dicalydones.[2]   To the remark already made (p. 94) on
the latter name, it should be added that it is as old at
least as the time of Ptolemy, who used it, in an older
form, as the basis of the adjective which he applies to
the ocean on the west of Scotland, when he terms it
Δουηκαληδόνιος, or, as it might perhaps be transcribed,
Dwicalidonios.   To return to the Verturian Picto-
Celts, it would seem that their country had not so
completely fallen under the power of the non-Celtic
races as that of the more or less Goidelic population

[1] See Skene's " Celtic Scoland," i. p. 87, &c.
[2] Amm. Marcell., xxvii. 8.

of the central part of Cismonlane Pictland; but the
northerners had sufficient command of the country
immediately beyond the Forth to have ready
access to the Roman province. Some of their hordes
came down from the direction of Dunkeld with
many Caledonians among them, anxious to join in
their plundering expeditions; some came from the
Mearns and from the land beyond the Mounth, and
all met among the Verturian tribes, who willingly
joined them, no doubt, and then steered them clear
of the end of the Roman Wall, the Latin name of
which they taught them for the first time. And
Gildas, though probably possessed of no close ac-
quaintance with the geography of the northern part
of the island, cannot be said to have inaptly described
the Picts as a transmarine people, emerging from their
coracles to attack the province from the north.[1]
This would be about the time when the Romans left
Britain to its fate : afterwards little or nothing is known
about the Picts until the time of St. Columba in the
sixth century, when the peoples of the north appear
again, occupying the same position, politically speaking, with regard to one another as before, that is to
say, the aboriginal race was still dominant. Bede[2]
tells us that they were ruled by a most powerful
king, called Brude mac Maelchon, who was in the
ninth year of his reign when Columba came over
from Ireland, about the year 563. Adamnan, a successor of St. Columba and his biographer, gives us

[1] Mommsen's "Chron. Minora," vol. iii. 14, p. 33.
[2] See Bede, ibid. ii. 4.

to understand that the saint, on finding at Brude's court the regulus of the Orkneys, whose hostages were in Brude's hands, asked the latter to commend to the protection of his vassal certain monks of his community, who were then on a voyage in the direction of those islands. So much of the extent northwards of Brude's dominion, which had its head-quarters at a place somewhere near the site of Inverness : southwards we know that it was too great for the Dalriad Scots of Cantyre to contend with, a circumstance which probably had a good deal to do from the first with Columba's mission to the king of the Picts. There remains Cismontane Pictland, from the Forth to the neighbourhood of Stonehaven. We are nowhere expressly told that this tract was under the government of Brude, but there is hardly room for doubt. The whole subsequent history of the Pictish kingdom implies it, and especially the fact that Gartnait, who succeeded Brude as king, and without a revolution as far as we know, fixed his head-quarters at a place on the Tay, which is supposed to have been Abernethy, whither Columba thought it expedient to follow him. Thus we seem to have to do with a kingdom which had not as yet one fixed capital, and though the southern part was in the long run certain to win the preference, the fact, that the head-quarters of the king were once in the north, clearly proves that the course of conquest had not been from the Tay northwards rather than from the Ness towards the sunnier south. Further, there is a characteristic of the Pictish kingdom, which very clearly points in the direction of the Ness, in the neighbourhood of which it always existed, and where it was last heard of : we allude to the so-called Pictish succession, which was vested in the mother, while the father did not count, so to speak. Among the results of the working of that custom, as observed in the history of the Transmontane Picts, may be mentioned the fact, that the sons of the same woman succeeded one another, and that, when they failed, the sovereignty passed to the sons of a sister ; also that no son of a previous king of the Picts is recorded to have ever been made king by them ; that his race on the father's side did not matter, there being among the kings whose names are preserved a Welshman and an Angle. Such a law can hardly be regarded as the result of any other than a low view of matrimony, which must have at one time prevailed among them, and of a backward state of society, in which a man's paternity was normally uncertain ; in fact, it would appear to have been the natural growth of some such system of group marriage as that so often mentioned by ancient authors, in various startling terms, as existing in Britain. In touching on this custom, we have already hinted that in all probability it can hardly have been Celtic, but that it is rather to be attributed to the descendants of the aborigines of the island. With regard to the Pictish succession this may be asserted with still more confidence : it may even be doubted that it was at any time Aryan, while it is certain that outside the Pictish range there is in the Celtic world scarcely a trace of it known to the history either of Brythons or

Goidels. So strange did it appear to the Irish, that a legend had been invented by them to account for it some time before Bede wrote his History, in which he speaks to the effect, that the Picts, having come in a few ships from Scythia without women, succeeded in persuading the Goidels to give them wives, on the condition that the Pictish succession should, in case of doubt, be vested in the mother rather than in the father.[1]

From the time of Brude mac Maelchon, who died in 584, down to the beginning of the eighth century, our knowledge of what passed in the Pictish kingdom is very slender and imperfect : in the first place we are met by the difficulty which attaches to the history of the indefatigable Aedan, the Scot whom Columba had made king of his Dalriad people in Britain. On the whole it appears that he was bent on strengthening the power of the Dalriads by giving them the lead of the Celts opposed to the Angles, and in the next place by compelling the Picts to make concessions to them. This is probably the explanation of the fact, that he is recorded to have made an expedition to the Orkneys in 580 or 581, and also of his part in the war of the Miati, when he seems to have fought a battle in which he lost more than one of his sons and a great number of his men ; it was that of Circinn, of uncertain site, in 596. This was, it may be guessed, a struggle on the part of the Dalriad Scots, together, possibly, with the Brythons

---

[1] Bede, ib. i. 1, delicately qualifies the story and says : *ut ubi res ueniret in dubium.*

of Fortrenn, against the domination of the non-Celtic Picts, it may have offered Aedan and his men an opportunity of dealing a blow at the power of the latter. He may, however, have been at the same time following up personal claims of his own, of which nothing is known, except that his war with the Miati or Mæatæ looks like the first of the series of attempts which eventually made his descendants masters of the kingdom of the Picts. He died in 606, and peace seems to have prevailed for a long time afterwards between the Picts and the Dalriad Scots, of the former of whom we have nothing of importance to say till we come to the great victory of the Northumbrian Oswiu in 665. It is not improbable that they had joined the Celtic hosts who acted with Penda ; so when he was defeated and slain, we find Oswiu, shortly afterwards, making himself master of the greater part of the Picts, as Bede states, meaning probably the inhabitants of Cismontane Pictland. In 672 the latter were aided in an attempt to throw off the Anglian yoke by a large force from the Picts north of them, but they did not succeed. The Picts then had for king a prince named Brude, son of Bile, who was on his father's side a Welshman from Alclyde, and we hear of him operating in the extreme north, where there would seem to have been a partial revolt : he besieged a stronghold in Caithness in 680, and devastated the Orkneys in 682. His activity had, however, not been confined to the north, as he laid siege to Dunnottar, in the Mearns, in 681, where he was probably engaged against the Angles ;

then we read of him meeting with success in Fortrenn
in 683, when he appears termed in Irish chronicles
king of Fortrenn.   At length Ecgfrith, who found the
Picts assisted by the Dalriad Scots, and probably suspected that they derived aid from Ireland, sent
an army thither, which cruelly ravaged the Irish coast
from Dublin to Drogheda in 684, and in the following
year he led his forces in person to the country of the
Cismontane Picts.   The result was the battle of Dún
Nechtain, supposed to be Dunnichen in Forfarshire,
where he was slain with nearly all his men : with this
victory of Brude ended Anglian rule beyond the Forth.
Brude lived till the year 693, and the next Pictish
king of any note was Nechtan, who began to reign in
706, and forced the ecclesiastical affairs of his kingdom
into great prominence.   We left Columba among the
Cismontane Picts, at the headquarters of Gartnait, by
whom he is said to have been so effectually supported
as to silence all opposition among the tribes on the
banks of the Tay.[1] What the nature of that opposition
may have been we are not told ; probably it arose no
more from those who were still pagans than from men
who mixed paganism with Christianity.   In so far as
the Goidelic and Goidelicizing people of that region
were Christians at all, their religious ideas had been
derived from the teaching of such previous missionaries as Nynias or Ninnian, who laboured also among
the Picts of Galloway as early as the year 397.

[1] " He subdued to benediction the mouths of the fierce ones
who dwelt with Tay's high king " : see Stokes's rendering of the
Eulogy of St. Columba, *Rev. Celt.* xx. 401.

Even when Columba was busy among the Picts on the Tay his contemporary and friend, Kentigern, appears to have gone on a mission beyond the Mounth ; and that Welsh missionaries had carried on work of a lasting nature among the Transmontane Picts is proved by a group of dedications in the upper valley of the Dee, among which are found Kentigern's own name and that of Ffinan, whose church in Anglesey is called Llanffinan, while his church in Scotland gave its name to Lumphanan, a place of some note in Pictish history. Columba's successors continued that saint's work, and by the eighth century they had doubtless gained great influence in the kingdom ; but it was a Scottic church under the rule of the abbots of Iona, and it probably succeeded to a considerably less degree among the Brythons of Fortrenn than in other parts of Cismontane Pictland, that is, among the Goidelic populations. Of the latter, those who were most devoted to it were probably the people near the Tay, where the founder himself had laboured under royal protection. The Columban Church had also done a great work in Northumbria, but it had come to an end there in 664, when the Angles conformed to Rome. The same thing now threatened it in Pictland under Nechtan.[1] He was at peace with the Angles of Northumbria, and, with their example before his eyes, he ordered the

---

[1] As to this name it is to be remarked that it was in Welsh Neithon, written Naiton by Bede ; for it is characteristic of the mixture of races we have here to deal with, that the names of their kings are handed down to us sometimes in a Goidelic form, and sometimes in a Brythonic one.

observance of Easter and the tonsure of the clergy to be regulated by the then practice of the Church of Rome. This took place in the year 710 at Scone, which is supposed by that time to have become the capital and the place of the coronation stone now at Westminster. The king had the assistance of Anglian priests to carry out the change, and the Columban clergy refusing to obey were expelled in 717, when they crossed Drumalban to the country of their Scottic kinsmen. It is highly probable, however, that they had many powerful friends among Nechtan's subjects who sympathized with them and began to oppose him. At any rate we find the king himself becoming a cleric in 724, possibly not altogether from choice, as he is found to have been succeeded by a king called Drust, who was supported by a party opposed to Nechtan. Both Nechtan and Drust were, we think, non-Celtic Picts; but the former seems to have derived his principal support from the country beyond the mountains, where the expulsion of the Columban clergy was perhaps less keenly felt, while the latter appears more identified with the Cismontane Picts of Angus and Mearn. The quarrel between the Picts is noteworthy as the prelude to the fall of the power of the aboriginal race in Cismontane Pictland, and the signal for the two Celtic peoples to compete for the succession.

The leading events in point were, briefly speaking, the following :[1]—In 725, Nechtan's adherents took a

---

[1] In this chapter we have in the main followed Mr. Skene in his "Celtic Scotland," vol. i., chaps. 6, 7, and part of the succeeding one.

son of Drust prisoner, which was avenged by Drust's putting Nechtan in chains in the year following. Then came a revolution and drove Drust from his throne, which was seized by a king called Alpin, in Welsh, Elphin. On his father's side he was a great-grandson of Domnall Brecc, the grandson of Aedan, king of the Dalriad Scots of Argyle : his name, which is possibly not Celtic, suggests that his mother was of the royal family of the Picts. At the same time that he ousted Drust, his brother Eochaid secured the throne of the Dalriad Scots for himself; but in Cismontane Pictland Nechtan again emerged into secular life to win back his throne, and the complication was aggravated by the appearance of another competitor for power in the person of Aengus or Angus, son of Fergus, or, as he was called by his Brythonic subjects, among the Men of Fortrenn, Ungust son of Wurgust. He was undoubtedly a Brython, while Alpin may be surmised to have identified himself with the more purely Goidelic peoples of the central part of Cismontane Pictland, and to have possessed whatever claims to power over them, if any, Aedan, the Dalriad Scot, had long before him. The first encounter happened in 728, between Ungust and Alpin, at a place not far from the meeting of the Earn and the Tay, where Ungust won the day and possession of the whole district west of the latter river. Alpin and his Goidels were afterwards totally defeated by Nechtan at Scone, when the latter found himself again king; but in 729 a battle took place between the hosts of Ungust and Nechtan, when the latter suffered so great a defeat that Ungust then became king of the Picts. The place where this happened, being on the banks of a loch formed by the waters of the Spey, indicates that Nechtan relied on the men of that district as his most faithful subjects.

The next event was a battle between Ungust and Drust, in which Ungust was again victorious, and Drust killed. Then Ungust's son, Brude, defeated Talargan, son of Congus, one of the leaders of Alpin's party, and forced him to flee to the Scots in Argyle. But Dungal, king of the Dalriad Scots, happening to find Brude in a church on Tory Island, near the coast of Donegal, violated his sanctuary and made him prisoner, which drew on the Scots an invasion by Ungust, who put Talargan to death, and forced Dungal to flee, wounded, to Ireland. Two years later, in 736, Ungust devastated the whole country of the Scots, destroyed their capital, together with other places, and made several of their princes prisoners. Such were the straits to which the Scots were brought that Alpin, who had fought against Ungust and Nechtan in Pictland, was forced to lead the portion of the nation of the Scots of which he was the head, into the land of the Picts of Manaw, with a view probably of drawing Ungust away from Dalriada. But he was met by Talargan, brother to Ungust, at the head of the Men of Fortrenn and there defeated with a heavy loss to his forces, at a place near the Avon. It is not very clear what the exact object may have been of the course adopted

by Alpin ånd his Scots in bursting into Manaw:
it has been supposed that Ungust, as king
of the Picts beyond the Forth, had stirred the
Picts of Manaw and Galloway to revolt against the
Angles of Northumbria, whose king, Eadberht, is
mentioned as engaged in war with the Picts in 740,
when the king of Mercia took advantage of his absence
to lay waste a part of his kingdom. It may be that
the Scots had been encouraged by the Northumbrians
to invade Manaw by a promise of co-operating with
them. After his defeat, Alpin was king of the Scots
for four years, which brings us to 740, when, after
leading his men into Galloway and completely
devastating it, he there met with his death in the
neighbourhood of Loch Ryan in 741. Ungust then
completed the crushing of the Scottic kingdom, and
the country thenceforth formed a dependency of the
Picts. The part of the Scots now seems to have
devolved on the Cumbrians of Strathclyde, a fact which
appears to require as its explanation that we should
suppose them to have previously arrayed themselves
on the side of the Scots against the Picts and the
Angles, who were now at one with the Picts. It may
be that the Cumbrians had also received among them
the remains of the army of the Dalriad Scots when
they were finally dispersed, and that they found
directed against them the power of Talargan, Ungust's
brother, on the southern coast of the Firth of Forth.
At any rate, we read of a battle in 744 between the
Picts of Galloway and the Cumbrians; and the latter
suffered from Ungust and Eadberht a combined

attack which led, in 750, to the annexation to Galloway of a part of their territory and to a battle between the Cumbrians and the Picts of Manaw under the same leader who defeated Alpin, namely, Talargan, who seems to have been the king of those Picts. The Cumbrians had the best of it, and Talargan was killed; but in 756 the armies of Ungust and of the Angles made for Alclyde, and the Cumbrians had to submit to the yoke of the Angles. In the meantime those who had supported Nechtan seem to have been gathering strength in the north, and Ungust had to contend with a king, called Brude mac Maelchon, a namesake of Columba's contemporary, whose rightful representative, according to the Pictish law of succession, he may be supposed to have been, at the same time that he was probably the heir to Nechtan's claims. He also was unsuccessful, and fell in a battle against Ungust, in the Mearns, in 752. The death of the latter is not recorded as taking place till the year 761, after a reign of about thirty years, in the course of which he had allowed the monastery of Cennrigmonaid or Kilrymont—that is to say, St. Andrew's—to be founded: the death of its first abbot is recorded under the year 747.

Ungust was succeeded by his brother Brude, king of Fortrenn, who died in the year 763. Then came Cinaeth, the son of Wredech, who had in 768 to give battle in Fortrenn to Aed Finn or the White: neither of them appears from his name to have been a Brython. Most likely Aed was a Dalriad Scot reviving the claims of Alpin, and trying to rebuild the kingdom of the

Scots in Argyle: he seems to have failed, and
Cinaeth reigned over the Picts until his death in 775.
He was followed by Alpin, who was probably his
brother: the latter died in 780, and during his reign
Aed Finn also died in the year 778. At the death of
Alpin, Talargan, a son of Ungust, ascended the
throne; but this was in violation of the law of Pictish
succession, which was probably foreign to the habits
of the Brythons, to whom he belonged. So we find
besides him another king, whose name was Drust,
and whose strength presumably lay among the Transmontane Picts that clung to the female succession.
He survived Talargan, who was slain in 782, and is
described by one chronicler as king of the Picts
this side of the Mounth. Drust, who probably
reigned beyond it among the other Picts, was undoubtedly not a Brython, and was succeeded by a
man who seems to have been a Goidel—Conall, son
of Tadg, who was attacked in 789, or the year after,
by the Brythonic king of Fortrenn, whose name was
Constantine, son of Ungust. Constantine, succeeding,
became king of the Picts, while Conall fled to Argyle,
where he tried to establish himself; but in 807 Constantine asserted his sway over that region; and here
it may be added that the hopes of restoring the
Scottic kingdom of the Dalriads in Cantyre or
Argyle had been fast vanishing: Fergus, the brother
of Aed Finn, had died in 781, while three years
later, in 784, the bones of the founders, the Sons of
Erc, were carried away from Iona to be buried with
those of the kings of Ulster at Taillten, in Meath.

Now the Scandinavian pagans made their appearance on the coasts of the British Isles in 793, which was followed by such terrible devastation, that the Columban community of Iona, which was supreme over the Columban churches, both in Britain and Ireland, betook itself partly to Kells, in Meath, and partly to Dunkeld, on the Tay, where Constantine built a church for them. He died in 820, and was succeeded by his brother Ungust, who had ruled under him for some years over the province consisting of the old kingdom of the Dalriad Scots of Argyle. He died in 834, and was succeeded, in violation of the Pictish rule, by the son of a previous king, namely, Drust, son of Constantine: so we find another king reigning at the same time with him, supported perhaps by the Transmontane Picts, as was usual with them in such cases: his name was Talargan, son of Wthol. They reigned three years, but a competitor arose in the person of Alpin, a representative probably of the previous Alpin, and champion of the claims of the same house. He was victorious in a battle in 834, but before the end of the year he was defeated and slain: tradition localizes the contest in the Carse of Gowrie and Fife. After Drust and Talargan came Uven or Owen, son of Ungust, who had ruled for thirteen years over the Scots of Argyle. As he was the son of a previous king, he probably reigned only over the Cismontane Picts: this lasted only for three years, from 836 to 839; for now there came over the affairs of Pictland a great change, which was ushered in by the Danes,

who had been engaged in plundering Leinster and
parts of Ulster.   They crossed to the north of
Britain, and succeeded in giving the Men of Fortrenn
battle, in which the latter suffered a crushing defeat.
The man who reaped the advantages of this expedition and probably the one who had planned it, was the
son of Alpin, the Scot defeated and slain in 834 : his
name was Cinaeth or Kenneth, and he is usually
known as Kenneth mac Alpin.   He followed up the
defeat of the Men of Fortrenn with such success that
he soon became master of the Dalriad province in
Argyle, where probably there were still many of his
Scottic kinsmen, and after a few years' struggle he
made himself king of the Picts.   His first year is
reckoned to have been 844; and he died in 860,
leaving his family firmly established in possession of
the kingdom.

One may say, that for more than one hundred
years, beginning with the victory of Ungust in 728,
no Goidel before Kenneth had been able to possess
himself for any great length of time of the kingdom
of Scone, as that of the Picts is sometimes called ; so
his reign may be said to have commenced a new
era, that of the supremacy, not so much of the Scots
as of the Goidels generally, over the Brythonic
populations and the aboriginal peoples of the country.
The changes which accompanied this revolution were
important—Kenneth completed, among other things,
the reinstating of the Columban clergy.   It had been
begun by Constantine when he gave Dunkeld to the
family of Iona, but now a church was built there for

the relics of the founder, St. Columba; and the abbot of Dunkeld was placed at the head of the Northern Church. The first of that description, styled bishop of Fortrenn and abbot of Dunkeld, is recorded as dying in the year 865. All this had, no doubt, been well earned by the Columban clergy, as they may be supposed to have been active supporters of the cause of Kenneth's family from the time of the earlier Alpin to Kenneth's triumph. Lastly, it may be mentioned, that, whereas the kings of Fortrenn, who were also over-kings of the Picts, had usually been on good terms with the Angles of Northumbria from the time Ungust made peace with Eadberht, Kenneth is described as repeatedly invading Saxony, which means the territory of the Angles, where he burned Dunbar and Melrose. As to his other wars, we read of the Brythons, probably the Cumbrians of Strath-clyde, destroying Dunblane, and of the Danes devastating Pictland as far as Dunkeld. Before leaving this reign it may be added that writers of a subsequent period term Kenneth the first king of Scots who reigned over Pictland, and his father Alpin is likewise called by them king of Scots. Historians have set themselves the task of discovering whence the said Scots came, and have guessed that there was a general rising everywhere of the remains of the Dalriad Scots in favour of Kenneth. It must be readily granted that he was on the father's side a Dalriad Scot entitled to be king of the Scots in the narrower sense of the word, and that some of them were probably to be found both in their old territory and elsewhere, who may have readily joined him. But surely the Scots sought for were always in the heart of Pictland on the banks of the Tay, the warmest adherents of the Columban Church, and the lineal descendants of the men who had undergone defeat with the earlier Alpin in 728. We hear of Kenneth and Alpin's Scots mostly because writers who used the Latin language called them *Scotti*. By this time the proper rendering of that word, however, is Gaels or Goidels, and the chronicles not written in Latin call them such, as does also the Pictish chronicle, though written in Latin, when it speaks of *Goedeli* instead of *Scotti*, in mentioning the succession established by them in the person of Kenneth's brother.[1] The accession of this family means, in a word, the supremacy of the Picto-Goidels over the other nations of Pictland, the Verturian Brythons, and the non-Celtic Picts, the former of whom now began rapidly to disappear, as a people, from history. It is right, however, to say that besides a certain Goidelic nucleus in the Tay valley and the Goidelic element among the ancient Dumnonii there was probably very little that could be racially described as Goidelic at all in North Britain: so the word Goidel comes largely to mean here one who spoke Goidelic and accepted the customs of the Goidel, for instance, in the matter of the Celtic succession as distinguished from the succession usual among the Northern Picts.

Kenneth was succeeded, not by his son, but by his

[1] Skene's " Chronicles of the Picts and Scots," p. 8.

brother Domnall or Donald, in accordance with the Celtic rule of succession known to history as tanistry, whereby Kenneth's son came in only after his father's brother. The establishment of this custom is spoken of in the Pictish chronicle as first effected in the time of Donald, and it is referred to in the passage already mentioned, as the Rights and Laws of the Kingdom of Aed, in allusion to the Dalriad Scot of that name who died in 778, after trying to set up the old kingdom of the Scots of Argyle. Donald's reign was a short one, as we find Constantine, son of Kenneth, beginning to reign in 863. Passing by quarrels with the Cumbrians, and struggles with the Norsemen, we find Constantine defeated by the Danes in a great battle in which he fell in the year 876, together with a great many of those who were most loyal to his house. He was succeeded by his brother Aed who died in 878, killed, it is said, by his own people, a statement which introduces a contest for the throne, in which the Brythonic element won again for a time a kind of victory. This took place in the person of Eochaid, son of Rhun, King of Alclyde, for the mother of Eochaid—his name is not recorded in its Brythonic form—was sister to Constantine and daughter to Kenneth. With him was associate d as his tutor and governor, a man whose name was Girg : it is given also as Girc, Grig, Girig, and Ciric. Whether the latter ever filled the office of king tradition does not clearly state, but it is noteworthy that it connects him with the district of the Mearns, while Eochaid was probably supported by the Brythons of

Fortrenn. Bernicia appears to have been now over-run by the Picts and the monastery of Lindisfarne plundered. Girg is said to have reannexed to the kingdom of Strathclyde the Cumbrian district south of the Solway, and also to have liberated the Picts of Galloway from the yoke of the Angles; but none of these things are authenticated, though they may well have taken place at this time, as North-umbria, after Eadberht ceased to reign in 758, and his son and successor shortly fell at the hands of his own people, passed out of the power of Ida's family into confusion, which was afterwards grievously deepened by the Danes. As to the Pictish kingdom we seem to have now to do with a coalition against the dynasty of Kenneth mac Alpin; and the real relation in which Girg probably stood to Eochaid was that of a non-Celtic king of Pictish descent, wielding the power of the Pictish nation, with Eochaid ruling among the Brythons of Fortrenn more or less subject to him. Lastly, these two kings of Pictland are represented as trying to strengthen their position by conciliating the Scottish Church, which they freed from the various exactions and services to which it had till then been liable. Even this, however, did not avail them against the Scottic, or, more accurately speaking, the Goidelic party, and they were expelled in 889, when Donald, son of Constantine, became king, and the succession was firmly re-established in the male line of Kenneth mac Alpin. Kenneth and his suc-cessors had hitherto been called kings of the Picts, while the country over which they ruled was the kingdom of Scone, or else the land of the Picts, for which *Pictania* and *Pictinia* were invented by the chroniclers; but in Donald's time, or not long later, this seems to have begun to get out of fashion; and we find one chronicle[1] in recording his death, which took place in the year 900, calling him king of Alban.

The next king was Constantine, son of Aed, who was brother to Donald's father. He reigned forty years, during which he tried to consolidate his kingdom by putting the different churches on a footing of equality as to their privileges and rights, at the same time that an end was made of the supremacy of Dunkeld, while the bishop of Kilrymont or St. Andrew's came to be called the bishop of Alban. Now at length Constantine's subjects began to get some rest from the Norsemen and the Danes; but they were destined ere long to have to fight with the king of England: as soon as Æthelstán, who began to reign in 925 found himself firmly established on his throne, he set about annexing Northumbria to his other provinces, and in 926 got possession of Deira, whence he expelled the Danish prince who had the upper hand there. The latter sought the alliance of Constantine: Æthelstán anticipated this by invading Alban by land and sea in the year 933, when his troops are said to have made their way as far north as Dunnottar in the Mearns and another place called Wertermor, by which was probably meant the plain of Fortrenn. Thus they would seem to have ravaged

[1] See the Annals of Inisfallen, in Skene's " Chr. of the Picts and Scots," p. 169.

two of the most important provinces of Alban:
three years later Constantine and his men, together
with the Cumbrians and the Danes from different
parts of Britain and Ireland, met in the north of
England at a place called Brunnanburh, and fought a
great battle with Æthelstán in 937, when they were
utterly defeated by the English. Æthelstán died
in 940, leaving his throne to his son Edmund, and
Constantine was succeeded in 942 by Maelcoluim or
Malcolm, son of Donald. He began his reign by
trying to assert his power over the peoples beyond
the river Spey, where considerable portions of the
country had long been subject to the Norsemen But
a more important event was yet to come; Northumbria had for some time been in the power of
Danish princes who were kings of Dublin, and
in the habit of deriving assistance from their kinsmen in Ireland. They had access to Northumbria
through the country of the Cumbrians, who seem to
have been only too willing to help them against the
Angles, as were also probably the Picts of Galloway.
So Edmund harried Cumbria in 945, and gave it
together with Galloway to Malcolm, on the understanding that he, who was connected by marriage
with Anlaf Cuaran, the most irrepressible of the
Danish Wickings who troubled the country at this
time, should give assistance to the English by land
and sea against the Danes. In 946 Edmund was
succeeded by Edred, who proceeded to reduce
Northumbria under his power; and, after various
contests in that kingdom, we read of it accepting

Edred's rule in 954: he then made it an earldom. As to its extent towards the north, the Pictish Chronicle tells us, that, in the reign of Indulph over Alban, from 954 to 962, the English gave Edinburgh up to him, so that he now ruled as far south on the eastern side of the island as the Lothian river Esk. But, instead of there being one earldom of Northumbria, Bernicia was made soon after 966 into an earldom and Deira into another. Then Kenneth, son of Malcolm, who was king of Alban from 971 to 995, among the first things he did, invaded the more northern earldom as far as the confines of Deira: this he repeated the year after, carrying the earl away as his prisoner; and it has been asserted that Edgar, the king of England, gave a great part of Bernicia to the king of Alban as a fief of his crown. But there is no proof, and the only fact which is tolerably clear is, that those northern kings who were in the habit of invading it, must have believed that they had some sort of hereditary right to it, the grounds of which are no longer known. In the year 1000 Æthelred, king of England, ravaged the country of the Cumbrians, but did not succeed in wresting them from the king of Alban; and we find them giving valuable aid to Malcolm, son of Kenneth, who reigned from 1005 to 1034, and continued his family's practice of invading Bernicia. This he did first in 1006, when he laid siege to Durham, and suffered a serious defeat. But now a great event occurred in the year 1014, to wit the battle of Clontarf, near Dublin, where the Danes of Ireland, and their allies from Britain and the smaller islands,

met with a crushing defeat. Their power was considerably reduced in consequence not only in Ireland
but in Britain also; and Malcolm was at length able
to extend his sway towards the north and north-west
of Scotland. In 1018 he succeeded, with the aid
of the Cumbrians, in bringing to the field such a
force for the invasion of Bernicia, that he gave battle
to the Northumbrians at Carham, near the Tweed,
and defeated them so completely that all the land of
the Angles north of that river was ceded to him, and
it became for the first time the boundary between
England and the northern kingdom. For this province he is said to have done homage in 1031 to
Cnut, the king of England. Malcolm died in 1034;
and he was the last male descendant of Kenneth mac
Alpin.

The kingdom then devolved on Donnchad or Duncan, the son of a daughter of Malcolm. He was an
unfortunate prince, whose troubles began with an
attempt by the earl of Bernicia to recover the district ceded by his predecessor to Duncan's grandfather, and by his invading Cumbria in the year
1038, which induced Duncan to lead a large army
to lay siege to Durham, where he met with a dis-
astrous defeat. He was still more unlucky beyond
the Forth, where, however, next to nothing is
known of his history. Since writers such as Simeon
of Durham altogether ignore him as king of Alban, it
may be doubted whether he ever possessed much real
power there; he died, probably, in the attempt to
acquire it, being slain in the year 1040 by Macbeth,

the head of the Transmontane Picts, who bore the title of mórmaer or grand steward of Moray. As the latter is said to have been Duncan's general, it would seem that Duncan had tried to conciliate him, and to attach to himself one who was practically independent of him. The circumstances under which Macbeth slew Duncan are unknown; but, as it appears to have happened at a place near Elgin, it may be regarded as the result of an attempt on Duncan's part to reduce him to submission : the result was that Macbeth mounted the throne of Alban and occupied it for no less than 17 years. For a long time the Norsemen had been in possession, not only of the Orkneys and Shetlands, but also of the north and west of the mainland : the most powerful of them at this time was one Thorfinn, who was on his mother's side, like Duncan, a grandson of Malcolm, from whom he had received the title of earl when he was very young. One of the first things Macbeth did was to try to force Thorfinn to pay tribute to him as king; and an old Norse story called the Jarla Saga,[1] which makes no allusion to Duncan, but speaks of Macbeth as Karl Hundason, or Karl Hound's Son, gives an account of the war which ensued. Not only did Macbeth's repeated attempts to conquer Thorfinn completely fail, but

---

[1] A critical edition of this and the other Orkney Sagas, prepared by Dr. Vigfusson for the Master of the Rolls, has been in type since 1875, but it is not yet published : thanks to the kindness of a friend, the author had the use of the Norse text some years ago.

the latter carried the war into Moray, nor did he cease before he had cruelly ravaged the country as far as Fife, when Macbeth may be supposed to have been obliged to come to terms with him. The sagas magnify Thorfinn's power, and speak of his possessing no less than nine earldoms in Scotland ; but the details they give tend to show that he had nothing much to do afterwards with Macbeth's kingdom, at least until the latter wanted his aid, and that he settled down to the ordinary life of a Wicking, spending his winters in the Orkneys, and his summers in harrying the western coasts of England, together with Wales and Ireland. Not only did Thorfinn continue at peace with Macbeth, but he was induced by the latter to give him very valuable aid in resisting the attack which the party of Malcolm, son of Duncan, was preparing ; the result was a great battle in 1054, but it fell short of dislodging Macbeth, who seems to have had the united support of the people of Alban, and it was only in 1057 that Malcolm, after having been in possession for some time of the country south of the Forth, was able to drive him over the Mounth and to slay him in battle at Lumphanan in Marr, or the district between the Dee and the Don. At Macbeth's death, the prince who should be mórmaer of Moray was set up as his successor, but he was killed after a few months by Malcolm at Essy in Strathbolgy, on the north-west boundary of the present county of Aberdeen.

Macbeth was not of the family of Kenneth mac Alpin, but his wife was ; for she belonged to a branch of it, the head of which Duncan's grandfather had thought expedient to kill, lest he might some day stand in the grandson's way to the throne: that Macbeth made the best of his wife's pedigree appears probable from the fact that, in a grant[1] of land by him and his wife to the Church, they are respectively entitled king and queen of Scots. But the descent of Macbeth's wife, and the lack of all historical proofs that he was a worse tyrant than the other princes of his time, do not suffice to remove the difficulty which historians have found in understanding how an usurper was allowed to seat himself so readily and so firmly on Duncan's throne. This is, however, a difficulty which is in a great measure of their own creating, as Macbeth was not a mere usurper; he himself probably considered that he inherited the right of Brude mac Maelchon and of Nechtan to the throne, a right which was even of older date than that of Kenneth mac Alpin. In the interval of nearly 200 years, from the beginning of Kenneth's reign to the death of Duncan, it is not improbable that the two Celtic races in Cismontane Alban had been rapidly amalgamating together: in fact, we read but little about the men of Fortrenn causing trouble to the kings of Alban after their great defeat by the Danes and Kenneth's accession; and it is remarkable that the crozier of St. Columba, which served the Goidels as their

[1] "Registr. Prior. S. Andree," p. 114, Skene's "Celtic Scot.," i. p. 406, and Reeves's "Culdees," pp. 125, 126. Compare Herbert in the "Irish Nennius," pp. lxxviii.-xc.

standard, is recorded to have been borne before
the men of Fortrenn in a battle in which they prayed
for his aid against the Danes in Strathearn and vanquished them. This was in the year 904, in the
reign of that Constantine who undertook to put
the churches of different origins on a footing of
equality within his kingdom. By the time of Macbeth, the Goidels and Brythons of Alban might,
perhaps, practically be treated all alike as Goidels.
But not so the non-Celtic tribes ; for, though the
Transmontane Picts had been able to rule down to
the Forth, the Celtic kings on the banks of the Tay
were scarcely ever able to exercise much power beyond the mountain barriers, and, though the Goidelic
language may have been steadily gaining ground
among the nearest non-Celtic tribes, the process of
amalgamating the two races must have been a comparatively slow and tedious one. This is fully borne
out by what we read ; for every now and then we
find the men of the Mearns acting as it were in
the vanguard of the Transmontane Picts against the
princes of the Kenneth dynasty who quartered themselves amongst them. Thus it was the former, probably, that put forward Girg in 878 and supported
him ; then Donald, son of Constantine, fell at Dunnottar in their country, in the year 900, though we are
not expressly told that they killed him ; but Malcolm,
son of Donald, is distinctly stated in the Pictish
Chronicle to have been slain by the men of the
Mearns at Fetteresso, in their country, in 954. They
had also probably something to do with the death of

Kenneth, son of Malcolm, which took place at Fetter-cairn, in the Mearns, in 995, through the treachery we are told, of Finnola, daughter of Cunchar, earl of the province of Angus : she is made to appear as the avenger of her only son, killed by Kenneth at Dunsinnan in the range of the Sidlaw Hills. Nor is it improbable that the men of the Mearns and the other Picts took a leading part in the wars of succession, of which we have glimpses in the year 997, when Constantine, son of Culen, was killed after he had reigned only three years; and in 1004, when another king of Alban, Kenneth, son of Dub, was slain. The chief of one branch of the Kenneth dynasty seems to have usually quartered himself in Fortrenn, while the other is repeatedly identified with the Mearns, which he most likely tried to treat as Fortrenn had been treated; but here the resistance was prolonged, probably owing to the aid the inhabitants derived from the Picts in their back-ground. In what light the dominant race regarded both Fortrenn and the Mearns may be seen from certain Irish legends calling them its sword-lands,[1] a term applied also in the Pictish Chronicle to the Mearns. At length we hear no more of the men of the latter district, but the antagonism probably continued between the people of Cismontane Alban and those beyond the Mounth : it was no doubt a much more languid antagonism, as the authority of the kings reigning over the former was seldom able to make

[1] See Skene's " Chr. of the Picts and Scots," pp. 10, 319, 329.

itself appear much more than a name in the north,
which may have required of the most powerful of
the northern Picts that he should content himself
with the title of mórmaer or grand steward.
Several of Macbeth's immediate predecessors seem
to have gone further, and to have claimed to be
independent of the king reigning in Cismontane
Alban : thus Finlaig, who was killed in 1020, is called
by one chronicler king of Alban ;[1] while another,[1]
who died in 1029, is called so by another chronicler.
Moreover, when Cnut received the homage of Malcolm,
he obtained that also of the Wicking at the head of a
petty kingdom in Argyle, and of a prince, whose
name is given in the Saxon Chronicle as Mælbæthe
or Mealbæaðe, which has been mended by some
into Macbeth. If, however, it is to be altered, it is
only into Maelbeth, a real name of the same class as
the former, and borne probably by a predecessor
of Macbeth's. Whichever of the two he was, he
appears to have regarded himself, and to have been
regarded by the king of England, as independent of
Malcolm ; and his dominions may be supposed to
have taken in all Transmontane Alban except a
part of Argyle, and a portion of the north which
was, together with the Orkneys, doubtless in the
power of the Norsemen at that time. So, apart from the
relations in which Macbeth personally stood to Duncan,
and of which we know next to nothing, his becoming
king in his stead was not so much an act of usurpation

[1] See the Annals of Ulster and T'gernach respectively in
Skene's " Chr. of the Picts and Scots," pp. 368, 377.

as a forcible assertion for a time, and that not a very
short one either, of the supremacy of his people over
those of Cismontane Alban. Of course the death of
Macbeth and his unfortunate successor, Lulach, did
not put an end to the aspirations of the northern
Picts. For a time, it is true, we hear little of them,
but in the reign of king David, Angus, the son of
Lulach's daughter—a succession not correctly Pictish
—having become mórmaer of Moray, made a formidable attempt to secure the throne of Scotland ;
but it ended in his defeat and death in the year
1130. Still later in the reign of David's grandson,
Malcolm, we read of severe measures being taken in
1160 to reduce to quietness the people of Moray,
and of grants of their lands being made by the king
to the barons by whom he surrounded himself.

The amalgamation already indicated of the Celtic
peoples of Alban during the period of nearly two
centuries from the accession of Kenneth mac Alpin
to that of Macbeth must have added to the importance of the Goidelic element in the kingdom ; so
its heads now began to have in Latin the title of
king of *Scotia* and of *rex Scottorum*, that is to say,
king of Goidels, though it is rendered oftener by
the ambiguous phrase "king of Scots." This,
it need hardly be said, had little to do with the
connexion of Kenneth and his ancestors with the
Dalriad Scots, as it seems to have become the fashion
only in the tenth century, and was followed in the
ensuing one, by Macbeth among others. But at the
same time that the name Goidel extended itself to all

peoples speaking Celtic in Cismontane Alban and the province of Dalriada in Argyle, the term Cruthni, or Picts may be supposed to have gained in definiteness of meaning by becoming more closely identified with the Transmontane Picts, who probably had the most right to it from the first. To what extent Goidels had interm xed with these descendants of the neolithic inhabitants of Britain it is impossible to say; nor is one as yet able to trace in Scotch topography the retreat, step by step, of their language, as it remains an unknown tongue. We find, however, that in Columba's time there were men of rank on the mainland opposite the island of Skye, with whom he could not converse in Goidelic, as there were also peasants of the same description in the neighbourhood of king Brude's head-quarters near the river Ness, while there is no hint that the saint found any linguistic difficulty in making his way at that monarch's court. So it would seem that Goidelic was already asserting itself in that district, and that it was not very long ere it had made much progress in the region east of the Ness, though the aboriginal language may be supposed not to have died out of the country for some time after the Danes and the Norsemen began to plunder these islands. That the Goidelic idiom vigorously spread itself in all directions under the Kenneth dynasty might be expected from the nature of the case; and as against the Brythonic dialects this is amply borne out by the topography of Scotland. A few instances, some of which will bring us south of the Forth, will

suffice to show the kind of evidence they afford.
Verturiones was probably the traditional form of
a Brythonic word, but the later one of Fortrenn
is Goidelic, and we do not even know what the
later Brythonic form may have exactly been, though
we seem to have traces of it in the *Werter-morum*
already cited from the pen of Simeon of Durham.[1]
Next may be mentioned the name of Kentigern,
which would be pronounced by his kinsmen in his
time Cunotigernios, or the like, in the first part of
which the Goidels discerned the word for hound and
called the saint *In Glas Chú* or The Grey Hound:[2]
though he was a Brython, and though the place where he
settled finally was in the land of the Cumbrians, it is
now known only by his Goidelic name of *Glas Chú*
as Glasgow.   Lastly may be mentioned the name of
the river Nith, called in Ptolemy's Geography *Novios*,
which, if Celtic, was the word for new in all the
dialects ; but the Brythons treated it as Novïos or
Noviios, and eventually made it into the Welsh
newydd, new ; and it is from some stage of this last
that we get *Nith;* but it could only happen through
the medium of the men who spoke Goidelic.   In this
instance they were probably the Picts of Galloway, but
the same thing appears to have occurred north of the
Forth in the name of a stream flowing into Largo Bay
in Fifeshire, called Newburn, but which is said to have
been formerly known as Nithbren.[3]

[1] See the " Mon. Hist. Brit.," p. 686, C., and note *k*.
[2] Pinkerton's " Vitæ Sanctorum Scotiæ," pp. 195-
[3] See Skene's " Celtic Scotland," i. p. 133.

So much for the triumph of the Goidelic element in the North: a word must now be said of its ultimate defeat and retreat to the Highlands. After the crown came again into the possession of Kenneth mac Alpin's descendants at Macbeth's death, it remained with them until the direct line became extinct by the death of the Maid of Norway in 1290, when it proved the bone of contention between the king of England and the Norman barons connected in the female line with the house of Kenneth—we have said Norman barons, for the dynasty had long since become English, and surrounded itself with a host of Normans, Angles, and Flemings. This may be said to have begun when Malcolm married Margaret, sister of Edgar Ætheling, the son and heir of the English king Edmund, after he had been obliged to flee with his mother and sisters to Scotland in 1068. The southern influence went on increasing until the court in the time of David, who began to reign in 1124 after being educated in England in all the ways of the Normans, was filled with his Anglian and Norman vassals. He is accordingly regarded as the first wholly feudal king of Scotland, and the growth of feudalism continued at the expense of the power and position of the Celtic princes, who saw themselves snubbed and crowded out to make room for the king's barons, who had grants made to them of land here and there wherever it was worth having. The result was a deep-seated discontent, which every now and then burst into a flame of open revolt on the part of the rightful owners of the soil; and it

smouldered long afterwards as the well-known hatred
of the clans of the Highlands for the farmers of the
Lowlands, of the Gael, as Sir Walter Scott puts it,
for the stranger and the Saxon, who was regarded as
having reft the native of the land which was his birth-
right. It was doubtless the force that finally welded
Celts and non Celts together into one people, known
to us in modern times as the Gaels of the Highlands
and Islands of Scotland. As to the language, we
read that when Margaret, in 1074, called a council
to inquire into the abuses which had crept into the
Church, Gaelic was the only language the clergy
could speak, so that King Malcolm, her husband,
acted as her interpreter. But the predominance of
the Celtic element seems to have passed away with
the reign of Donald Bán, who, though brother to
Malcolm, allowed the Scots, when they made him
king in 1093, to drive out all the English whom his
brother had introduced ; but after some intervals of
power he was defeated in 1097 by Malcolm and
Margaret's son Edgar, under whom, together with
his brothers, the English element was much more
than reinstated, as every encouragement was held
forth by them and their feudal successors to Englishmen, Flemings, and Normans to settle in Scotland.
At the time, however, of the War of Independence,
Gaelic appears to have still reached down to Stirling
and Perth, to the Ochil and Sidlaw Hills, while north-
east of the Tay it had as yet yielded to English or
Broad Scotch only a very narrow strip along the coast.

One of the lessons of this chapter is that the

Goidel, where he owned a fairly fertile country, as in
the neighbourhood of the Tay, showed that he was
not wanting in genius for political organization ; and
the history of the kingdom of Scotland, as modelled
by Kenneth mac Alpin and his descendants, warns
us not to give ear to the spirit of race-weighing
and race-damning criticism that jauntily discovers, in
what it fancies the character of a nation, the reasons
why that nation has not achieved results never fairly
placed within its reach by the accidents either of
geography or history. Considering, also, how little
the general tenor of recent study has taught one
to expect from the non-Aryan races of Europe, it is
worth while recalling the testimony which history
bears to the political capacity of the aboriginal inhabitants of Britain, in that part of it where they
were able to hold their own ; for the kingdom which
Kenneth mac Alpin wrested from the Brythons of
Fortrenn was, so far as can be gathered, neither
Celtic nor Aryan in its origin.   The trouble the
non-Celtic Picts were able to give the Romans and
the Romanizing Brythons has often been dilated
upon by historians, who have seldom dwelt on the
much more remarkable fact, that a power, with its
head-quarters in the neighbourhood of the Ness, had
been so organised as to make itself obeyed from the
Orkneys to the Mull of Cantyre, and from Skye to
the mouth of the Tay, as early as the middle of the
sixth century.   It is important to bear this in mind
in connexion with the question, how far the earlier
Celtic invaders of this country may have mixed with

the ancient inhabitants, since it clearly shows that there was no such a gulf between them as would make it impossible or even difficult for them to amalgamate. It is but natural to suppose that the Goidelic race has been greatly modified in its character by its absorption of this ancient people of the Atlantic seaboard.

CHAPTER VI.

THE ETHNOLOGY OF EARLY BRITAIN.

THE most ancient name now supposed to have been
given to these islands was that of Cassiterides, and to
Britain that of Albion.   The latter occurs in a treatise
respecting the world, which used to be ascribed to
Aristotle : it is now regarded as the work of somebody who lived later.   We then meet with it after a
long interval in the Natural History written by Pliny,
who died in the year 79 : he only remarks that
Albion was the name given this country when all the
islands of our group were called Britanniæ ; but it
continued to be the habit of Greek writers, even long
after his time, to treat Britain simply as one of a
number of islands, to all of which they applied the
adjective Bretannic, or, according to their more accurate spelling, Pretanic.   After Britain had been divided
and sub-divided, by the Romans, they not unfrequently
spoke of the province in the plural as Britanniæ, but
Pliny could not have had that in his mind : most
likely he was thinking of the Πρετανικαὶ Νῆσοι of Greek
authors.   There is, however, another allusion to Britain
which seems to carry us much farther back, though it
has usually been ill understood.   It occurs in the story
of the labours of Hercules, who, after securing the cows
of Geryon, comes from Spain to Liguria, where he is
attacked by two giants, whom he kills before making

his way to Italy. Now, according to Pomponius Mela, the names of the giants were Albiona and Bergyon, which one may, without much hesitation, restore to the forms of Albion and Iberion, representing, undoubtedly, Britain and Ireland, the position of which in the sea is most appropriately symbolized by the story making them sons of Neptune or the sea-god. The geographical difficulty of bringing Albion and Liguria together is completely disposed of by the fact that Britain and Ireland were once thought by Greek and Latin writers to have been separated from Spain and Gaul by only a very narrow channel ; not to mention that it is hardly known how far Liguria may have reached towards the west and north, or even whether the Loire—in Latin, Liger—may not have got that name as a Ligurian river : it is described by Vibius Sequester as dividing the Celts from the Aquitanians.[1]   In some other allusions to this story nothing is found that can be made out to refer to Ireland, and in one of them the second giant is called Ligys, who doubtless represented the Ligurian race. In some form or other the story can be traced as far back as the time of the Greek tragedian, Æschylus,[2] in the sixth century before the Christian era, though it is impossible to say when the names of the giants who attacked Hercules were introduced, or when they assumed the forms which may be guessed from the manuscripts of Mela. Even in the time of Pliny, Albion, as the name of the island, had fallen out

[1] See Elton's " Origins of English History," p. 25.
[2] It is met with in a fragment of the " Prometheus Unbound."

of use in the case of Latin authors ; but it was not so
with the Greeks, or with the Celts themselves, at any
rate those of the Goidelic branch ; for it is probably right to suppose that we have but the same
word in the Irish and Scotch Gaelic *Alba*, genitive
Alban, the kingdom of Alban or Scotland beyond the
Forth.   Albion would be a form of the name according to the Brythonic pronunciation of it, and between
the latter and Alban there is precisely the same difference
of vowel as one finds between the genitive of the Latin
word *oratio*, prayer, namely *orationis*, and the *orthan*
which the Irish made of it when they borrowed
it into their own language.   It would thus appear
that the name Albion is one that has been restricted
to a corner of the island, to the whole of which it
once applied.   If so, we ought to be able to
indicate an intermediate point in this retreat, and we
can : in a work associated with Cormac, a learned
Irishman of the ninth century, the name Alban is
found given to a part of Britain which extended to
the Ictian Sea or the English Channel ;[1] nor does
the author of it appear to have been the only Irish
writer [2] who has spoken of Alban as reaching so far.
Cormac goes on to specify that within his Alban were

[1] " Cormac's Glossary," published in English by Stokes (Cal-
cutta, 1868), *s v.* Mug-éime, p. 111.

[2] See the MS of Duald Mac Firbis, quoted by Reeves in
his Adamnan's Life of St. Columba, p. 145.   Add to these
instances a passage to which Dr. Stokes has called my attention
in the Book of Leinster, fo. 29a, line 43, where the peoples of
Alba are described as Saxons, Welshmen, and Picts : see
also the verse of the *Duan Albanach* quoted in " The Welsh
People," p. 115.

situated the town of Glastonbury and an unidentified fort of the Cornish Brythons. Thus it would
seem that at the time he referred to, approximately
the end of the Roman occupation, the name Alban
meant all those portions of the west and north of
Britain which his kinsmen, the Goidels of this island,
had been wont to call their own. The name has
not been identified for certain in the dialects of the
Brythons, and it is probable that they were not the
race that gave it to the island ; it is more likely that
they only learnt it from the Goidels whom they found
in possession. It need hardly be added that its
meaning is utterly unknown, in spite of guesses both
new and old : possibly the word is not Celtic.

Next comes the question whence the name Britain
is derived. This, together with the Medieval Welsh
Brytaen, is to be traced back to the Latin form,
which was most commonly written Britannia : and
this in its turn appears to have been suggested to the
Romans by *Britanni*: the Greeks adopted it but slowly
and sparingly. When they did use it the spelling was
ordinarily that of Βρεττανία. On the other hand, the
Welsh is *Ynys Prydain*, " the Island of Prydain,"
which is not to be regarded as etymologically connected with it, but rather as a variant of *Prydyn*,
which will be brought under the reader's notice by
and by. Its people were known to the Romans as
Britanni, and this term it was that suggested the
word Britannia to denote their country, which would
seem to have come into existence not long before
the time of Julius Cæsar, when Britain first began

seriously to occupy the heads and arms of the
Romans; at any rate, Cæsar was one of the first
authors to make regular use of the term, though it
occurs once in the writings of Diodorus Siculus, who
lived in his time and that of Augustus, spending
much of his life at Rome; but he wrote in Greek, and
in this matter he followed as a rule the custom of
his countrymen, while we find Cicero, as well as his
brother, who accompanied Cæsar to Britain, using
the word Britannia so freely as to suggest that they
knew of no other name for it. As we have thus
traced *Britain* to the Latin *Britannia*, and the
latter to the Latin name of the people, it will be
asked what about that name itself? Its oldest form,
as used by the Romans, was *Britanni*, which they
regarded as belonging to the set *Britannus*, *Britanna*,
Britannum, to which might be added *Britannicus*,
and the like. Here the practical identity between
the Latin and Greek forms makes it probable that
it was from or through the Greeks of Marseilles that
the Romans first heard of these islands. This is not
all, for the Latin *Brittanni* and especially the Greek
Βρεττανοί, have their exact counterpart in the Medieval
Irish plurals Bretain, genitive Bretan, which had at times
to function as the name both of the Brythons and of
the island. It is to be noticed that neither Βρεττανοί
or Britanni, nor the Irish Bretain has anything corresponding to it in the dialects of the Brythons themselves. From whom, then, did the Greeks hear the
word which served as the basis of their names for
Britain and its people? It cannot have been from

the Brythonic peoples of the south-east of the island,
or any, perhaps, of the Gauls of the Continent : it
was probably from the natives of the south-west who
brought their tin to market, and in whose country the
only Celtic speech in use was as yet Goidelic.   But,
while the earliest allusions of the ancients to Britain
take us back near the time of Pytheas, there is no
distinct evidence of any direct communication existing
then, or for a long time afterwards, between Dumnonia
and the Continent.   This brings us to the conclusion already stated, that the people of the south-west
conveyed their tin eastwards to some point on the
coast, to be there sold to foreign merchants ; the
latter were probably, in the main, Greek traders from
Marseilles.   When, however, the Romans came to
Britain they learnt the name which the Brythons gave
themselves in the south-east of the island, and this
was not Britanni or Brettani, but Brĭttŏnes, singular
Brĭtto.   It is the name which all the Celts who have
spoken a Brythonic language in later times own in
common ; among the Kymry it becomes Brython,
which is one of the names they still give themselves,
and from which they derive the word Brythoneg,
one of their names for the Welsh language.   This,
in old Cornish, was Brethonec, and meant the
Brythonic dialect of Wales and Cornwall after
Goidelic had been chased away, while in Breton the
word assumes the form Brezonek, and means the Brythonic language spoken in Lesser Britain.   So, when
one wants to speak collectively of this linguistic group
of Celts from the Clyde to the neighbourhood of the

Loire, confusion is best avoided by calling them by
some such name as Brythons and Brythonic, leaving
the words Britain, British, and Britannic for other uses,
including among them the exigencies of the Englishman, who, in his more playful moods, condescends to
call himself a Briton. The traditional Latin spelling
of the earlier name seems to have been incontestably
Britanni, while both the Brythonic and the Goidelic
forms, also the French *Bretagne*, prove beyond doubt
that it was etymologically entitled to the *tt* allowed to
the other form Brittones, though some editors are
pleased to treat this as Brītones, for which there seems
to be no special reasons but their own perversity : *Brittones* occurs often enough as the spelling in ancient
manuscripts, and usually in inscriptions. The word
is first used in Roman literature by Juvenal and
Martial; but the more the Romans became familiar
with Britain and its leading Celtic peoples the more
the form *Brittones* may be said to have gained on
that of *Britanni*, and it seems to have reacted on
the spelling of the latter and the kindred word
Britannia, which began to be not unfrequently written
with *tt* in the time of Commodus. This continued
on the coins of that emperor and his successors
until the victory over Britain ceased to be commemorated by such means in the time of Carausius,
whose coins in consequence give us no information on
this point. A rare medallion[1] of Commodus goes so

[1] There is one, we believe, in the British Museum, and Sir
John Evans possesses another, which he kindly allowed the
author to inspect some years ago.

far as to give us the theoretically correct spelling
Brittania, with the consonants as given by Greek
writers; but the change of spelling is probably not
to be ascribed to their example so much as to the
analogy of the synonymous *Brittones* or *Brettones*.
From the writings of such men as Bede, Nennius,
and the chroniclers, the form *Britanni* may be said to
have been driven out by that of *Brittones* or *Brettones :*
of the two the latter alone can have been regarded
by them as a living word, the other, *Britanni*, having
passed away with the Roman occupation and the
Roman empire.

So much as to the spelling and the history of these
words, but what did they originally mean ? The
usual way to explain them is to suppose them of
the same origin as the Welsh *brîth*, spotted parti-
coloured, feminine *braith* and to find in them a reference to the painting or tattooing of the body already
alluded to more than once.   Any one, however, who
knows the elements of Celtic phonology will at once
see that *brîth*, and *braith*, which are represented in Old
Irish by *mrecht* or *brecht*, can have nothing to do with
Brython or the related forms. So far as we know, the
only Celtic words which can be of the same origin
with them are the Welsh vocables *brethyn*, cloth, and
its congeners. In a manuscript of the ninth century
we meet with the simpler Welsh form brith,[1] which
would now be written bryth, and as it there enters

---

[1] See the Welsh glosses published by Stokes in the "Transactions of the Philological Society for 1860-1861," p. 210, and in
Kuhn's "Beitræge," iv. p. 393.

into the plural compound mapbrith, and occurs as a gloss on the Latin word cunabula, meaning a baby's swaddling-clothes, the singular implied must have been either *brath* or *breth* The connexion may be seen still more clearly on Irish ground, where *bratt* or *brat* means a cloth, a cloak, or a sail, and *brattán*, a little cloak, while from the former a derivative *bretnais* was formed, which in Cormac's time, had two distinct meanings: when the root-word was taken simply as relating to cloth or clothing, *bretnais* meant a thing connected with clothing—namely, a brooch ;[1] but when it referred to the national name of the Brythons it meant a thing connected with them— namely, their language,[2] which in the case Cormac was speaking of, happened to be the Brythonic tongue of the people of Cornwall in his time. It would, then, appear that the word Brython and its congeners meant a clothed or cloth-clad people. But a national name of such a nature would have little meaning unless they had lived some time or other near another people that wore little or no clothing, or else clothing of a very different material and make. If the first people called Brittones could be regarded as the first Celtic invaders of Britain, the name might be regarded as meant to distinguish them from the neolithic natives whom they found in possession, and whose clothing may have consisted of the skins of the animals they killed ; but as no Goidels, in the lin-

---

[1] It may, however, be that *bretnais* in this sense is a compound, meaning a dress fastening or the like.

[2] Stokes's " Cormac," s. v. " Mug-éime," p. 111.

guistic sense of the word, are found to have been
called Brittones either by themselves or by the other
Celts within historical times, there is no reason why
the name should not be treated as exclusively belonging in Britain to the non-Goidelic branch of the Celts
of the second invasion.   Who, then, were the people
whom the Brythons did not consider cloth-clad or properly clothed ?   They could hardly have been Celts of
any kind, as the art of making cloth of some sort was
known on the Continent, even to the earliest of them
to land here.   In fact, the words we have cited supply
the proof, and it would have been worth our while, had
space allowed of it, to show how original Aryan *gv* or
gw, a partly labial combination, yields the simple labial
b in the Celtic languages ; how it is simplified, with the
guttural hardened to *c* or *k*, in the Teutonic ones, which
allows us to equate Irish *bó* with English *cow*, and to
regard the old Welsh *brith* alluded to and the Irish *bratt*
as etymologically one and the same vocable with their
familiar English equivalent *cloth*, the German kleid,
cloth, a garment, and the old Norse klædi, of much
the same meaning; and how the last-mentioned language possessed in a genitive plural klædna the same
kind of derivative as the Welsh *brethyn*.   One might
then widen the circle of comparison and introduce
the old Irish word *bréit*, a strip of any woollen cloth,
a kerchief, which implies, according to the ascertained course of phonetic decay in Goidelic speech,
an older form, *brenti:* both the latter and *bratt*
have their equivalents in the Sanskrit group of
words connected with the verb *grath* or *granth*,

to tie or to wind up, which, as it falls decidedly
short of the more developed idea of weaving, strikingly
suggests that the Aryan nations of the West did not
simply retain a civilisation which some would trace to
the far East, but that they were in some respects in
advance of it. So among the useful arts practised by
Celts and Teutons long before any of them had
reached the shores of the Atlantic was that of
weaving, however rude it may have been. In other
words, the race with which the Brythons contrasted
themselves to their own satisfaction, when they began
to give themselves that name, was probably some
of the aboriginal tribes whose home they invaded on the
Continent; for there are reasons to think that the
name belonged to the Brythons before they came to
this country. That is to say, remnants of that people
are supposed to show traces of their existence in
Gaul in historical times. Thus Pliny speaks of Continental Britanni who seem to have lived on the banks
of the river Somme, and it is thought that most or all
of the regiments termed Brittones in the Roman
army in Britain were natives of Gaul.[1] Procopius
also, a Greek writer of the sixth century, gives a
very fabulous account of an island called Brittia,
which he distinguishes from Britannia. One writer
on this difficult subject, M. de Vit, identifies Brittia
with Jutland, and supposes Brittones from beyond
the Rhine to have shared in the advance of the Teu-

[1] See Pliny's Hist. Nat. iv. 106, also "Das Römische Heer,"
by Hübner in "Hermes," xvi ; and M. de Vit s communication
in the "Bullett. dell' Inst. d Corrisp. Arch." (Rome), for 1867,
p. 39.

tons on Gaul, and to have settled in Brittany. That
is doubtful, but it is a fact, though never noticed,
that Brittia must have been a real name, as it is
exactly the form which would result in that which is
the actual Breton name of Brittany—namely, Breiz :
this last is the shortest, and cannot be derived
from any known form of the kindred name of
our country or of its people, and thus tells not a
little against the tradition that Brittany was first
colonized by Brythons from here ; not to mention the
fact that there is some difficulty as to whence those
fugitives could have come, seeing that if they set out
from the nearest parts of this country, that is, from
Cornwall or Devon, they would most likely have been
Goidels, so that the language of the Bretons would
now probably be a Goidelic dialect, and not the
comparatively pure Brythonic speech it is. This view
would give Breton an importance not usually attached
to it.

The soundest division which can be made of the
Celtic family rests on an accident of Celtic phonology.
It is that of the change of *qu* or *qv* into *p*, which is
found to have taken place in some of the Celtic
languages, but not in all, at the same time that
it is known in languages other than Celtic. Thus,
while Latin retained the older complex in the words
quinque, five, and *equus*, a horse, the Greeks differed
among themselves, some saying πέμπε for five, and
some πέντε, some ἵππος for a horse, and some
ἴκκος : while the Romans said *quatuor*, four, and
quum or *quom* when, some of the other Italians said

petur and *pon*. The Celts differed in much the
same way, since all the Brythons, whether Welshmen
or Bretons, agree in using *p* (liable to be softened
into *b*), as did the Gauls also, as far back as we can
trace them, in all their names excepting a few like
Sequani and Sequana; the Goidels, on the other
hand, whether in Ireland, Man, or Scotland, never
made *qv* into *p*, but simplified it in another way
by dropping the *v*, and making *q* into *c* (liable to
be modified into the guttural spirant *ch*) : this took
place in the sixth or the seventh century. In the old
Ogam inscriptions of Ireland the *qv* is represented by a
symbol of its own, and not only there, but in those of
Wales, Cornwall, and Devon. Thus on both sides of St.
George's Channel the most important key-word which
the ancient epitaphs supply us with is *maqvi*, the
genitive of the word which has yielded the Goidels of
the present day their *mac*, a son, and has taken in
Welsh the form *ab* (for an older *map*) of the same
meaning. The inscriptions in question from Wales
and Dumnonia may, roughly speaking, be assigned
to the sixth century, though some of them may be of
the fifth and some of the seventh : the remarkable
point about them is that the little Celtic which they
yield us usually agrees both in the matter of the *qv*
and in other respects, with the language of the Goidels
rather than with Gaulish, Welsh, Old Cornish, or
Breton. Who, then, were the Celts, of whose language
the epitaphs in question give us a few samples?
The question has been variously answered : some
would say that they were invaders from Ireland, the

Scots, in fact, who made descents on the coast of Britain about the end of the Roman occupation and afterwards; but the evidence to that effect is not yet abundant, while the fact that the Romans had not even a single company of soldiers to defend either Wales or Cornwall is significant. Some would say that they were the ancestors of the Welsh and of the Celts of Cornwall and Devon, and that their language was an early form of what has since become known as Welsh and Cornish : that is to say, the Celtic of the Ogam inscripti ns in the course of time underwent changes which shaped it into the dialects we call Welsh and Old Cornish. Years ago this was the view taken by the author, but a more thorough understanding of the inscriptions, together with additional information, has forced him to give it up in favour of the following, namely, that the Celts who spoke the language of the Celtic epitaphs were, in part, the ancestors of the Welsh and Cornish peoples, and that their descendants have changed their language from Goidelic to Brythonic. In other words, they were Goidels belonging to the first Celtic invasion of Britain, of whom some passed over into Ireland, and made that island also Celtic. At that point, or still earlier, all the British Islands may be treated as Goidelic, excepting certain parts where the neolithic natives may have been able to make a stand against the Goidels ; but at a later period there arrived another Celtic people with another Celtic language, which was probably to all intents and purposes the same as that of the Gauls. These later invaders called themselves Brittones and Belgæ, and

seized on the best portions of Britain, driving the
Goidelic Celts before them to the west and north of
the island.   Now it is partly the monuments of these
retreating Goidels of Britain that we have in the old
inscriptions, but partly perhaps those also of Goidelic
invaders from Ireland.   For it is true that their Goidelic
idioms, which were at length supplanted by the ever-
encroaching dialects of the Brythons, formed practically the same language as that of the Celts of
Ireland, of Man, and of Scotland.   Thus we are left
without any means of distinguishing in point of speech
between the ancient inhabitants and their invading
kinsmen from the sister island.

We shall now try further to show what portions of
the island were occupied by the Brythonic and the
Goidelic Celts respectively, about the beginning, say,
of the Roman occupation.   Setting out from the Isle
of Wight, we find that the Dumnoni of Devon and
Cornwall are proved by their epitaphs[1] after the Roman
occupation to have been Goidels, in so far as they were
Celts at all, for in point of blood they consisted
largely, perhaps, of the non-Celtic natives, and the
language of the latter can hardly have died out in the
district near the Land's End at the time when it got
its name of Belerion, which Ptolemy gives it ; since it
is possibly not an accident that Belerion is an early
form which would yield, in old Irish, *bélre*, later, *bérla*.
This is the word the Irish employ for language, usually
a language not their own and particularly the English
tongue.   Now whether Belerion meant a tongue in

[1] See Hübner's " Inscr. Brit. Christ.," Nos, 3, 17, 24, 25, 26.

the linguistic sense or merely a tongue of land it is evidence of Goidelic occupation, and it goes back to the time of Posidonius and Cicero : see pages 8, 45 above. As to the Durotriges, to the east of the mixed people of Dumnonia, it is difficult to determine their nationality. On the whole, however, they also seem to have been Goidels, a conclusion suggested, among other things, by the name of their town, Dunion, which differs from the Gaulish *dūnon.* Welsh din, a town or fortress, just where it comes near its Irish equivalent *dún,* genitive *dúne.* In that case no part of the country west of the Dorsetshire Stour and the Parret is presumably to be regarded as Brythonic. North of the Bristol Channel, the Severn and its tributary the Teme probably formed the boundary, the country within those rivers being divided between the Silures, who had the south-east, and the Demetæ, who had the south-west. Both these peoples may, like other Goidelic states, have, to a certain extent, absorbed an earlier, non Celtic, neolithic population ; but as against the Brythons we must treat them in point of language as Goidelic, and leave the question of origin mainly to those who study skins and skulls. The rest of what is now the Principality of Wales, together with the portion of the West of England adjoining, is usually supposed to have been occupied by the Ordovices ; but this powerful people, which we assume to have been Brythonic, overshadowed a Goidelic population occupying the north-west corner of the Principality, including Mona and the mainland within the Clwyd, the Dee, and the Mawddach, which

reaches the sea at Barmouth.   At some earlier stage
in the Brythonic advance it may be gathered that
the Ordovices owned no land north of the Dee or
within its bend, and that the old earthworks of Caer
Drywyn, north of the Dee, and overlooking the small
town of Corwen, were probably a stronghold of the
Goidels against the Ordovices of Mid-Wales, who
formed, as it were, a wedge reaching the sea between
the Mawddach and the Dovey, and completely sever-
ing the Goidels of North Wales from those towards the
Severn se1: their country may, roughly speaking, be
identified with the Powys of later times, and that name,
which probably meant merely a settlement, may be
looked at as a very old one.   On the shores of
Cardigan Bay several points may be indicated which
successively marked the advance southwards of the
Ordovices.   They seem first to have conquered the
coast from the Dovey to the Wyrè, a small river which
reaches the sea some miles south of Aberystwyth,
in Cardiganshire, together with a corresponding extent of country inland, all included in the old
bishopric of Paternus or Padarn, whose name is
now best known in connexion with his church
of Llanbadarn Fawr, near the same town.   The
Wyrè marks the boundary of a Welsh dialect, peculiar
to the northern part of Cardiganshire : it has much
in common with the dialects of Merionethshire and
Montgomeryshire, while it differs in certain particulars
from those of Demetia.   Later, the remainder of what
is now Cardiganshire was conquered as far as the
neighbourhood of the Teivi by Keredig, as mentioned

in a previous chapter. This happened in Christian times, so that the displacement of the inhabitants does not seem to have been very great, which is in a measure proved by the local dialect being in most respects the same as that of the rest of Demetia. David's name figures among the dedications in the district as it does more to the south, while the tombstone of a man of importance in Keredig's kingdom, probably a ruling prince, stands at Pembryn, overlooking the sea some distance north of Cardigan : his name was Corbalengi, and the inscriber has styled him an *Ordous*, meaning probably thereby one of the Ordovices.

East of the Ordovices the whole breadth of the island was occupied by the Cornavii and Coritani, the former of whom possessed a strip of country extending from the neighbourhood of the Worcestershire Avon, along the eastern bank of the Severn, and continued in a sort of an arc of a circle dipping into the sea between the Dee and the Mersey : it is possibly from the peninsula with which their territory began that this people had its name of Cornavii, just as the south-west of Britain and the north-west of France both terminate in a Cornish district, as did also the north of Scotland : compare the Welsh word *corn*, of the same meaning and origin as the Latin *cornu*, and the English *horn*. North of the Mersey and the Humber most of the country, as far as the Caledonian Forest, belonged to the Brigantes. The Parisi in the region of the Humber and the Tees appear to have been independent of them, as were also

probably the Novantæ, whose territory may have
embraced all the country west of the Nith and
south of the Ayr, as it undoubtedly included the
promontory of the Novantæ, whereby the Mull of
Galloway is supposed to have been meant. The nam of
the Nith in Ptolemy's time was Novios, and possibly it
is from it that this people got the name of Novantæ,
given them probably by Brythons, in much the same
way as the Setantii may, perhaps, have been so termed
from their living near the river Seteia. To the east
and north-east of the Novantæ dwelt the Selgovæ,
protected by thick forests and a difficult country.
Possibly they have left their name in the modern
form of Solway to the moss and to the firth so called
The word probably meant hunters, and the people to
whom it applied may be supposed, not only to have
been no Brythons, but to have been to no very great
extent Celtic at all, except, perhaps, as to their
language, which they may have adopted at an early
date from the Goidelic invaders : in a great measure
they were most likely a remnant of the aboriginal inhabitants, and the same remark may be supposed to be
equally applicable to the Novantæ. It would not be
surprising, then, to find that they acted together, and,
on looking into the later history of the Roman
occupation, we certainly seem to detect them as a
people who gave the province a great deal of trouble.
They lived between the Walls, and possibly appeared
in later history as Atecotti. Everything points
to the conclusion that these were either the Selgovæ
or the Novantæ, or rather the aggregate of them,

and not least significant is the fact that the word
Atecotti appears to have meant old or ancient,
and marked them out as a people of older standing
in the country than the Brythons, to whom they
possibly owed that name. The struggle in which they
took part against the Romans ended in their ultimately
retaining only the country behind the Nith, where
the name of the Novantæ becomes, in Bede's mouth,
that of the Niduarian Picts, known as the Picts of
Galloway for centuries afterwards. We return to the
Brigantes, whose name probably denoted a league
of several peoples, or a dominant people ruling over
a considerable territory containing a number of
different tribes, among whom may be mentioned the
Setantii, in what is now probably Lancashire. The
Votadini occupied a part of Lothian and the coast
down to the southern Wall. They must have come
sooner or later under the power of the Brigantes, as
it is in this district that the latter bequeathed their
name to Bernicia : see page 113 above. Whether
they extended their sway also to the Dumnonii, we
have no means of ascertaining. These last inhabited
the country between the Novantæ, the Selgovæ, and
the Votadini on the one hand, and the mouth of the
Clyde and the Forth on the other, together with an
extensive tract beyond those rivers, including the
Northern Manaw or Manann, and reaching to the
Earn—possibly to the Almond—and to the neighbourhood of Loch Leven in Fifeshire. The
southern portion of the Dumnonii, inhabiting as they
did what was later the nucleus of the kingdom of the

Cumbrians, may be regarded, like the other Dumnonii, as Goidels who adopted Brythonic speech; but the Votadini were of Brythonic race, and are always treated as such in Welsh literature, where their name becomes Guotodin and Gododin; they disappeared early, their country having been seized in part by the Picts from the other side of the Forth, and in part by Germanic invaders from beyond the sea. But to return to the outlying portion of the Dumnonii, when the wall from the Clyde to the Forth was built they were cut off from their kinsmen included in the Roman province ; and possibly it is they who figure in history as Boresti and Verturiones, or at any rate who supplied a ruling class in the country of the Verturiones. They formed the advanced posts of the Brythons, and they had given hostages to Agricola, and possibly to Severus, not to mention that their name of Verturiones may have meant the people of the land of the fortresses in allusion, either to stations[1] occupied by the Romans in their country, or to earlier works of their own construction, intended for the defence of their borders against other tribes.

We have already suggested the position of the Caledonians, who were Picts. They, together with the Vacomagi, flanked the country of the Verturiones or Men of Fortrenn, on its northern boundary ; but how far both Pictish peoples were influenced by the Goidels of the Tay Valley it is hard to say, especially as the latter seem to have been there from early times, a conclusion forced upon us by the absence of any

[1] See Skene's " Celtic Scotland," i. p. 74.

certain historical indication, how or when they reached the Tay.   The position of the Vacomagi has already been touched upon; so has that of the Tæxali, and that of the Vernicomes.   The remaining peoples of the North, all probably non-Celtic in point of race, and mostly, perhaps, in that of language, were the following, as enumerated by Ptolemy:—The Epidii occupied most of the sea-board from where the Leven discharges the waters of Loch Lomond into the estuary of the Clyde, to the neighbourhood of Ben Nevis, and it is to them that the Epidian Promontory belonged: by this Ptolemy is supposed to have meant the headland now called the Mull of Cantyre. Their name looks as though it had been one given them by a Brythonic peope, and had meant horsemen, though they dwelt in a region where one would have rather expected coracles: its Brythonic appearance is, perhaps, only due to an accident, as we seem to have practically the same word in the name of the islands called Ebudæ, which, together with the neighbouring ones, from Tiree to Arran may have all belonged to them, though Ptolemy calls only one of them Epidion, identified by Dr. Skene[1] with the Isle of Lismore: it may have been that of Jura   Beyond the Epidii, and inhabiting the west as far, presumably, as Cape Wrath, come three or four peoples, called by Ptolemy respectively Cerones, Creones, Carnonacæ, and Carini.   At first sight we are tempted to regard he four names as merely clerical variants of a single one, but such a

[1] "Celtic Scotland," i. p. 69.

view is not countenanced by the still greater variety of
the modern names, some, at least, of which may be
supposed connected with some of those recorded by
Ptolemy : witness those of the lochs—Crinan, Creran,
Carron, Kearon, Keiarn, and a good many others
involving the same consonants, and belonging to the
western Highlands, but better known to the angler
than the historian. The region from Cape Wrath to
Duncansby Head may be said to have been the home
of the Cornavii, so called for a reason which has
already been suggested as a matter of conjecture.
The south-eastern side of the present counties of
Caithness and Sutherland was divided between two
peoples, called the Smertæ and the Lugi. Lastly, the
coast from the neighbourhood of the Dornoch Firth
to the confines of the Caledonians, belonged to a
nation called the Decantæ. Most of these tribes of
the west and north were probably allies or subjects of
the powerful twin people of the Dicalydones.

Now that we are dealing with Ptolemy's account of
the north of the island, we may add a few words respecting the remarkable feature of Scotland known to
the ancients as the Caledonian Forest. It was called
in Latin Caledonius Saltus or Silva Caledonia, and
in Welsh literature Coed Celyddon or the Wood
of Calidon : Ptolemy, who terms it Καληδόνιος
Δρυμός, by which there is no occasion to suppose
him to have meant the chain of mountains called
Drumalban, says that it was above the land of the
Caledonians, whence the usual and erroneous idea
that it must have been in the Western Highlands, in a

region where one would hardly, perhaps, have expected
to find it at all. The mistake has arisen from failing
to realize Ptolemy's point of view : among other peculiarities of his description of the geography of Britain,
he began from what he considered the most northern
point of the island. And as he somehow made a
mistake in his map of Scotland, and twisted eastwards
what should have been north, his most northern point
of Britain turns out to have been the headland of the
Novantæ : it is thence that he seems to have surveyed,
as it were, the whole island. Beginning at that
corner he enumerates the features of the coast until
he reaches Cape Wrath, and from the same place he
commences his description of the western coast southwards to Cornwall. He follows the same plan in
enumerating the peoples inhabiting the country, and
from his point of view the Vacomagi, who, like the
Caledonian Forest, have sometimes been transported
to the west because he states them to have been
above the Caledonians, fall into their right place,
and into possession of their towns, some of which
cannot easily be removed very far from the shore of the
Moray Firth. Similarly interpreted, the Caledonian
Forest is found to have been located by Ptolemy
where there is every reason to suppose that it really
was—namely, covering a tract over which we are told
that a thick wood of birch and hazel must once have
stretched, that is, from the west of the district of
Menteith in the neighbourhood of Loch Lomond across
the country to Dunkeld.[1] It is this vast forest that

[1] Skene's " Celtic Scotland," i. p. 86.

probably formed in part at least the boundary between the Caledonians and the Verturiones or the mixed people of Fortrenn.

We have already made some use of linguistic facts in trying to determine the nationality of some of the peoples brought under the reader's notice, and now we would bring them together in the compass of few words. In doing so the place of importance is claimed for Celtic proper names which involve the consonant p. In the Greek language, for instance, this sound comes from two sources : thus in πατήρ it corresponds to the p in the Latin pater and the Sanskrit pitar, and to f in their English equivalent father : in this instance the Greeks had perpetuated the original Aryan p. But in the Celtic languages it is found to have been one of their characteristics that they eventually got rid of this Aryan consonant, so that the Irish word for father is not *pathair*, but *athair*, and the Celtic preposition corresponding to the Greek παρά, appears in Welsh as *ar*, and is given in Old Gaulish as *are* in the name of the cities termed by Cæsar *Aremoricæ*,[1] from a Gaulish word which is in Welsh *mor*, sea : this latter, with the prefix, went to form the adjective applied to the states on or by the sea in the north-west of Gaul, but a shorter form became usual, yielding Brittany the name of Armorica it sometimes bears. Greek, on the other hand, had words with a p from another origin, such as πέντε or πέμπε, five, in which that consonant corresponds to the qu of the Latin *quinque*. Some of the Celtic lan-

---

[1] " Bell. Gall.," v. 53 ; vii. 75 ; viii. 31.

guages likewise supply us with a *p* of this origin, but
not all of them, the Goidelic dialects having never
made *qv* or *qu* into *p*.   The Welsh word corresponding to πέμπε and *quinque* is now *pump*, and it
must have been somewhat similar in Gaulish, in which
the name of the cinquefoil is recorded as *pempedula ;*
while in Old Irish, which reduced its early *qv* into *c*,
the fifth numeral was *côic*.   When we have, then, a
presumably Celtic word containing *p*, we presume on
the whole that we are dealing with one of the languages
of what has been called the Gallo-Brythonic branch of
the family, and not of the Goidelic one.   Passing by
such place-names as Præsidium and Prætorium as
clearly Latin ; Procolitia, Petrianæ, and Spinis as not
improbably Latin ; and such others as Durolipons as
possibly in part Latin, we have the following left,
which appear to come either from a Gallo-Brythonic
language, or from that of the non-Celtic aborigines of
the island :—

(1.) Mons Granpius or Graupius, from which the
     great battle where Agricola defeated Calgacos
     and his Caledonians took its name.   It is
     thought to have been on the tongue of land
     at the meeting of the Isla with the Tay.

(2) Corstopiton or Corstopilon, supposed to be
     Corbridge in Northumberland.

(3.) Epeiacon, the name of which has led to its
     being identified with Ebchester ; it has also
     been placed at Lanchester and Hexham.
     Ptolemy's figures, however, point rather to
     Keswick in Cumberland, but the name seems

to signify a place for horses or cavalry, which appears to be the case also with Vereda, a station mentioned in the Antonine Itinerary and identified with Castle-Steads at Plumpton Wall, near Old Penrith, in the same county : it may be that the two names denoted one and the same town.

(4.) Maponi, given by the anonymous geographer of Ravenna as the name of a place in Britain, and meaning probably the Fane of Maponos,[1] a god equated with Apollo on a fine monument at Hexham ; he was also probably the Mabon spoken of in the Mabinogion.[2]

(5.) Parisi, the people in the neighbourhood of the Humber.

(6.) Petuaria, the name of the town ascribed to the Parisi by Ptolemy, the auxiliaries from which are termed *Petuerienses* in the Table of Dignities. It may have been at Patrington or Hedon.

(7.) Pennocrucion, which has been identified by some with Stretton, by others with Penkridge in Staffordshire : wherever it was, the name, which was a common one, survives in that of the latter town.

(8.) Prasutagos, king of the Eceni, and husband of Queen Boudicca.

(9.) Toliapis, at the mouth of the Thames, and now

[1] The Berlin " Corpus Insc. Lat.," vii. No. 1345.

[2] Oxford Edition, pp. 124, 128-32, 140, 141, 159 ; Guest's Edition, ii., pp. 225, 226, 234, 235, 286, 287, 300, 301.

called the Isle of Sheppey, though no longer surrounded by the sea.

(10.) Rutupiæ or Ritupiæ, identified with Richborough in Kent.

(11.) Octapitaron, the name given by Ptolemy to St. David's Head : it comes most likely from the forgotten language of the non-Celtic inhabitants, and it occurs just in the vicinity of St. David's or Mynyw, called in the Welsh Chronicle *Moni Iudeorum*, which contains an allusion probably to the same people : we may add that an old legend speaks of Sts. Teilo and David as opposed there by a Pictish prince called Baia or Boia,[1] a name which occupies a place of importance in the story of the Déisi in the Book of the Dun Cow.

(12.) Leucopibia, the name of a place somewhere in Galloway.

(13.) Epidii, a name which we have already treated as akin with the name of the islands called Ebudæ.

It has already been hinted that some of the names given by the ancients to non-Brythonic peoples may, nevertheless, be themselves Brythonic, the reason being that the Romans came more in contact with Brythons, and got more of their information from them than from the other populations. This may possibly be the explanation of such a name as Leucopibia. Among the more evident instances may

---

[1] See the "Liber Landavensis," pp. 94, 95, and the "Lives of the Cambro-British Saints," pp. 124-126.

be mentioned that of the Caledonians, who are called by ancient authors Caledonii and Caledones, in both of which the stem Caledon would seem to belong to Brythonic, rather than to Goidelic, in which it would be Calidin or Caliden, as proved by the later forms. The difference of declension may be represented thus : the Goidelic inflections in point went on the same lines as Latin words like *virgo*, a virgin, genitive *virgin-is*, nom. plural *virgin-es*, while the Brythonic dialects gave the declension an evenness which did not originally belong to it, by repeating the vowel of the nominative singular in some or all of the other cases, as if we had in Latin *virgo*, *virgonis*, and so on, which in fact we sometimes have, as when the unattested form *hemo* yields an accusative *hemonem* for the more usual *hominem* corresponding to a nominative *homo*, man. Another instance offers itself in the name of the Decantæ of northern Scotland, which is practically the same as that of the Decanti of Deganwy, near Llandudno, in North Wales, a place called *Decantorum arx* in the Welsh Chronicle. In both instances Decant- was probably the Brythonic pronunciation of Decn̥t-, which in the mouths of Goidels, who regularly rid themselves of the nasal in such cases, became at a comparatively early date the Decet- or Decēt- of the inscriptional name of Mac-Dechet on ancient monuments in Devon, Anglesey, and Ireland, among them being one of the largest early monuments of the kind in the British Islands, that standing on rising ground near a bay of the Kenmare River in the south-west of Ireland. It is doubtful whether the name of the Novantæ is not

likewise to be regarded as a merely Brythonic one, but
it is less so in the case of a town of the Selgovæ : we
allude to Carbantorigon, on the eastern bank of the
Nith, for it is not impossible that we have the same
name abbreviated in the CARVETIOR of a Roman inscription on a stone at Penrith, in the neighbourhood
of Carlisle, commemorating a man. who had held a
quæstorial office in the place it points to.   If so, either
a Goidelic language or a non-Celtic one was in use
among the Selgovæ at the time the epitaph in question was carved.   It is in their country that was
probably situated the place called *Blatobulgion* in the
Antonine Itinerary, and supposed to have been near
Middlebie Kirk, not very far from the river Annan,
in the county of Dumfries.

In some instances another means of distinguishing
between Brythonic and the other languages of Britain
is supplied by the consonantal combination *cs* or *x*
usual in Gaulish, but long ago reduced in the
Brythonic dialects into *ch* and *h* : while in the
Goidelic ones it was made somewhat later into *ss* or *s*.
Now, about a dozen Latin words with *x* have been
borrowed into Welsh, and in none of them has the
x been reduced to *ch*, but in all to *is* or *s*, as also in
the word *Sais*, a Saxon in the sense of Englishman.   It would seem that the change from *x* into
ch was obsolete before the ancestors of the Welsh had
adopted the Latin words in question, or even, perhaps,
before they had been much in contact with the
Romans.   Among the instances which concern us
here may be mentioned the Gaulish *uxel-* which

appears in Welsh as *uchel*, high ; while in Irish and
Scotch Gaelic it is *uasal*, high (in the metaphorical
sense of high-born, noble or gentle) : the Brythonic form of this word is probably that which
we have in the name of the Ochil Hills, in the
country of the ancient Verturiones. It is remarkable,
on the other hand, that most of the early names
with *x* belong to districts which have before been
pointed out as non-Brythonic. First may be mentioned the people called Tæxali, already spoken of.
Then comes the mouth of a river Loxa, that can
hardly be any other than the Lossie which falls into
the Moray Firth in the land of the Vacomagi. Coming
down South along the east of the island, we miss
all names with *x*, nor do we find any in the
south until we reach the country of the Dumnonii.
There Ptolemy mentions a high town or high fort,
called Uxella, and gives the estuary where the Taw
and the Torridge meet the name of Vexalla. Proceeding northwards, we come across a doubtful instance
between Pennocrucion and Vriconion, which the
manuscripts of the Antonine Itinerary, where it is
mentioned, variously call Uxacona, Usoccona, and
Uscocona, and we stop finally in the neighbourhood
of the Solway Firth. There, in the country of the
Selgovæ, Ptolemy supplies us with another high town,
called by him Uxellon, which must have been close
to the mouth of the river Nith. But this is not all,
since there was another high fort or high town, called
Uxelodunon or Uxelodunion, situated at the mouth
of the Ellen, on the coast of Cumberland, not far

from the Derwent. Hence it may be inferred that, about the time of the coming of the Romans, a non-Brythonic people still possessed the shores of the Solway as far south as the river Derwent. Nay, possibly most of the lake district down to Morecambe Bay and Kendal, or still farther south, was peopled by a mixed race of Goidels and non-Celtic aborigines; for Kendal has been sometimes supposed to be the site of the ancient Concangii, the name of which is probably non-Celtic, and reminds one vaguely of the De-ceangli, near the Dee, of that of the Gangani, after whom Ptolemy names the westernmost point of Carnarvon-shire, and of that of the other Gangani, placed by the same geographer in the west of Ireland. After the building of the Roman Wall, by which those south of it were severed from their kinsmen north of it, the former probably soon lost their national character-istics and become Brythonicised, while the Selgovæ remained perhaps to form, with the Novantæ, the formidable people of the Atecotti, who afterwards gave Roman Britain so much to do, until their power was broken by Theodosius, who enrolled their able-bodied men in the Roman army, and sent them away to the Continent, where no less than four distinct bodies of them served at the time when the Table of Dignities was drawn up. They were a fierce and warlike people, but by the end of the Roman occupation they seem to have been subdued or driven beyond the Nith, and within the dyke[1] which was, probably about that time, made from opposite the end of the Roman

[1] See Skene's "Celtic Scotland," i p 108.

Wall across the upper parts of the valleys draining
themselves into the Solway, so as to end at Loch
Ryan : here the language of the inhabitants down to
the sixteenth century was Goidelic.

There are a few facts of another order which are
to the point here, and foremost among them may be
mentioned, that the later Brythons, whether such by
blood or merely by adopting a Brythonic language, as
in the case of those of Cornwall and of parts of the
north and of the south of Wales, agree in possessing
legends about a great hero whom they call Arthur.
Whether he was from the first a purely imaginary
character in whom the best qualities of the race were
supposed to meet, or had a solid foundation in the
facts of a long-forgotten history, it would be difficult
to say ; but the popular imagination of the Brythons
had fully developed his attributes before the twelfth
century. He appears as the ideal champion of the
race, donning the armour of a Christian general
to lead the Brythons to war against the pagan
invaders, whether Picts or Germans. The fortunes
of the Brythons were his concern, and their wars were
his wars, so that their great battles were believed to
have been fought under his command ; nay, he was
related to have with his own hand slain in each conflict
a marvellous number of the foe. Sometimes, however, he is dimly seen in the background as a grand
figure that does not descend into the arena : thus a
Welsh poem[1] in a manuscript of the 12th century,
describing the feats of valour of the Dumnonian

[1] Skene's " Ancient Books of Wales," ii. pp. 37, 38.

prince Geraint in a battle fought probably with
Ine of Wessex, speaks of Geraint's men as the men of
Arthur : this was a long while, be it marked, after the
time when Arthur is supposed to have lived.   Now
and then he even found his way into the chronicles ;
but when that happened it was a good while after the
date of the event in which he was supposed to have
been concerned.   Thus, according to Nennius, he it
was that led the Brythons in the important battle of
Badon Hill ; but Gildas, who felt a great interest in
that battle, partly because it was fought in the year
in which he himself. was born, says nothing whatever
about Arthur there or anywhere else.   Had that
Kymric Jeremiah lived a century or two later, he
might have described Arthur's feats of superhuman
prowess there at length.   The Celts of Brittany
regard Arthur as their own, so do those of Cornwall,
though they have now adopted the language of their
English neighbours, and so do the Kymry of Wales,
while a most urgent claim has also been advanced
in favour of the district between the Roman Walls.
This is quite natural : Arthur belongs to them all,
wherever Celts have spoken a Brythonic language,
from the Morbihan to the Caledonian Forest.   It is
characteristic of such popular creations that they
localize themselves readily here and there and everywhere in the domain of the race in whose imagination
they live and have their growth : the topography of
Brythonic lands has no lack of Arthur's Hills, Arthur's
Seats, Arthur's Quoits, Round Tables, and other be-
longings of his and his followers.   The results of the

search made into Scotch topography by those who have undertaken to find the home and cradle of Arthur in the north are partly puzzling and partly instructive. Passing by the abundant traces of him in the topography of the district between the Roman Walls, one fails to find any in the Brythonic country between Stirling on the Forth and Perth on the Tay, while one gets interesting instances in Strathmore and Forfarshire ;[1] but it is as hard to believe that Arthur is not to be discovered in Fortrenn as it is to find any evidence of a Brythonic occupation extending to the neighbourhood of Forfar, and the subject deserves to be further studied. On the other hand, place-names, show that wherever the Goidel carried his language he also peopled the country with the creatures of his own story. Most of Scotland beyond the firths, including the district between the Earn and the Tay is found to have been, topographically speaking, possessed by Finn, Oisín, Diarmait, and the other widely-ranging heroes of that group, who belong no less to Scotland than to Ireland, being in fact, as universally Goidelic as Arthur and the Knights of the Round Table are the creatures of Brythonic story. If Arthur is to be treated as historical, the historian must look at him much in the same light as he does at Charlemagne, with all the legends that have gathered round his name. He will in that case find that the hero whom the Welsh sometimes call King Arthur, and sometimes Arthur the Emperor, falls

[1] See Stuart Glennie's " Arthurian Localities" (Edinburgh, 1869), pp. 36-40.

readily into the place and position of a successor of the Count of Britain ; and in favour of that view might be cited the fact that Arthur's name might be explained as the Welsh form which the Kymry gave to the Latin *Artorius*.[1]   This would not be enough to prove that he was of Roman origin, though it could not help reminding one of the case of Aurelius Ambrosius.

[1] So far as we know, the credit of having first pointed this out belongs to Mr. Coote : see his " Romans of Britain," pp. 10, 11, 189, 190.

CHAPTER VII.

THE ETHNOLOGY OF BRITAIN.

(*Continued.*)

So far we have tried to draw the outlines of an
ethnological map of Britain : we now pause to fill in
a detail here and there where data happen to offer
themselves. Cæsar tells us that the inhabitants of
Britain in his day painted themselves with a dye
extracted from woad ; by the time, however, of
British independence under Carausius and Allectus,
in the latter part of the third century, the fashion had
so far fallen off in Roman Britain that the word *Picti*,
Picts, or painted men, had got to mean the nations
beyond the Northern Wall : the people on the
Solway were probably included under the same
name, though they went also by the special designation of Atecotti. Now, all these Picts were natives
of Britain, and the word Picti is found applied to
them for the first time, in a panegyric by Eumenius,
in the year 296 ; but in the year 360 another painted
people appeared on the scene. They came from
Ireland, and to distinguish these two sets of painted
foes from one another, Latin historians left the
painted natives to be called Picti, as had been the

custom before, and for the painted invaders from
Ireland, they retained, untranslated, a Celtic word,
possibly of the same meaning, or nearly the same
meaning, namely, *Scotti.* These older peoples, however, were known by a common name, which described
them in Celtic as painted men. Rather we should
say it did more : it connoted the embellishment of
the person, which the tattooing was supposed to
effect. This word was Cruthni,[1] which is found
applied equally to the painted people of both islands,
though one detects somewhat of a tendency on the
part of the chroniclers to draw a distinction, the Irish
Picts being more persistently called Cruthni, Latinized
Cruthenii or Crutheni, while the compound Cruithen-
tuath or the nation of the Picts, was mostly appro-
priated to the Picts of Britain north of the Forth, who
were also termed Piccardach, suggested by the Latin
Picti, Pictones, Pictores, all of which terms and more
have been used in reference to them. The eponymus
of all the Picts was Cruithne, and we have the corresponding Brythonic form in Prydyn, the name by
which Picts and Pictland or Scotland once used to
be known to the Kymry. An earlier Welsh form of
Prydyn is Priten, and later ones are Prydein and
Prydain ; for our island is in Welsh Ynys Prydain
" Prydain's Island " or Island of the Picts, pointing to
the original underlying the Greek Πρετανικαὶ Νῆσοι or
" Pictish Isles." This, under the influence of the name

[1] It occurs as *Cruthne* in the gen. plural in the Book of the
Dun Cow, fol. 70a ; late writers, however, prefer the adjectival
form *Cruithnig* ; nom. singular, *Cruithnech.*

of the Brythons, Βρεττανοί, became at last Βρεττανικαὶ
Νῆσοι, that is to say, " Brythonic Isles " The Picts have
sometimes been called in Welsh literature, *Gwyddyl
Ffichti*, Goidelic Picts, or Pictish Goidels, *Ffichti* is
not the regular rendering of *Picti* into Welsh, and
it is not, we think, found in manuscripts earlier than
the fourteenth century, so that this clumsy translation
of *Scotti Picti* has not the importance which has sometimes been ascribed to it. The words Cruthni and
Prydyn are derived from *cruth* and *pryd* respectively,
which mean form, and an Irish shanachie [1] has rightly
explained the former as meaning a people who painted
the forms (crotha) of beasts, birds, and fishes on their
faces, and not on their faces only, but on the whole
of the body. Herodian states that they did not
wear clothes lest they should conceal the pictures.
This agrees with Claudian's vivid description of
Stilicho's soldiery, scanning the figures punctured
with iron on the body of the fallen Pict, and with the
much later reference to the term Cruthni, which we
seem to have in Isidore of Seville's words in the sixth
century, when he wrote that the Scotti were named
in their own tongue from their painting the body,
since, as he went on to say, they were tattooed by
means of iron points and ink, with the marking of
various figures.[2]

---

[1] Duald Mac Firbis, quoted by Todd in a note on the Irish
version of Nennius, p. vi. ; see also Herodian iij., 14, § 8.

[2] For this and other passages in point see Skene's " Chronicles
of the Picts and Scots," pp. 393-395, also p. 137.

The word Scotti[1] itself, as already hinted, appears
to have referred to the same habit, as we have in
Welsh the kindred words—*ysgwthr*, a cutting, carving
or sculpturing, and *ysgythru*, to cut, lop, prune, to do
the sculptor's work; but the word also occurs meaning
to dye or paint, though it is not quite clear whether
this latter be not a signification derived from that of
carving or sculpturing, by some such intermediate step
as that of tattooing, or embossing, or mosaic work.
Thus the word Scotti would seem to mean simply
painted men, or else—and this is, on the whole, the
more probable view—it meant persons who were cut,
scored or scarred. That would, at first sight, seem
a forced explanation of the name, but it will be found,
that, though the people who tattooed themselves re
garded it as a way of beautifying their persons, others
who did not practise it usually took quite the contrary
view of the effect. Among the latter may be cited the
legates of Pope Adrian, who, in reporting[2] to him
their proceedings in Britain, in 787, speak of God as
having made man beautiful, and of the pagans of
this country as "having by a diabolical impulse added
to him most foul scars," and they further remark that,
"if anyone endured for God's sake this injury of
being dyed, he would therefore certainly receive a
great reward." Such a name, then, as Scotti, if we
are not mistaken as to its meaning, is probably not

---

[1] The word occurs for the first time in Ammianus Marcellinus's
account (xx. 1) of an invasion of Roman Britain by the Scots
and the Picts in the year 360.

[2] Haddan and Stubbs, "Councils," &c., iii. p. 458.

one which that people gave itself : it is to be traced, rather, to the Brythons of Roman Britain, and the Welsh words cited favour this view. Moreover, the fact has usually been overlooked that it is a term which has practically only come down to modern times as the Latin word for natives of Ireland or their descendants. So the Welshman or the Irishman, who would speak in his own language of a Gwyddel or Goidel, rendered it into Scottus as soon as he had occasion to write Latin; and from that was formed in due time Scottia or Scotia, as the name for Ireland instead of Hibernia. It is needless to say that the word Scotia has no formation corresponding to it in any Celtic language : it is found used first by Isidore, but by the end of the seventh century Adamnan, a native of Ireland, employs it in writing Latin. Eventually, the old name reasserted itself. and the new one, having passed over into Scotland in the modern sense of the word, took root in its new home, and was fully established there during the War of Independence. The term Scotti was made in Irish into Scuit, but this is hardly ever to be met with in Irish literature, and its appearance there is probably only due to the importance of *Scotti* in Latin. Among other things it was too tempting not to associate it with Scythia, and hence there sprang up a number of tales relating how the Irish came from that country to Ireland ; this was, of course, only a part of the crop of etymological speculations, which not only connected the Picts with the Gaulish Pictones and Pictavi whose names survive in those of Poitiers and Poitou, but with any other people to whom the adjective *pictus* had been applied by Latin authors. Thus Vergil's allusion[1] to the Geloni in the line,

"Eoasque domos Arabum pictosque Gelonos,"

did not fail to lead to the identification with the Irish of more than one tribe descended from Hercules.[2]

But to whom did the name Scotti originally apply before the indiscriminate use of the word as the Latin equivalent for the plural Goidil? Supposing we have made an approach to the true meaning of the word, it could only have denoted those of the Irish who continued the old fashion of tattooing themselves: when those of a corner of the island got to be known as Cruthni, or Picts, most of the inhabitants of Ireland must have abstained from the practice of tattooing their persons. Whatever the meaning of the word Scotti may have been, there is no reason to think that it originally denoted most or all of the people of Ireland, for as far back as we can penetrate they have never been known to the Kymry but by the name Goidel, in Welsh Gwyddel. Now, the portion of Ireland best known to history as Pictish was a pretty well defined district, consisting of the present county of Antrim and most of that of Down. The northern half or so of the former was the home of the descendants of Riada or the Dál-Riada, whence the Dalriad Scots of Argyle, while another tract of that Pictish peninsula belonged to the descendants of

---

[1] "Georgics," ii. 115.
[2] See the "Irish Nennius," pp, xxxix. 49,

Araide and Fiatach or the Dál-nAraide and Dál-
Fiatach, who continued to be commonly known as
Cruthni for a long time. But this only represents a
last stage of the Cruthnian shrinkage, for the Ivernian
people of Ulster, called not only Cruthni, but also, and
more commonly, Ulaid, " Ulidians or Ultonians," and
Fír Ulaid, " Ulidians Proper or True Ultonians," to
distinguish them from the Goidelic conquerors of
Ulster, are said to have in early times possessed Tara
under their famous king, Ollam Fodla. In a more
historical period we find them retreating northwards,
and making Emain Macha, '' the Navan Fort " near
Armagh, their headquarters. A long time afterwards
they are again in retreat, to wit, to the corner of
Ul-ter east of Loch Neagh and the river Bann. To
this they were forced by the Goidelic conquests
made from Meath by the Three Collas, who wrested
from them the whole of Ulster from Loch Neagh
westwards, slew their king, and razed their capital.
This decisive war, with the crowding of the Fír Ulaid
into the north-east corner of their territory, is placed
by the Four Masters in the year 327, and if that date
is even approximately correct, one can hardly doubt that
the Scotti, joining the Picts of Britain in 360, (p. 243)
hailed from the narrowed realm of the Cruthnian
Ulaid. We may take it that they had begun to come
across years earlier, but that in the year 360 they had
arrived in such numbers as to prove a serious danger
to the province. Once, however, these Cruthnians
had learned the way into the heart of the Roman
province, other adventurers eager for plunder may

have joined them, or taken routes of their own, though Gildas distinctly states that the Scotti set out from the north-west. This agrees well with the fact that where Netherby now stands, to which the waters of the Solway once reached, there was at one time a Roman station called by the significant name of *Castra Exploratorum*, or the Camp of the Scouts; that at Netherstall, near Maryport, at the mouth of the river Ellen in Cumberland, where Uxelodunon stood, there was in the time of Hadrian a fleet under the command of M. Mænius Agrippa, whose name appears in several inscriptions from that neighbourhood; and that later, when the Selgovæ had been disposed of, the remainder of the non-Brythonic people on the Solway were enclosed by a rampart from the end of that firth to Loch Ryan,[1] as already mentioned at p. 235 above. It is probable that it was in their country the Irish invaders usually organized their expeditions southwards all the time they continued to come over.

It has, however, been sometimes supposed that it was in Wales the Irish invaders habitually landed. They may have done so occasionally, as in the case of the Déisi, the date of whose coming to Dyved is, nevertheless, uncertain: we may say toward the end of the third century. But it is highly improbable that it was the usual resort, as it was a country neither rich in booty nor easy to penetrate. Besides, had Wales been much exposed to such visitations, it would be in the highest degree remarkable that not a

[1] Skene's ' Celtic Scotland," i. 108.

single regiment of soldiers was located there by the Romans at the date of the compiling of the Table of Dignities, all being quartered in the north or the south-east of the province. Welsh tradition has been invoked to prove the invasion of Wales from Ireland in the fourth and fifth centuries, and medieval travesties of the history of the incursions of the Danes, especially those settled at Dublin, have been blindly brought forward in evidence. This is too fruitless a subject to discuss at length, and an instance or two will serve to show what has been sometimes done :—" Anlach, son of Coronac," is moved back to this period by writers who do not detect in him the well known Dane, Anlaf Cuaran, and, similarly, the leader of the Goidels in their last battle with " Caswallon Lawhir," is called Serrigi or Sirigi, possibly a corrupt form of some personal name torn out of a Latin context, while Caswallon turns out to have been a Welsh prince of the tenth century, and not the father of Maelgwn in the sixth. In both instances the name was Cadwallon before it was improved into that of the ancient general, Cassivellaunos, who fought against Julius Cæsar. There are many more similar pitfalls into which Welsh legendary history is wont to lead the unsuspecting. What has usually been regarded as evidence for the invasion of Wales from Ireland proves on examination to be no such thing ; but the references we have made to the Déisi of Dyved will prevent the conclusion from being drawn, that no evidence of the kind exists at all. However, the author finds the data so slender, and the difficulties iuvolved so considerable, especially as to determining which of the Goidels of the West of Britain represented the ancient inhabitants, and which of them were invaders from the sister island, that he must content himself with merely warning the reader that the question is answered in different ways, some scholars being of the opinion that all Goidelic peoples in Britain are to be traced to Ireland. He prefers to think that the Goidels of the districts in point were partly of the one origin and partly of the other: in any case, Goidels they were, and their language continued to exist in Wales down to the end probably of the seventh century, possibly somewhat later in out-of-the-way corners of the country. To fix the time of its utter disappearance would be impossible, but Dr. Hübner, the greatest German epigraphist who has studied the inscriptions of Britain, places one[1] of them, written in Latin and Goidelic, and found on the south of the Teivi, near Cardigan, among those which he assigns to the seventh or possibly to the eighth century, the classification being mainly based on the forms of the letters used.

When those of our early inscriptions, which are non-Roman and begin to date soon after the departure of the legions, have their localities marked on a map of Wales, it is found that hardly any of them occur in what was the country of the Ordovices: they may be said to crowd together in the tract within the Clwyd, the Dee, and the Mawddach in North Wales, while in South Wales they form two groups;

[1] " Inscrip. Brit. Christ.," No. 108.

an eastern one around a line drawn from Brecon to Neath in Glamorgan; and the other, the more important one, in the district west of the basin of the Towy. All the inscriptions belong to Christian times, but it is not to be concluded that the people of the epigraphic area were converted to Christianity before those of the rest of the country. For not only were Cunedda and his people Christians, but it was by members of the former's family, or by men who enjoyed its protection, that Christianity was mainly, so far as we know it, spread among the Goidels; and, even if they were Christians previously, it is from the Cunedda saints that the organization of the Church in Wales has come down to us, so that whatever Christianity existed among the Goidels before their labours, was so completely covered by the latter as to have been almost wholly forgotten. Thus, so far as we know, St. David was the first who systematically undertook to Christianize the people of Dyved or Demetia; he was grandson to Keredig, who gave its name to Keredigion and was son of Cunedda. Next comes Kentigern, who founded the bishopric of St. Asaph: he did so under the protection of Cadwallon, Maelgwn's father; and it was under the auspices of Maelgwn himself, that Daniel, or, as he is called in Welsh, Deinioel, became the first bishop of Bangor in Arvon, whither he came from the great monastic establishment at Bangor on the Dee. We have, then, to look elsewhere for the explanation of the comparative lack of inscriptions in the Brythonic area of Wales, and we are forced to believe that it arose from a difference in the manner of burying the dead. Among the first things to strike one is the fact that the country of the Ordovices is almost wholly devoid of those rude stone structures called cromlechs, which are found to crowd together in the same districts as the inscriptions, especially in the island of Mona and the county of Pembroke: the conclusion darkly suggests itself that it was the same race that set up the cromlechs and erected the maenhirs or longstone monuments of the Principality. Probably we should not be far wrong in considering the maenhir to be as old, to say the least of it, as the cromlech, and merely a less elaborate way of attaining the same object, that of commemorating the dead ; but the relative age of these is a question which archæology cannot be said to have seriously considered, or even perhaps clearly formulated, though it undertakes to distinguish the burial-places of the Celts from those of the pre-Celtic peoples of Britain, the former having the round barrows assigned to them, and the latter the long ones. This may be correct in the main, and it may be that the archæologist has no data to help him to more exact results, but he should bear in mind that his study of the tombs falls short of the historian's wish so long as he cannot tell the resting-place of a Brython from that of a Goidel, and both from those of the neolithic native. The two last would seem from the latest archæological investigations to have buried in long barrows, but some of those barrows contain the dead placed with care to sit grimly in their subterranean houses, while others disclose only the huddled bones of men and beasts, as though they

were the remains of cannibal feastings.   Can they be
ascribed to the same race?   If so, what was the
meaning of the revolution which took place in their
mode of burial, and what did it signify as regards their
religious belief?

As to the people of the Belgo-Brythonic branch,
who were not given to the erection of great stone
monuments, there is no difficulty in supposing them
to have continued in Christian times their use of the
barrows, of which so many scores are known clus-
tering around the ancient temple of Stonehenge, and
in other parts of the country. Now, the mound of
earth which we call a barrow or a tumulus, offered no
great opportunities for the writer of epitaphs, but the
maenhirs did : it may be assumed that, when the
Goidels became acquainted with writing and had the
example of the Romans before their eyes, they not unwillingly began to imitate them in having their monuments lettered. But a survey of the latter, both in
Britain and Ireland, gives one the impression that their
chief consideration was still the size and durability
of the stone used ; it might be inscribed or not, that
was an afterthought and a luxury unknown to their
ancestors.   But, in case any writing was indulged in,
the language in this country was usually Latin, which
seems to have continued to be the official and learned
tongue. In about two dozen instances, however, the
Goidelic language was used mostly to accompany
a Latin version, and written in a peculiar character
called Ogam. Possibly that kind of writing was invented by a Goidelic native of Siluria or Demetia, who,

having acquired a knowledge of the Roman alphabet, and some practice in a simple system of scoring numbers, elaborated the latter into an alphabet of his own fitted for cutting on stone or wood. From South Wales we might presume it to have been introduced to Ireland, especially the south and south-west ; and, on the other hand, to Devon, but rather sparingly so far as one can discover, to Cornwall, and more sparingly still to North Wales, while the Ogams of Scotland need not be discussed, as they seem to be mostly of later introduction, showing traces of the influence of manuscript writing on parchment. The argument from numbers points to Ireland as the country where Ogmic writing was invented, and it must also be admitted that there are certain features of the Ogam alphabet which Latin letters cannot have suggested. It is emphatically the work of a grammarian, who is possibly to be regarded as representing the linguistic science of the more learned class of Druids in ancient Erin.

Looking at the Ogam epitaphs of Ireland, of which more than 200 are said to have existed, and most of which are still extant, chiefly in the counties of Waterford, Cork, and Kerry, one finds that, though they belong to Christian times, the burial-places in which they occur are frequently unconnected with churches, and used only for interring unbaptized persons, or else no longer used at all : thus it would seem that they are the old pagan burial-places, continued in use in Christian times by a Christian people. The stones are, in many instances, the objects of a reverence bordering very

closely on worship, a state of things of which we find
a trace in the Welsh legend[1] about St. David splitting
with a stroke of his sword the capstone of the cromlech
in Gower, called Maen Cetti, in order to show to the
people that it had no divine attributes : thereupon they
are said to have been converted to his religion. But
the belief in such stones was probably far too deeply
rooted to be readily got rid of, and the Church
possibly had no difficulty in making them arti-
culate witnesses to a kind of merit recognised by a
class of inscriptions in Wales, dating usually about
the eighth century or later, and having nothing
exactly corresponding to them in any other part of
western Christendom.   One, for instance, runs thus :—
" The cross of Christ : Enniaun made it for the soul
of Guorgoret ; " and another thus :—" In the name
of God the highest begins the cross of the Saviour,
which Samson, the abbot, prepared for his own soul
and for that of Ithel, the king," &c. Another one, however, near Bridgend has been supposed to be of the
beginning of the seventh century, and it runs thus :—
" Conbellini set up this cross for the soul of his scitlivissi." The last word is unmistakably Goidelic, and
must have meant a man who acted as an emissary or
scout.   But this class of inscriptions is not to be
severed from another which is still better known, especially in Ireland.   It may be illustrated by the following specimen from Gwnnws in Cardiganshire :—"Whoever shall have read this name let him give a blessing
on behalf of the soul of Hiroidil, son of Carotinn,"

[1] Iolo MSS., p 83.

the name alluded to being a figure forming a sort of
wheel-cross supplemented by the monogram of Christ
x p s[1].

As regards the older inscriptions, they seem to
show that by the sixth century the Ordovices had
carried their Brythonic speech into the district north
of the Mawddach, and even into that portion of the
modern county of Carnarvon which consists of the
old deanery of Eivionydd, and looks, as it were, towards Harlech; but the country from the Mawddach
to the north of Eivionydd was made up of Ardudwy
and Eivionydd, which together are sometimes called
Dunodig, from Dunod, a son of Cunedda, who is
said to have conquered it from the Goidels. How far
Brythonic speech had then penetrated into the neighbourhood of Snowdon it is impossible to say; but
traces of an Ogam inscription have recently been discovered near Brynkir in Eivionydd, and there is a
well-known bilingual epitaph which was found as far
east as Clocaenog, near Ruthin, in the basin of the
Clwyd. In South Wales most of Cardiganshire was
probably still Goidelic, though it had long been conquered by the Cunedda family under the rule of Keredig.
But not only had all the country north of a line from
the Wyrè to the bend of the Wye near Talgarth, in
Brecknockshire, or thereabouts, become Brythonic
by this time, but the Goidelic country south of it
seems, if we may trust the indications afforded by the

[1] The inscriptions are respectively Nos. 73, 62, 67, and 122
in Hübner's "Inscrip. Brit. Christ."; see also Westwood's
"Lapid. Walliæ," pp. 144, 145, plate 68.

inscriptions, to have been severed into two regions,
of which the one lay west of the Towy, and the other
on both sides of a line drawn from Brecon to Neath,
in Glamorgan.   More exactly speaking, the latter consisted of two distinct districts, a southern one between
Cardiff and Loughor, and a northern one in the upper
valley of the Usk, with Brecon as its central point,
and taking in the old deaneries of Brecon, probably
the ancient patrimony of Brychan, who has so large a
place in Welsh hagiology.   Both he and his numerous offspring may have been more Goidelic than
Brythonic, though they were allied in various ways
with the Cunedda family.   The country east of these
two districts, from the hills of Brecknock and the
lower course of the Taff, seems to have become
Brythonic : when and how, it is very hard to say.   It
was brought about partly, perhaps, by the influence
of the nearest Brythonic tribes east of the Severn, as
suggested by the fact that one of the most important
inscriptions of ancient Glamorgan commemorates a
prince called Bodvoci,[1] a name at once Gaulish and
Brythonic, which had been in esteem among the
Dobunni, on whose gold coins it figured before they
submitted to the Roman yoke.   It was partly due
also, no doubt, to conquests by the Ordovices in the
direction of the mouth of the Severn.   The history
of these conquests, however, is lost, but attention has
already been called to the power of Maelgwn over
all parts of South Wales, and we have possibly a proof

[1] See Hübner's " Inscrip. Brit. Christianæ," No 71, and
Rhys's " Lectures on Welsh Philology," p. 86.

of the southern advance of the Ordovices in Dinas
Powys, the name of a place in the vicinity of Cardiff.
The epigraphic map, if we may use the term, further
suggests that the eastern Goidelic districts were cut
off from connection with the western one by a
strip of Brythonic land, reaching from the country
of the Ordovices to the basin of the Towy, and
down the eastern bank of that river to the sea.
This, it will be seen, would include the district of
Kidwelly, from which, together with Gower, Nennius[1] expressly mentions the driving out of the
Goidels by Cunedda and his sons.   But Welsh tradition sometimes ascribes the expulsion to Cunedda
and Urien of Rheged, and sometimes to the latter
alone.   The districts in question are specified
to have been Gower and Kidwelly, together with
Carnwyllon and Iscennen, between the Tawè and the
Towy, together with its tributary the Cothi.[2]   Nennius
mentions .Urien as one of the four kings of the
Brythons opposed to Hussa, who began his reign
over Bernicia in the year 567.   The reason for his
leaving the North is probably to be sought in the
feuds which culminated in the great battle of
Arderydd in 573, when the combatants on both sides
are surmised to have been Celts.   The conquests of
Urien in the land of the southern Goidels do not
appear to have formed an integral part of the Cunedda
legend, so we seem to be at liberty to place them
in this part of the sixth century.   It is needless to

[1] Mommsen's " Chronica Minora," iii. 14 (p. 156).
[2] Iolo MSS., pp. 70, 71.

say that they were hardly undertaken without the
leave of the over-king of the Cunedda dynasty. These
measures may have been called for by the Goidels
trying to make fresh conquests, and Urien, who
could, for some reason or other, be spared from the
North, may have been made use of to crush them with
his following of Brythons. In any case the result must
have practically put an end for ever to the aspirations
of the Goidels in South Wales, if they had any. There
are other indications to the same effect, especially
in the legendary life of St. David, written by Rhy-
gyvarch, bishop of St. David's, in the latter part of
the eleventh century. We are there told of a severe
struggle[1] between the saint and the prince called
Boia. This Pagan chief, sometimes called a Scot
and sometimes a Pict, was, of course, discomfited
by the miracles said to have been wrought by David :
in due time both he and his wife came to a bad
end, which may be taken to mean that the saint was
backed to such an extent by the power of the Cunedda
family, to which he belonged on the father's side,
that local opposition was of no avail against him. The
king of Demetia in Gildas's time is by him called (in
the vocative) *Vortipori*, a non-Goidelic name, which
may be regarded as evidence of Brythonic influence in
the country : the name appears in the Nennian genealogies in the Welsh form of *Guortepir*, borne by a son
of Aircol, whose name must be the Welsh reduction
of the Latin *Agricola*. Aircol's father was *Triphun*,

---

[1] It has been alluded to at p. 231 ; see also "Cambro-Brit.
SS.," pp. 117–143

which also seems to be a non-Goidelic name, but
Triphun and his Sons are said to have been the
princes of Demetia at the time of St. David's birth.
During some part of King Triphun's reign, Keredigion
seems to have been ruled by Sanctus or Sant, the
son of Keredig, and the father of St. David : according to the legendary life of his son, Sant had become a
monk, and gone to Demetia, where he met the nun
who became the mother of St. David : the incident is
easier to understand if we suppose him to have been
at the time not only king of Keredigion, but possessed
of power enough in Demetia to enable him to do
there much as he liked. In any case, the king of
Demetia does not seem to have had much authority
left to him as against the princes of the house of
Cunedda. The ancestors of Triphun had possibly
made the best of the situation by adopting the religion
of the dominant race, and allying themselves by
marriage with the Cunedda dynasty. However that
may be, the princes of his house affected non-
Goidelic names, though they derived their origin
from Ireland, being, as they were, descended from
the Déisi exiles. The proof of this is to be found in
the agreement between their pedigree as given in the
legend of the Déisi and in the Nennian Genealogies.[1]

[1] The former is given in the Bodley MSS., Laud Misc. 610,
and Rawlinson B. 502, already alluded to, and the latter in the
Harleian MS. 3,859, where the portion of Triphun's genealogy
which should show the Irish descent is replaced by a fabrication
which includes as his remote ancestors both Maximus and Constantine. It will be found printed in the pedigree of Elen wife
to Howel the Good, in the preface to Williams' " Ann. Cambriæ.," p. x. See also the "Arch. Cambrensis," 1892, p. 64.

We are reminded by it that the words of Nennius as to
the expulsion of the Scotti are not to be interpreted too
literally ; for, as their princes in Dyved were allowed
to remain, it is not likely that the clansmen were
driven out of the country.   The power of the Goidels
here had probably been broken ever since the conquests of Keredig, who was doubtless the *Coroticus* of a
letter[1] of St. Patrick, in which the saint holds him up
to detestation on account of the cruelty of his men
towards certain converted Goidels whom they had
taken captive.   To revert to St. David, it is important
to bear in mind that he was probably a Goidel, on the
mother's side : this explains, at least in part, why his
labours were always directed to the Goidelic districts,
and also why men from Ireland came to sit at his feet.
It, moreover, gives a meaning to a curious passage in
his life, which describes how Gildas's preaching in
Demetia was, once on a time, brought to an abrupt
end by the mysterious influence of the greatness of
David, even when he happened to be present only in
embryo.   The story seems to make the difference between the two men in point of age too great; but the fact
it dimly sets forth is that Gildas, who was a Brython of
the Brythons, could not hope for the same following
among the Goidels as a man, who to his connexion
with a powerful Brythonic family added probably a
native's knowledge of Goidelic speech and complete
sympathy with everything Goidelic except Goidelic
paganism.   But it is in Cadoc that we find David's

[1] Published by Haddan and Stubbs in their " Councils and
Eccles. Documents," ii. pp. 314–319.

most formidable rival. Cadoc, like his brother saint, may have been connected by blood with the house of Cunedda, but whether that was so or not, he seems to have had the support of Maelgwn, its redoubtable head; and, like David, he seems to have possessed the qualifications calculated to make his ministration acceptable to the Goidels. The reputation, however, which he has left behind him is rather one for learning and wisdom ; while churches dedicated to David are to be found here and there in all parts of South Wales, except that which formed the old diocese of St. Padarn.

The Brythonic people, who may be presumed to have buried in barrows, have left us an inscription in Montgomeryshire, and another in Merionethshire, in both of which the deceased is said to have been placed in a barrow or mound—*in tumulo :* the same expression occurs also in an epitaph not very far from Edinburgh, and another near Yarrow kirk, in the county of Selkirk. This contrasts with the great majority of the epitaphs from the Goidelic parts of Wales and Dumnonia, in which we are simply told that the deceased "lies," *jacit*, or "lies here," *hic jacit.* There are, however, a few of the former description on Goidelic ground or on its boundaries : one such occurs in Cornwall, one or possibly two in South Wales, and there is a curious one in Carnarvonshire in which the dead man is said to lie in a *congeries lapidum* or cairn of stones.[1] All the above interments belonged, probably,

[1] See Hübner, Nos. 125, 131, 211, 209, 7, 52, 234, 136; compare also Kuhn's " Beitræge," iii, p. 73, where Stokes gives Gaulish and Irish parallels.

to Brythons, or were made under the influence of the
Brythonic fashion which was spreading among the Goidels. Compared with the other and more numerous epitaphs, they are on an average longer and fuller, more in
accordance with the Roman custom, and characterized
by a greater variety of formula, which would seem to
show that they appertained to a people more given to
writing than the Goidels can have been, though the
latter made more frequent use of it in honouring the
dead. It is probably with these Brythonic burials
that we have to class the grass-grown cairn, removed
in 1832, in the immediate neighbourhood of Mold, in
Flintshire. The spot was called Bryn yr Ellyllon
"the Elves' Knoll," and it was believed in the
country around to be haunted by a spectre in gold
armour. When more than 300 loads of stones had
been carted away the workmen came to a cist with
the following contents: (1) The skeleton of a tall
and powerful man placed at full length. (2) A richly
embossed gold peytrel[1] (French *poitrail*) or brunt for
a pony of about 12 hands like the famous Welsh
breed of the present day : it measured about 3 ft. 7 ins.
by a central depth of 8½ ins., and was mounted on a
copper plate provided with a fringe of coarse cloth.
(3) Some three hundred amber beads. Traces of
something made of iron are said to have been
detected, and two or three yards from the cist was
found standing a cinerary urn full of ashes. The

[1] It is one of the treasures in the British Museum : see Read's
Guide, pp. 149-51, and Boyd Dawkins's Early Man in Britain,
pp. 431-33.

burial belongs to the end of the Bronze Age, when cremation was not entirely obsolete in this country, and when gold cannot have been scarce. We should probably not be wrong in attributing it to the time of the Roman occupation. On the whole, the duty of commemorating the dead among the Celts may be supposed to have devolved on the bards to whom we are probably indebted for the seventy or more stanzas devoted to this object in the Black Book of Carmarthen, a Welsh manuscript of the twelfth century.[1] The last of them, strangely enough, has to do with a grave in the same neighbourhood of Mold, and it runs as follows when freely rendered into English : nay, it is not impossible that one of its references is to him of Bryn yr Ellyllon.

> Whose the grave in the great glade ?
> Proud was his hand on his blade—
> There Beli, giant Benlli's son, is laid.

A word now respecting the people whom the Celts found in possession of the island when they came here : little is known for certain about them, though a good deal may be inferred, as we have frequently had occasion to suggest. From the nature of the case the first Celtic invaders, that is to say, the Celts of the Goidelic branch, were those who had most to do with the aborigines, and it may be doubted whether the Brythons and Belgæ ever came much in contact with them. So when they adopted Celtic speech and habits, it was those of the Goidels they learnt and not of the Brythons ; and, looked at from the opposite

[1] See Skene's " Four Ancient Books of Wales," pp. 28-35.

point of view, it is hardly open to doubt that the
Goidelic race was profoundly modified in many
respects by its absorption and assimilation of the
indigenous element. Indeed, it has been well said
that "the term Goidelic should strictly be confined
to the mixed population of Aryan and non-Aryan
language in possession of the country when the
Brythons arrived."[1] It is here, in fact, we are to look
for the explanation of a good deal of the difference of
speech between the Welsh and the Irish, not to
mention that the study of the skulls of the present
inhabitants of the British Islands, and of their physique
and complexion, has convinced anthropologists that
we still have among us a large number of men who
are at least in part the descendants of non-Aryan
ancestors. In fact we seem to detect their influence
on the Goidels even within the narrow circle of their
ancient inscriptions. The subject is a difficult one,
and we can only touch it superficially. The full
Aryan proper name was of the class to which such
instances as the Greek Θεό-δωρος and Δωρό-θεος
belong, from θεός, god, and δῶρον, a gift; and abundance of names compounded in the same easy way
are to be found in every Celtic language; besides
these the Goidels have others which are not com-
pounds, and to which the other Aryan languages

[1] See Read's Guide, p. 2?. This text could be readily illustrated by indicating some of the differences between the oldest
Goidelic of Ogmic epigraphy and the non-Gaulish Celtic of the
Coligny Calendar, for which see the Rev. Celtique, xix. 213-23,
plates i.-vi., and Nicholson's ' Keltic Researches," pp. 116-28.

offer few parallels. An instructive instance is such a
name as Maelumi or Mael-Umi, the slave or servant
of bronze, which possibly testifies to a national devotion to the bronze sword, a weapon which the ancient
Irish regarded as inspired and capable, among
other things, of giving the lie to the perjurer : *mael*
means shorn or tonsured, and here refers, probably,
to the tonsure with which the Goidels were familiar
as denoting servitude, even before the Church introduced a somewhat different observance among
them. They went on forming Christian names in
the same fashion, as may be learned from such well-
known instances as Mael-Padraic, Patrick's slave, and
Gille-Crist, Christ's servant, Anglicized respectively
into Mulpatrick and Gilchrist.[1] Another word used
in the same way was *mug* or *mog*, a slave, as in
the proper name, Mog-Nuadat, Nuada's-Slave, where
Nuada—in Welsh, Nudd and Lludd, better known in
English as Lud—was a name of the god of the sea.
Irish legend makes Nuada Necht husband of the
Boyne, and the Silurians worshipped the god under
the name of Nodens or Nudens, in a temple of
Roman make at Lydney, on the western bank of the
Severn. To the same class belongs Mog-Neid or
Mog-Nét, Nét's-Slave, in which the name of *Nét* was,
according to Cormac, that of a god of war of the
pagan Goidels. More correctly speaking, he seems to
have been a war-god of the non-Celtic race in both
Ireland and Britain ; for an inscription in the county

[1] See page 73 of this volume, and compare Semitic names
like *Abdiel* and the like,

of Kerry gives the name without a case-ending, and
so marks it out as a probably non-Celtic word : it
is worthy of notice that the man's name Mog-Nét,
appears in the eighth century among the Transmontane Picts of Alban as evidence that the amalgamation
of the same races had begun there also. It occurs
reduced to Moneit in one of the chronicles as the
name of the father of Biceot, one of the officers of
Nechtan when he was defeated by Ungust in 729 near
the waters of the Spey. The Kerry monument[1] to
which we allude introduces us to another remarkable
class of names, for it is found to commemorate a man
called Nét's-Hound son of Rí's-Hound. The latter
is probably to be distinguished from Rói in Irish
literature, in the name of a well-known legendary
hero, called Cú-Rói mac Dairi, or Daire's son Hound
of Rói. Rí was possibly the name of one of the
gods of the non-Celtic race of the Ivernians or Erna
of Munster, as was also most likely Corb, whence
such names of men as Mog-Corb, Corb's-Slave, and
Cú-Corb, Corb's-Hound, were derived. Plenty more
of this dog nomenclature could be produced from
Irish literature, such as Cú-Ulad, the Hound of the
Ultonians, where we take *hound* to mean Guardian or
Champion ; and so in other cases. Macbeth is also
possibly a name of the same class. It was current in
Ireland as well as in Scotland, and was sometimes

---

[1] See Brash's " Ogam Monument," p. 175, and plate xvi. ;
the reading is *Conu Nett moqvi Conu Ri ;* compare also the
Hebrew *Caleb*, dog.

treated as purely Goidelic, meaning Son of Life[1]; but such an abstract interpretation is discountenanced by *Maelbeth*, which was likewise used in both islands, and must have meant the Slave of Beth. That this last word meant some dog divinity or dog-totem, is suggested by the probable identity of Macbeth —not of Duncan, as we think—with the Hundason, or Hound's-Son, of one of the Orkney Sagas which relate to their time. In that case Maelbeth would be a partial translation into Gaelic of the name, which, completely rendered into it, produced the *Maelchon*[2] we have more than once mentioned in connection with the Pictish kings; this at any rate, meant the Hound's Slave. Similarly Macbeth, put wholly into Goidelic, would be Mac-Con, or the Hound's Son, which occurs as the name of a legendary prince, whose sway was not confined to Ireland, but extended, according to Cormac, to the part of Britain in which Glastonbury stood. Mac-Con may, perhaps, be regarded as representing the whole non-Celtic race of these islands. It would occupy too much space to go into the details of this question, but enough has been said to make it probable that the dog was a most highly respected totem or god of that race, and also

[1] It is right, however, to say that this interpretation is countenanced by the fact that it is matched in Irish by a " Son of death."

[2] The nominative would be *Mael-Con*, and the full genitive might be expected to be Maile-Chon; but, as in certain other instances of the same kind, we have never met with the longer form, except in Bede's Hist. iii. 4. where it is written *Meilochon* in three syllables.

to call to mind the words of Herodotus, who would seem to have heard of such a people when he speaks of a race called the Kynesii or Kynetes ; both of these terms have a look of Greek words meaning dog-men. His first mention of them comes in the second book (c. 33), where he speaks thus :—" The Celts are outside the Pillars of Hercules, and they border on the Kynesii, who dwell the farthest away towards the west of the inhabitants of Europe." The other passage occurs in the fourth book (c. 49), where he speaks in the same way, mentioning the Celts as the farthest away towards the setting of the sun, with the exception of the Kynetes. So far as the words of Herodotus go, one might suppose that the race he had in view was a non-Celtic one of Britain and Ireland ; but later writers, such as Avienus, locate them in the west of the Spanish peninsula, which suggests a still more important inference—namely, that there existed in Herodotus's time a Continental people of the same origin and habits as the non-Celtic aborigines of these islands. What the name of the latter was in this country we are not quite sure, but in Ireland it was Ivernii in Ptolemy's time ; and he mentions a town there called Ivernis, and a river Iernos. To these may be added various forms of the name of the island, such as Juvenal's *Iuuerna*, for which the Romans more usually substituted *Hibernia* ; the *Iverna* of a graffito to be seen till lately in the Palace of the Cæsars in Rome ; the Irish *Hériu* or *Ériu*, accusative *Hérinn* or *Érinn* ; and the Welsh *Iwerddon* ; not to mention Ἰέρνη, mulcted of its *v* or *w* by Greek pronunciation, just as in Irish itself an early *Iverijo* has yielded *Hériu*, while the name of the *Ivernii* appears as *Ierni*,[1] *Erni*, and *Erna* in Irish literature, which musters that people latest and strongest in Munster.[2] It may be added that the fact of our having the same word as the Goidelic name of Ireland used also as that of the river Earn[3] in Scotland, suggests that one would, perhaps, not err greatly in applying the term *Ivernii*, or Ivernian, to the non-Celtic natives of Britain as well as of the sister island, where their eponymous ancestor of cognate name was called Ier, Iar, Er, Ir. He is eclipsed by Emer ; and the legend makes the whole Irish people[4] descend from two brothers, of whom Emer was the one, and much to their credit Airem (genitive Airemon) the other, whose name means a ploughman ; for he represented the Aryan farmer who introduced agriculture, however rude, among a people of hunters or shepherds, and he is, moreover, described as the first in Ireland, except the Fairies, to yoke cattle for work. This is in harmony with what is stated in the old Irish Laws, that in Erin all law emanated from the Féini or the waggon-men,

---

[1] This important form is to be inferred from *ier diernaib* (Iver de Iverniis), in " Lebar na h-Uidre," p. 99*a*.

[2] Loch Erne derives its name from another source, namely from the ancient people called by Ptolemy Ἐρδινοι, accented Ἐρδῖνοι in Müller's text, though most of the MSS. seem to read Ἐρδινοι.

[3] See Berchan's prophecy in Skene's " Chr. of the Picts and Scots," pp. 84, 88, 98 ; also a confused bit of geography cited in Reeves's " Culdees," p. 124, where *sraith hirend* must refer to Strathearn.

[4] See Fiacc's Hymn in Stoke's " Goidelica," pp. 127, 131.

whence it was sometimes called Féineachus.¹ As the
Celt was destined to have the upper hand over the
Ivernian, the legend makes Airem slay Emer, and
seize on the southern half of the island, which was
supposed to have been the latter's kingdom ; but the
two races agreed in being warlike, so the two brothers
are described as the sons of a soldier or warrior,
whom the legend therefore calls Míl in Irish, and
Miles in Latin, whence the so-called Milesian
Irish. This soldier sometimes had his own name,
*Galam*² or *Golam*, meaning likewise a warrior or a
brave man, from the word *gal*, passion, violence,
valour, of the same origin as *Galli*, the alternative
designation of the Continental Celts, the meaning of
which we have suggested at p. 2 above. But the
simple division of Ireland between the two ancestors
of the Irish proved insufficient for the legend-mongers,
since there were descendants of Emer and Ir in the
north as well as in the south : the legend became com-
plicated with an Emer son of Míl, and an Emer son
of Er or Ir : the latter was to be the father of the
northern Ivernians. These last partly succumbed to
Goidels from Meath, represented eventually by the
northern O'Neils, and they partly retreated as already
mentioned (pp. 94, 246) beyond the Bann to what
was afterwards known as the country of the Irish
Picts or the Scotti proper : there they resisted
the advance of the Goidels, though some of them

¹ See the "Senchus Mór," i. pp. 52, 116.
² See O'Curry's "MS. Materials of Ancient Irish History,"
p. 447, and the Book of Leinster, fol. 4a.

eventually found it necessary to seek a permanent home in Britain, namely in Argyle. Next to Munster this land of Dalriada, Dalnaraide, and Dalfiatach remained probably the most thoroughly Ivernian and the least Celtic in the island. It was found necessary to expand the story about Míl in another direction by giving him an uncle to bear the name of Ith and account for several places in Ireland called Mag-Ithe or the plain of Ith. This was probably non-Celtic, and it entered into the name of the Scotch island of Tiree, known formerly as Tirieth and *Terra Hith*. It is most likely the same name which we have met in that of the Lothian town of Iudeu mentioned by Nennius and in that of the Judic people of the district around St. David's (see pp. 134 and 152 above).

At what time the Ivernian language became extinct in Ireland it is impossible to discover, but in Munster it appears to have not long been dead when Cormac wrote a sort of glossary in the ninth century, and alluded to it as the *Iarn* or iron language ; for, owing to an accident of Irish phonology, both *isern-*, the early form of the Celtic word for iron, and *Ivern-* must become *iarn* in the later stages of the language, so that Cormac believed that in *Iarn* he had the ordinary Irish word for iron, or affected so to believe in order to proceed to explain that it was so called on account of the difficulty of seeing through it, owing to its darkness and the compactness of its texture. He has, however, recorded two words which he regarded as belonging to that language—namely, *fern*,

anything good, and *ond*, a stone. But these, together
with Nét, Corb, Ri, and similar vocables, which may
be suspected of being Ivernian, have hitherto thrown
no light on the origin of the language. Should it
turn out that the historians, who without hesitation
call our Ivernians Iberians, and bring them into
relationship with the Basque-speaking people of
France and Spain, are right in doing so, one could
scarcely wonder that Cormac considered Ivernian a
dark speech. In the north of Ireland that idiom may
have been extinct in the time of Adamnan ; and
Columba in the sixth century cannot have known it,
which, nevertheless, does not prove that there were
no peasants who spoke it there in his time. However that may be, Adamnan mentions a name into
which *ond*, a stone, possibly enters—to wit, that of
Ondemone, a place where the Irish Picts were beaten
by the Goidels in the year 563 : it seems to have
been near the Bann, between Loch Neagh and the
mouth of that river. As for Britain, one of the
most thoroughly non-Celtic portions of it south of
the Clyde was probably that of the Selgovæ or
hunters in Roman times, and later the more limited
Pictish district beyond the Nith, but there is nothing
to prove that the inhabitants had retained their non-
Celtic tongue down to the sixth century, or that
they had lost it before the Roman occupation. North
of the Firths it is otherwise, as we have indications
in Adamnan's Life of Columba that the language of
the aborigines was still a living tongue. Adamnan
wrote a little before the close of the seventh century,

and his work has come down to us in a manuscript
of the eighth. Now Columba, about whom he wrote,
came from the north of Ireland, and spoke the
Goidelic language : he passed over to the new settlement of the Dalriad Scots in Cantyre in 563, when
he was forty-two years of age. Shortly afterwards he
had the island of Iona given him, where he established his religious house, over which Adamnan pre-
sided in a later age. Not long after Columba
came over to Britain he crossed Drumalban on
a mission to Brude, king of the Picts, who had his
stronghold in the neighbourhood of the river Ness,
not far, probably, from its mouth. To him and his men
Columba appears to have had no difficulty in making
himself understood. But when, as we are told, he was
in the province of the Picts, probably a little later but
in much the same district, we read of him preaching
to peasants or plebeians by interpreter. At another
time he happened to be in the island of Skye, when
a boat arrived with two young men who brought their
aged father to be baptized by Columba. This time
also he preached by an interpreter, though the convert
bore the Celtic name of Artbranan, and is described
as the chief of the Geonians (better perhaps Genunians), called by Adamnan Geona Cohors, in which
we have possibly the name of a people of the mainland, called Cerones in the manuscripts of Ptolemy's
Geography. They had their representative among the
seven legendary sons of Cruithne in that one of them
called Ce. The use here made of the word *cohors*
has already been noticed (p. 91) as a rendering of the

Goidelic word *dál*, which is proved to have been applied by the Goidels to the people of that region by the term Dalar, which it suggested to the Norsemen as a name for the Western Highlands : it has been the custom of historians to try to derive it from the Dalriads of Cantyre. The question now arises as to what was the language of the people whom Columba could cnly address by an interpreter. There were in north Britain two groups of Celtic dialects, the Goidelic and the Brythonic ; but there is no reason to suppose that the peasants near King Brude's palace were Brythons, and still less probable is it that those who visited Columba in Skye were of that race. It has usually been supposed that they merely differed from the missionary Scot in speaking a Goidelic dialect, which was not his ; but such a view does scant justice to the devotion of the early saints of Ireland to their work, and there is no reason whatever to suppose that they could not speedily master dialectal differences, which were at most of no very important nature in that early age. So far from this being the case, the usual silence as to interpreters suggests that it was not a rare thing for Goidels to master the language of the Brythons, and the latter that of the former, so far as to be able to make their way in one another's country, though it must have given them infinitely more trouble than any dialect closely akin to their own. It remains, then, that the language of the people who could not understand Columba was not Celtic : in all probability it was that of the ancient inhabitants. In the district in which

the power of the Picts grew into a considerable state,
where the remarkable succession, known as Pictish,
obtained and lasted longest, it appears that Goidelic
was unintelligible to the peasants in the sixth century, while in the west, opposite Skye, even men of
rank among the Picts could be found who knew
no Goidelic, though they had begun to adopt Goidelic
names, just as, in Wales, many a man has the English
name John Jones, though he cannot speak English
or pronounce his name in the English way. Here
may also be mentioned Argyle, as it is found variously
called Oirir Gaithel, Airer Gaethel, and Arregaethel,
meaning the region belonging to the Goidels or
Gaelic-speaking people, just as Airer Dalriatai
meant the country of the Dalriads : to give the
word Argyle its full meaning, it must be supposed
that, at the time it came into use, the Picts to the north
of the district properly so called were as yet not
Goidels : that is to say, that they still had a language ot
their own.   Bede enumerates [1] the peoples of Britain,
in whose languages Christianity was taught in his
day, as being the Angles, the Brythons, the Scotti
(that is to say, the Goidels), the Picts, and the Latins.
But so far as regards the Pictish language, the sig-
nificance of his words is sometimes explained away
by supposing it to have been a Celtic dialect lying
somewhere between Brythonic and Goidelic, but
rather nearer the latter.   There is, however, no reason
to suppose that to have been Bede's view ; for in the
case of English, he was content to let the language of

[1] " Hist. Eccl.," i. 1.

the Angles stand for all the dialects without mentioning here, for instance, that of the Saxons.   For a long
time, probably before Pictish or Ivernian wholly died
out, it was loaded with words borrowed from Celtic ;
but there is no ground whatever to suppose that it otherwise resembled Celtic or any other Aryan tongue ;
and if what we have surmised as to the name Macbeth
should prove well founded, it would tend to show
that the non-Celtic speech did not become completely
extinct till the restoration for a time, in the eleventh
century, of the Pictish kingdom, in the person
of the king of that name.   The subject cannot be
here gone into at length, but we may say that there
are data which tend to prove that the non-Celtic aborigines spoke what was practically one and the same
language in both Britain and Ireland.   Moreover, we
are inclined to believe that it has left its influence on
Goidelic, and it may be presumed, that where the
ancient inhabitants were unable to hold their own,
they were not extirpated by the Goidels but gradually
assimilated by them.   At first the Goidel probably
drove the Ivernian back towards the west and
the north, but, when another invasion came, that
of the Brythons, he was driven back in the same
way; that is, he was, forced, so to say, into the
arms of the Ivernian native, to make common
cause with him against the common enemy.   Then
followed the amalgamation of the Goidelic and
Ivernian elements ; for wherever traces of the latter
are found we seem to come upon the native in the
process of making himself a Goidel, and before

becoming Welsh or English in speech he first became Goidelic, in every instance south of the Clyde. This means, from the Celtic point of view, that the Goidelic race of history is not wholly Celtic or Aryan, but that it inherits in part a claim to the soil of these islands, derived from possession at a time when, as yet, no Aryan waggoner's team had approached the Atlantic ; and it is, perhaps, from their Kynesian ancestry that the Irish of the present day have inherited the lively humour and ready wit, which, among other character- istics, distinguish them from the Celts of the Brythonic branch, most of whom, especially the Kymry, are a people still more mixed, as they consist of the Goidelic element of the compound nature already suggested, with an ample mixture of Brythonic blood, introduced mostly by the Ordovices. As for Welsh, in Wales, it is, roughly speaking, the Brythonic language as spoken by the Ordovices, and as learned by the Goidelic peoples overshadowed by them in the Princi- pality. This harmonizes with the actual distribution of the four chief dialects of spoken Welsh, which are those respectively of the Ordovic land of Powys, of Siluria or Gwent, of Demetia or Dyved, and of Venedot or Gwynedd.

Skulls are harder than consonants, and races lurk behind when languages slink away. The lineal des- cendants of the neolithic aborigines are ever among us, possibly even those of a still earlier race. On the other hand, we can imagine the Kynesian impatiently hearing out the last echoes of palæolithic speech ; we can guess dimly how the Goidel gradually silenced the

Kynesian; we can detect the former coming slowly round to the keynote of the Brython; and, lastly, we know how the Englishman is engaged, linguistically speaking, in drowning the voice of both in our own day. This intrusion upon intrusion of one race on another renders it very hard to treat intelligibly of such a people, for example, as the Welsh, at any rate without repeatedly making the wearisome round of circumlocution; thus, one may happen to be dealing with them chiefly in an anthropological sense as Brythons, and as distinguished from Goidels, while one may be understood to be looking ethnologically at them as forming certain well - known linguistic or political aggregates, which, in point of race, consist of mixed groups of Brythons, Goidels, and non-Aryans. We are not sanguine enough to suppose that the possibility of misunderstandings of the nature here indicated has been successfully avoided in these pages. All we can reasonably expect the reader's mind to retain, is a certain impression of a somewhat confused picture of one wave of speech chasing another and forcing it to dash itself into oblivion on the western confines of the Aryan world. That we should fondly dream English likely to be the last, comes only from our being unable to see into a distant future pregnant with untold changes of no less grave a nature than those which have taken place in the dreary wastes of the past.

APPENDIX.

— ❖ —

NOTES ON SOME OF THE NAMES IN THE TEXT.

AθθEDOMAROS, p. 36. The second part of this name, *māros*, is supposed to be the same word as the Welsh *mawr*, great, large, Irish *már* or *mór*, and it enters into a great many Celtic names. With regard to the other part, it is first to be observed that some of the Gallo-Brythonic Celts of antiquity lisped their *ss* in certain positions into δδ or θθ; but this habit was neither general nor has it come down into Welsh. The genitive of *Aδδedomaros* is read *Assedomari* in an inscription found in Styria (Berlin " Corpus Inscr. Lat.," iii. No. 5,291); and a Welsh name, partly identical, is met with in a Welsh MS. of the twelfth century as *Guynnassed* (see Skene's " Four Ancient Books of Wales," ii. p. 32), which would now be written *Gwynasedd*. But the number of Welsh words that should throw light on the meaning of *asedd* is somewhat embarrassing ; first comes *asen*, a rib, plural *eis*, ribs, also the roof beams which run the length of a house ; then we have an *asedd*, which would, at first sight, seem to be the word wanted, but is probably a collective plural of *as-en*, standing for an earlier *ansiia;* lastly may be mentioned *aseth*, which may be a variant of the same word as *assedo:* it means a spit or spear. Thus *Aδδedomaros* would appear to mean one who is great as to the spear, and *Gwynasedd* would be, so to speak, Whitespear. The related forms are Gothic *ans*, a beam, O. Norse *áss*, a pole, a main rafter, a yard ; also probably the Latin *asser*, a beam, pole, or stake. It would thus appear that *aðð* and *ass* in the name in question stand for an earlier *ans*, and this has an important bearing on the interpretation of other old names. A different theory has been proposed by the learned professor, M. d'Arbois de Jubainville, in his work, entitled "Études Grammaticales," pp. 32*-38.*

ADMINIUS, p. 34. The form *Amminus*, which is the one on coins, shows that *Adminius* is a Latinizing of *Amminios* under the influence of the notion that the name began with the prefix *ad*.

ALAUNA, p. 161. We have possibly the same name in the Welsh *Alun*, borne by a stream that joins the Dee not far from Chester, and there is a Coed *Alun* near Carnarvon.

ALLOBROX, p. 140. *Allobrox*, pl. *Allobroges*, appears in that form as the name of a Celtic people in Gaul. It is likewise read *Allobrogae*, a word thus explained by an ancient scholiast on Juvenal, viii. 233 :—"Allobrogae Galli sunt. Ideo autem dicti Allobrogae quoniam *brogae* Galli agrum dicunt, *alla* autem aliud ; dicti autem Allobroges quia ex alio loco fuerant translati " (see Jahn's "Juvenal," p. 303, and Diefenbach's "Orig. Europ.," s. v. *Allobrogae*). So the *allo-* of this name goes with the Greek ἀλλο-, as against the Latin aliu-s ; for the Gallo-Brythonic Celts agreed with the Greeks in making *lj* into *ll*. *Brox*, *broges*, and *brogae* are represented in Welsh by *bro*, a district or country. The Irish form *mruig*, more frequently *bruig*, has been ascertained to be the same word as the English *march*, and German *mark*, a boundary or district. Probably the Latin *margo*, edge or boundary, is from the same source. The old Gaulish had made *mr* into *br*, as Welsh has in *bro*, which enters also into the Welsh word *Cymro*, a Welshman, pl. *Cymry*, for *Com-brox* and *Com-brog ii* respectively. The vowel of the second part varied in Welsh as in *troed*, foot, *traed*, feet, since the Welsh word for a Welshwoman is *Cymraes*, and for the Welsh language *Cymraeg*, implying early forms, *Combragissa* and *Combragica*. The national name, *Cymro* seems to have been confined to the Kymric Celts, though the Bretons sometimes give the simple *brô* the sense of compatriot; and, whether the Kymry have ethnologically anything to do with the *Cimbri* or not, the names have absolutely nothing in common, in spite of what charlatans continue to say to the contrary.

ANTEθRIGUS, p. 37. The coins give *Antedrigus*, *Anteθ*, and other abbreviations ; so I have ventured to regard the name as *Anteðrigus* of the *U* declension : the meaning of the compound is obscure.

ATECOTTI, pp. 56, 91, 222. This seems to be the most correct spelling of the word, as it is probably to be resolved into Ate-cotti, the latter element being practically identical with the Cornish word *coth*, Breton *coz*, old or ancient. *Ate* is the early form of the prefix which appears in modern Welsh as *ad*, *at*, in such words as *adgas* or *atcas*, odious, from *cas*, hateful. With *Atecotti* as meaning ancient inhabitants, compare the Irish *Tuath Sen-Chenebil* and *Tuath Sen-Érann*, the tribe of the Old Race, and the tribe of the Old Ivernians respectively, in the lists of Irish tribes in O'Curry's "Manners and Customs of the Ancient Irish," vol. i. pp. xxviii., &c.

ATREBATES, p. 10. It is also treated as *Atrebatii*, which has been resolved into *Ad-treb-at-*, and derived from *ad-treb*, whence the Irish verb *attrebaim*, " I dwell or inhabit," and the Welsh *athref* in the term *tir athref,* whereby was meant the land immediately around the dwelling. Thus it appears that *Atrebates* meant inhabitants, but probably in the special sense of farmers or homestead men. It may be added that the Welsh word *tref* has its equivalents in the English *thorp,* German *dorf,* and their congeners.

BELISAMA, p. 68. The meaning of the name is unknown, but in point of form the word seems to be a superlative like *Uxama :* this occurs in the name of a Gaulish town in Spain called by Ptolemy *Uxama Barca,* which would in Welsh be *Barca Uchaf* or Upper Barca, literally, in accordance with Celtic idiom, Uppermost Barca. Possibly *Auximum* (now *Osimo*), a town of the Piceni, may be compared.

BITURIX, p. 65. The plural was Bituriges, and the name of the people is now perpetuated by the town of Bourges : it seems to have meant *Weltherrscher* or world-kings, *bitu* being the same word which we have in the Welsh *byd,* world, Irish, *bith,* gen. *betho.*

BLATOBULGION, p. 233. This is a curious name, and the following notes may be of interest:—The story of Branwen, daughter of Llyr, describes Bran, her brother, leading a host to Ireland and on the point of being received into a spacious palace by the Irish, when one of his brothers, having gone before, found that they had two hundred bags in different parts of the building containing each a warrior ready for battle : he asked the Irish what was in each bag (*bol*), and they persistently replied that it was meal (*blawd*). He went round, and quietly killed all the soldiers in the bags by squeezing each man's skull between his fingers : then he sang an *englyn* on the kind of meal he found in the last of the bags ("Mab.," iii. pp. 95, 96 ; 120, 121). On the Irish side we have the account of the battle of *Dúnbolg,* in Wicklow, published by O'Donovan in his edition of the "Four Masters" under the year 594, when, according to some, it took place. This story makes a provincial Irish king, Bran Dub, conquer the King of Erin by passing in the night into the latter's camp with a large number of wild horses and some thousands of oxen bearing hampers on their backs. The hampers were supposed by the sentinels to be full of food for the King of Erin, but they contained armed men, who presently attacked the camp, and tied small bags full of stones to the tails of the wild horses to increase the confusion. The result was the utter defeat of Bran's enemies, and that the place came to be called the fort of sacks or *Dún-bolg*. Treated as Celtic, *Blatobulgion* must have literally meant the Meal-bag, and it consists of early forms of the words cited from the Mabinogi of Branwen. It is, however, possible that *bulgion, bolg*, and *bòl* in all the foregoing instances are not words of Celtic origin, and that they had another meaning. The name in the Itinerary used to be treated as two words ; but it occurs only once—namely, in the ablative case—and we have no hesitation in reading *Blatobulgio* instead of the unintelligible *Blato Bulgio* of the editors. This is another happy suggestion for which we are indebted to Dr. Henry Bradley. Another Blatobulgion has been identified in the neighbourhood of St. Andrews : it is now *Blebo*, representing older forms *Blabo, Blabolg, Bladebolg, Blathbolg*. For this I am indebted to Mr. W. J. N. Liddall, who has published it in his "Place-names of Fife and Kinross" (Edinburgh, 1896). p. 10.

BORESTI, pp. 89, 95. It is difficult not to regard the first two syllables of this name as the Brythonic equivalent of the word *forest*, which comes to us from the Low Latin *foresta*. The Boresti were very probably the same people as the Verturiones ; and in

84 CELTIC BRITAIN.

that case they formed the outlying portion of the nation of the Brythons, and dwelt on the outskirts of the Caledonian Forest.

BOUDICCA, p. 66. This or *Bōdicca* is doubtless the most correct form, with the *c* doubled for a diminutival name: the ordinary Boadicea is the gibberish of editors. The name occurs as *Bodicca* in a Roman inscription found in Africa (Berlin, "Corpus Inscr. Lat." viii. No. 2877), and *Bodiccius* is read in an inscription commemorating a man belonging to a cohort of *Brittones* in Pannonia (iii. No. 3256). But *Boudica* or *Boudicas* is the spelling in a Roman inscription found in Spain (ii. No. 455), and the name Budic was not an unusual one formerly in Brittany. It is commonly supposed that they are all of the same origin as the Welsh word *budd*, benefit, advantage, and *buddugol*, victorious, so that *Boudicca* might perhaps be equated in point of meaning with such a Latin name as *Victorina*.

BRIGANTES, pp. 30, 39, 113. Some would have it that this name meant mountaineers or hill-men from the same origin as the Welsh *bre*, a hill, and *bryn*, the same. But there are other words which seem to offer a better explanation, such as Welsh *bri*, renown, eminence, *braint*, privilege, formerly written *bryeint* for *brigeint*·, representing an early *brigantia* or *brigantion* according as the word was fem. or neuter. From the stem *brigant-* was formed an adjective *brigant-in-*, which was reduced in Cornish to *brentyn* or *bryntyn* : it meant noble, free, privileged, the contrary of *kêth*, enslaved, while in Welsh it became *brëenhin*, now *brenhin*, a king, which has nothing to do with *Brennus*, though old-fashioned philologists still fancy it has. Phonologically *brigant-* in all these words is the Gallo-Brythonic form of a common Celtic *brignt-* which, with the nasal regularly suppressed, we have in the Irish name Brigit (for *Brignti* of the *i* declension), St. Bridget or Bride. On the whole, then, *Brigantes* would seem to have meant the free men or privileged race as contrasted with some other people.

CALEDONES or CALIDONES, pp. 165, 232. The nominative singular has been discovered as *Caledo* on a bronze tablet found a few years ago at Colchester : see " The Proceedings of the Society of Antiquaries," Series II., vol. xiv., p. 108; also "The Proc. of the Soc. of Antiq. of Scotland," xxxii. 326-30, and " The Welsh People," p. 46. The reading of this very important find is (subject to the correction of *si* into *stri*) :—

DEO · MARTI · MEDOCIO · CAMP
ESIVM [*sic*] · ET VICTORIE ALEXAN
DRI · PII FELICIS AVGVSTI · NOSI [*sic*]
DONVM · LOSSIO · VEDA · DE · SVO
POSVIT · NEPOS · VEPOGENI · CALEDO.

Caledo is probably of Pictish origin, and its meaning is unknown : the Celtic etymologies usually proposed for it will not bear examination. Probably the η in Ptolemy's Καληδόνιοι did not mean a long vowel : at any rate no such quantity is countenanced by the forms extant in Celtic, whether Gaelic or Welsh. This brings us to *Caledonia*, which was presumably a word like Britannia, made by the Romans from the national name Caledo. The latter probably yielded in Goidelic a genitive *Caledinas*, whence Caildenn in Dúnchailden or Dunkeld, and in early Brythonic a corresponding Calidonos, now Celyddon as in *Coed Celyddon*, the Caledonian Forest.

CALGACOS, p. 89. This seems a preferable spelling to Galgacos, as the word, if perchance Celtic, may be derived from the same origin as the Irish word *colg* or *calg*, a sword ; but another etymology is suggested by the Irish word *celg*, cunning, treachery : compare the

name of the Irish hero called *Celtchar na Celg* or
C. of the Wiles, in an Irish poem to be found in
Windisch's "Irische Texte," p. 215.

CALLEVA, pp. 24, 29. This possibly meant a town
in the wood, and is to be explained by means of the
Welsh collective *cell-i*, a wood, a copse : the simpler
form *cell* meant a grove as in *cell o ysgaw*, a grove of
elder, but it has been ousted by and confounded with
the other *cell*, which is the Latin *cella :* the Irish word
was *caill*, a wood. If this guess be right, it would
suggest that the first syllable of the present name
Silchester stands for the Latin word *silva*.

CAMULODUNON, p. 26. The locative occurs on
coins as Camuloduno. *Dunon* is the word which
makes *dīn*, a fortress or town in Welsh, and the whole
name seems to have meant the town of Camulos, who
appears as one of the gods of the Gauls. His name
also seems to enter into the proper name *Camelorigi*
on an early inscribed stone in Pembrokeshire, and
Camuloris on a lead coffin found in Anglesey : see
"Lect. on Welsh Phil.," pp. 364, 400.

CARATÂCOS, p. 35. The Romans wrote *Caratacus*,
and the editors have made it into *Caractacus*, which
is gibberish. The abbreviations CARAT and CARA
have been found on coins : see Sir J. Evans's " Additional coins of the Ancient Britons," pp. 252-5, pl. xii.
xx. The name is well-known in Mod. Welsh as
Caradog, and in Irish as *Carthach*, genitive *Carthaig*,
perpetuated in an Anglicized form by the Irish
families that call themselves *McCarthy*.

CARAUSIUS, pp. 93, 240. The name probably
became popular in Britain : at any rate we find it on
an early inscribed stone at Penmachno, near Bettws
y Coed. Etymologically speaking, we are tempted
to identify it with the Irish Cú-Rói, which seems to
have meant "the Hound of the Plain or of the Field,

probably the field of battle,' from the Irish feminine
róe, *rói*, 'a level plain,' of the same origin as Latin
rus, *rūris*, 'the country." The early Celtic base
would accordingly be rovesiā (Stokes's " Urkeltischer
Sprachschatz," p. 235), and the name Cú-Rói would
represent Kuō-rovesiāis or Kuō-rovesi-ēs, of which
Ca-rausi-us would seem to be an adaptation with the
unaccented *kuō* shortened into *cŭ* or *cŏ*. The further
change from unaccented *cŏ* to *cŭ* is detected in Latin
in the case of *Conovium*, 'Conway,' which has been
found (in the ablative) as *Kanovio* on a Roman mile-
stone : see Holder s.v.

CARBANTORIGON, p. 233. This may be taken to
be a somewhat fuller spelling of Carbantorion,
much in the same way as we have had *Bergyon* for
Iberion. The Geographer of Ravenna writes simply
Carbantium.

CARTISMANDUA, p. 39. It is also found written
Cartimandua, and the second element seems to be
the same as the first part of the name *Mandubratios*,
and we have it in such Gaulish ones as *Viromandui*
and *Epomanduoduron*.

CASSI, pp. 17, 28. Supposing the *ss* to stand here
for an earlier *ns*, the name might be taken to be
connected with the Gothic *hansa*, a band or host,
German *hanse*, a league, whence the name of the
Hanse Towns. The word Cassi in that case appears
to have meant allies or confederates : see *Veneti*.
The tribal idea of a common ancestor had perhaps
given, or been giving, way to the more purely political
one of alliance and mutual defence : see also *Catti*,
and *Aδδedomaros*.

CASSITERIDES, p. 204. M. Salomon Reinach infers
that, as the Greeks derived their word for copper
from the Greek name of Cyprus, and similarly in
the case of several others of their names of metals,

κασσίτερος 'tin' comes from a national name underlying *Cassiterides*. Does Celtic literature supply any clue to that name? We are inclined to think that it does—to wit, in the feminine noun *Cessair*, genitive *Cesra*, which occurs in Irish legend, and as to which one may say that Irish phonology permits our supposing the early form of the nominative to have been *Cassitari-s*, later *Cestari-s*, *Cessair :* so much as to the form. Ireland is sometimes found called Cessair's Island (Curry's "Courtship of Momera," p. 155), and a story occurs which represents Cessair and her followers landing in the south-west of Ireland shortly before the Flood. So she may be inferred to have been an early ancestress or eponymous goddess of a pre-Celtic population there ; but we want a people bearing her name in common in Ireland and Britain, or, at any rate, in the southern portions of both islands. In other words, we want a story which brings Cessair nearer to South Britain, and such a one offers itself in the Book of Leinster, fo. 21[b], 22[a]. It is to the effect that the early Goidelic king Ugaine the Great had twenty-five sons and daughters, whose names turn out to be no other than the names of plains and districts, of which nearly one-half belong to Leinster and most of the rest to Connaught and Munster. Now the name of the mother of Ugaine's children is given as Cessair, which confirms the conjecture that she represents the pre-Celtic populations of Ireland, with whom the Celtic element was beginning to amalgamate in Ugaine's time. Thus it is but natural to suppose the pre-Celts to have originally reached Ireland from the nearest shores of Britain, and for a considerable time subsequently to have owned the same national name in the colony and the mother country. Now it is to such a period somewhere in the second millennium before the Christian

era that we should refer κασσίτερος. We offer this
as a mere conjecture supplementary of the view
advocated by M. Reinach. See his paper in "L'An-
thropologie" for 1892, pp. 275-81, Rhys's letter concerning it in *The Academy*, Oct. 5, 1895, also "The
Welsh People," pp. 59-61.

CASSIVELLAUNOS, pp. 15, 248. The reading adopted
by the best editors of the Latin texts in which the
name occurs is Cassivellaunus, but we are not sure
that the *ll* is any more warranted here than in *Uxelodunon*, to be mentioned later. The whole name
would seem, in accordance with what has already
been guessed with regard to *Cassi*, to mean a ruler of
the league or a tribe-king; for Vellaunos probably
meant a prince or one who reigned, the root being
the same as that of the Welsh *gwlad*, Irish *flaith*
(pp. 67, 138), English, *wield*, German, *walten*, to
rule, and probably also that of the Latin *valere*, to be
strong. The epigraphic instances in point are the
following : — (1.) VELLAVNIVS in an inscription at
Caerleon (Berlin "Corpus Insc. Lat." vii. No. 126).
(2.) CATVALLAVNA, describing the nationality of a
woman married to a Palmyrene husband and buried
at South Shields ("Ephemeris Epigraphica," iv.
p. 212, No. 718*a*): the inscription commemorating
this Catuvellaunian lady is in somewhat rustic Latin,
and the compound has dropped the formative vowel
of the first element in the compound, so that *Catu-
vellauna* is here read *Cat-vallauna*. (3.) VELAVNI,
the name of an Alpine people ("Corpus Insc. Lat.,"
v. No. 7817, 45). (4.) VELAVNIS, the nominative of a
man's name in two inscriptions found in Spain (iii.
Nos. 1589; 1590). (5.) VALAMNI, the genitive of a
man's name on an Ogam-inscribed stone from the
county of Cork, and written in Mod. Irish *Follamhain*, in the family name *O'Follamhain*, which

English spelling simplifies into *O'Fallon*. The forms with *val* for *vel* represent probably a somewhat later stage of pronunciation among the Brythons than the others do, and the Goidelic *Valamni* further suggests that they and the Gauls had already begun to soften *mn* into *vn*, so that it would, perhaps, be more correct to write Cassivellavnos. Welsh tradition before the time of Geoffrey of Monmouth probably knew little of Cassivellaunos : his name was shaped, after the analogy of *Cadwallon* and the like, into *Caswallon*, which was then not unfrequently substituted for the former in quasi-historical writings. *Cadwallon*, however, is most likely a name very differently formed, standing, as it may be supposed, for *Catuvelio*, genitive *Catuvelionos :* a Brythonic *velio*, *velionos*, would in Irish be somewhat of the form *feliu*, *felenn* or *foliu*, *folann*, and we have a derivative from it in the Irish verb *follnaim*, I reign. Besides an early Brythonic *velio*, there was probably a *velatros*, of the same meaning : it is postulated by the Welsh name *Cadwaladr*. Most likely all these names are to be kept distinct from the *valos* implied by such a name as *Cadwal*, identical with the German *Hathovulf*, and meaning battle-wolf, where Welsh *wal* is to be equated with the *wolf* so common in German and English proper names : this *wal*, in its turn, has derivatives in *an*, such as *Buddwalan*.

CATTI, p. 29. The view that *Catti* was the name of a people depends on its being identical with *Cassi ;* for *Catti* might also be the genitive singular of a personal name, since we have the nominative *Cattos* on a Gaulish coin : see *Cassi*.

CATURIGES, p. 30. The word is made up of *rīges*, the plural of *rīx*, a king, and *catu*, of the same origin as the A.-Sax. *heatho-*, war. In Irish it is *cath*, and in Mod. Welsh *cad*, where it means a battle. The name would accordingly signify battle-kings or war kings.

CATUVELLAUNI : see *Cassivellaunos* and *Caturiges*.

CELTÆ, p. 2. This word is sometimes explained as the equivalent of the Latin *celsi*, in the sense of tall men; but *celse nati* would be a preferable interpretation. Better would be the German word *held*, a hero, and, better still, the O. Norse *hild-r*, which not only meant war, but was also the name of one of the Valkyrias, regarded as the handmaids of Woden as god of war, while it entered into many proper names like *Hildibrandr* and *Brynhildr*. According to M. d'Arbois de Jubainville, the Norse *Hild-r* was nothing but the masculine *Celta*, borrowed and treated as a feminine : see "Les Celtes" (Paris, 1904), p. 172. Perhaps in any case we have related forms in Lith. *kalti*, to strike, to hammer as a smith, *perkalti*, to strike through, Latin *percellere*, to strike, smite, to beat down. Lastly, it is possible that the word should be regarded as resembling *Brittones* in point of meaning (see p. 213), and that we should connect it with the Irish word *celt*, dress or raiment, whence the Scotch word *kilt*.

CENIMAGNI, pp. 17, 28. The conjecture that *Cenimagni* stands for *Ecenimagni* would require, to establish it, that one should assign the meanings of both parts, *eceni* and *magni*. This is unfortunately difficult to do; but it may be supposed that *ecen-* is to be equated with the Welsh word *egin*, which now has no other signification than that of sprouts or germs of a blade-like form, and one may surmise that it originally connoted sharpness, as its etymology is probably the same as that of the Latin *acuere*, to sharpen, *acies*, edge, sharp edge. In that case, *Eceni* originally referred to some sort of sword or knife, and the word *magni* was added to particularise it; but in

what sense is not evident. For *magn·* would probably yield in Welsh *maen*, which is perhaps to be
identified with the Welsh word *maen*, 'a stone.'
Provisionally, then, the whole term would mean the
Men of the Knives of Stone ; in that case it is clear
that the qualifying term might frequently be dispensed with, when the people would be simply called
Eceni. This, in fact, would be a sort of Celtic
parallel to the name of the Saxons, supposed to be so
called from their use of the knife they termed *seax*.
A part of the Gaulish people of the Aulerci was also
called *Cenomani ;* so, perhaps after all, the safest view
to take is to consider this to be practically the same
name as that of our *Cenimagni*, and the British people
so named to have been a Belgic tribe, to whom no
other allusion has been found. Lastly, if we treat
Eceni as the whole name, it would probably be more
correct to consider it to have been of the more
derivative form *Ecenii*, meaning men armed with
blades, let us say swordsmen.

COGIDUMNOS, p. 79. Tacitus has *Cogidumno* in
the dative, and all that is legible of the name in
the inscription is GIDVBNI for the genitive Cogidubni,
with *bn* for the *mn* of the MSS., an interchange which
is very common, and suggests that both *mn* and *bn*
had already been softened into *vn*.

COMMIOS, p. 10. The meaning of this name is
uncertain, but we have a simpler form of the same
origin in the Gaulish *Comus*, with which the *Comux*
of an old British coin is probably identical, with *x*
for *s*, which was not very unusual : see *Tincommios*.

CONBELLINI, p. 254. The reading of this vocable
is now certain : it is possibly the same name as
Cunobelinos, or rather a Goidelic derivative from it.

CONCANGII, p. 235. The other names with which
this seems to range itself are Gangani and Deceangli,

the latter being the name which is suggested by the abbreviations *Decea, Deceang, Deceangl* on pigs of lead found in Cheshire and Staffordshire: see the Berlin "Corp. Insc. Lat.," vii. Nos. 1,204, 1,205, 1,206, with which compare No. 1,207 found in the country of the Brigantes, in the West Riding of Yorkshire: it is said to read *Brig.*

CORITANI, pp. 30, 106. This name may have been derived from pre-Celtic inhabitants, who possibly survived in the inaccessible districts near the Wash, which reached formerly almost to where Cambridge now stands. Add to this that we are reminded of the Pict as far south as the Kettering district in Northants, where there is a place called Pytchley, formerly *Pihtes leá*: see Kemble's "Codex Diplom." 443 (Ap. to vol. iii.); also Wilson's "Prehistoric Annals of Scotland," i. p. 287: compare p. 313 below. According to another reading of Ptolemy, the people's name was not *Coritani*, but *Coritavi;* but it is not so well supported, and we give the preference to the other.

CORNAVII, pp. 30, 221. The Welsh *corn*, a horn, was probably a *U* stem like the Latin *cornu*, but in other cases the *u* may have been diphthongized so that the genitive, for instance, may have been *cornovos*, from which an adjective was formed, making in the singular *Cornovios* or *Cornavios*, and in the plural *Cornavii*. In Cormac's Glossary the Cornavii of Dumnonia are called *Bretain Cornn*, or the Brythons of the Horns, if, indeed, the south-west corner of Wales be not what was meant. In an account of the Danes and Norsemen flocking together for the struggle which ended with the battle of Clontarf, some are said to have come from the Corn-Britons of St. David's, and allusion is there made to another *Corn*, which may possibly have been the headland between the Dee and the Mersey, which was in the possession of the Danes at one time. See Skene's " Celtic Scotland," i. p. 387.

CUNEGLASOS, p. 122. This is given by Gildas in the vocative as Cuneglase, which he asserts to have meant in Latin *lanio fulve*, the tawny butcher. The element, *cune*, is more usually met with as *cuno* or *cuna*, as in *Cuno-belinos* and *Cuna-lipi*. The reason for the variation is that the formative vowel was even then but slightly pronounced : later it disappeared altogether, leaving these names in the forms *Conglas* and *Conbelin*, whence later *Cynlas* and *Cynfelyn*. The meaning and origin of *cuno* are obscure; but Gildas may have had in his mind the Welsh word for a dog, which is now *ci*, plural *cwn*, though in his time it was probably *cū*, genitive *cūno(s)*, and what he renders *lanio* may well have meant, considering the mood he was in, a champion or great warrior. The corresponding Teutonic vocable was *hun*, the meaning of which is also obscure, though that of giant has been suggested. The following Celtic names in point have their exact equivalents in the list of Old German ones :—*Cunoval-i* (Mod. Welsh, *Cynwal*), *Cunalip-i* (which would be in Mod. Welsh *Cynllib*), and *Cuno-mor-i* (Mod. Welsh, *Cynfor*) = *Hunulf, Hunlaif,* and *Hunmar*.

CUNOBELINOS, p. 26. This name has been in vogue among the Welsh, by whom it has been successively written *Conbelin* and *Cynfelyn*. The first element, *cuno*, is mentioned under *Cuneglasos*, and the other seems to consist of the name of the god *Belenos* or *Belinos*. Continental inscriptions equate Belinos with Apollo; he was worshipped by the Gauls, and probably also by the Brythons, though we do not happen to have any votive tablets that would prove it. But the supposition is favoured by the fact of his name entering into that of *Cunobelinos*, which hardly stands alone, as the well-known Welsh name *Llywelyn* probably represents an early compound *Lugubelinos*.

DECEANGLI, pp. 81, 293. The reading formerly adopted was *inde Cangos*, while the sense requires *in Deceanglos*, which is suggested by the abbreviation *Deceangl* on the pigs of lead already alluded to. The question of the locality of this people is a very difficult one; but one thing which makes for the district between the Dee and the Clwyd, is that it produces lead, and bears in Welsh the name of *Tegeingl*, which shows some similarity to the name here in question. It would still further remove some of the difficulty if we could suppose the Deceangli to have inhabited the country on both banks of the Dee.

DECANTÆ, DECANTI, pp. 226, 232. These are virtually, no doubt, one and the same name; but that of the people from whom Deganwy was called *arx Decantorum* in the Welsh Chronicle differs slightly from *Deganwy*, since this last appears to represent a related form *Decantovion*, or the like. It is possible that Tacitus's words, already mentioned, *in Decangos*, should be emendated into *in Decantos*, which would bring the Roman army to the neighbourhood of the Conwy. Lastly, one should compare *Decantæ, Novantæ*, and *Setantii*, the two former of which Mr. Nicholson derives respectively from the Celtic numerals for 10 and 9, see his " Keltic Researches," pp. 18, 19.

DEIRA, p. 114. The origin of the Welsh *Deivr* or *Deifr*, from which this name comes, is obscure, but it may be presumed to derive directly from a form *Debria* or *Dobria*, and to be identical with the Welsh word *deifr*, waters. This leads us to suppose that the district got its name from the many rivers that meet in its south-western corner; and the reader may compare the following line in Arinbiorn's Lay: *i Ioforvik úrgom hiarli*, " over the wet land of York." (Vigfusson and Powell's "Corpus Poeticum Boreale," i., pp. 272, 538.)

DEMETÆ, p. 81. The name is of unknown meaning; the district is called in Modern Welsh *Dyved*, written *Dyfed;* beside the personal name *Dimet*, in the Nennian Pedigrees, we have its genitive as Demeti in an early inscription near Haverfordwest: see Rhys's "Lect. on Welsh Phil.," p. 277.

DEVA, p. 68. This word originally denoted the river, or rather the goddess of the river, for *Deva* is only the feminine corresponding to a masculine dēvo-s, a god; but, when the old terminations were dropped, *dēvos* and *dēva* assumed the same form, and this, according to rule, yielded in Old Welsh *doiu* or *duiu:* later it was written *dwyw*, as in *dwywol*, divine, which is now *dwyfol*, of the same meaning. The semi-vowel was either dropped or made into *v* (written *f*): so Modern Welsh has *meudwy*, a hermit, meaning literally (like the Irish *céle dé* or Culdee) God's slave, and the river is *Dyfrdwy*, rarely *Dyfrdwyf*, which means the stream of the goddess. In the Harleian MS. 3859 we find this river mentioned at fol. 195a, as a part of the boundary of the dominion of Cunedda and his Sons,—"Hic est terminus eorum a flumine quod vocatur *dubr duiu.* Usque ad aliud flumen *tebi.*" In another version, inaccurately printed in the 'Lives of the Cambro-Brit. SS." (pp. 97-101), it is similarly called *dubyr dviv.* How Deva came to be the name of Chester or the *Castra Legionis* (whence the Welsh *Caer Lleon*, Chester) is not clear; possibly it was at first the camp *Ad Devam*, or "by the Dee," just as another station was called *Ad Ansam;* but for the camp of the legion on the Dee, Ptolemy, at any rate, had a distinct name, consisting of the derivative *Dēvana*, though he was somewhat wide of the mark in his idea of the position of the place.

DICALYDONES, pp. 94, 166. See Δουηκαληδόνιος.

DIVICIACOS, p. 31. The name appears in some of the manuscripts of Cæsar as Diviciacus, and Gaulish coins prove that to have been the correct Latin form : it is of the same origin, doubtless, as the Gaulish name Divico (Cæsar, de Bell. Gall., i. 13).

DOBUNNI, p. 29. This name occurs in the genitive singular as that of a man mentioned on an early-inscribed stone now at Tavistock : see " Lect. on Welsh Phil.," p. 400.

DOMNOCOVEROS, DOMNOVEROS, p. 40. The difference between these two terms was probably one of form alone, *domnoco* being a derivative from *domno ;* see the remarks on *Durolipons*, where a possibly parallel case is mentioned. It is possible, however, that *Domnocoveros* should be analysed *Domno-coveros.* The *domno* of *Domnoveros,* more usually *dumno* or *dubno,* is probably the same word as the O. Irish *domun,* world ; but it is possible that it meant the smaller world of the tribe before meaning the world in a wider sense. That this was the case seems to be favoured by its fitting into the place of *cassi* in such names as *Cassivellaunos,* by the side of which we have *Dubnovellaunos :* compare also *Dumnorix,* which seems synonymous with *Toutiorix,* Welsh, *Tudri,* king of the tribe or of the people. The second element, *vero-s,* in *Domno-vero-s,* is probably the word for man, Welsh *gwr,* O. Irish *fer,* Latin *vir.* So it is possible that *Domnoveros* meant the man of the people ; but the point cannot be established by means of our present data.

Δουηκαληδόνιος, p. 167. This form is particularly interesting, as showing the Celtic pronunciation of the feminine numeral, which appears in the MSS. of Amm. Marcellinus, as the *di* of his peculiar spelling *Dicalydones :* in Modern Welsh it is *dwy,* and in Irish *dí*, Sanskrit *dvē*, two. But what the implied noun was is not evident, or whether the compound referred in the first place to two peoples or two tracts of country inhabited by them on the two sides, let us say, of the waters of the river Ness and the lochs connected with it. The inference we draw in either case is that the Dicalydones were a twin people, consisting of the Vacomagi and the other Caledonians.

DUBNOVELLAUNOS, p. 27. The forms in the Ancyra inscription are incomplete, both in the Greek and the Latin versions : the former still shows ΔΟΜ//Ο///-ΛΛΑΥΝΟΣ, which was probably Λομνοβέλλαυνος, with the Greek softened β for the Celtic *v*. This would explain why the Latin is found to read DVMNO-BELLA////, and it is a good instance of the utter impossibility of saying, from the use of Latin *b* in foreign names, whether *v* or *b* was the sound meant. See *Iverna* and *Trinovantes;* also *Domnoverōs* and *Cassivellaunos.*

DUMNONII, pp. 43, 155; 161, 223. There were two peoples so called, the one in the south-west of the island, and the other in the north. The latter are frequently called Damnonii, but their real name is clearly identical with that of the other, as two Roman inscriptions exist, in which the northern Dumnonii are referred to as *Civitas Dumnon* and *Civitas Dumni* ("Corpus Inscr. Lat.," vii. Nos. 775, 776), the latter of which would seem to stand for a genitive plural *Dumnionum*, with a nominative singular *Dumnio*, while the Welsh *Dyfneint*, Devon, must be the result of a false etymology, though it recals the *Dumnuntiorum* of one of the MSS. of the Antonine Itinerary. Both southern and northern Dumnonii were presumably outlying tribes of the earlier Celtic invasion of Britain, and only continued in common a name probably once popular among all Goidels ; but the northern Dumnonii, called also Dumnogeni (in an

old inscription at Yarrow), and conveniently located
for invading Ireland both in front and from behind,
carried it to that country. Witness Inber *Domnann*,
the old name of Malahide Bay, north of Dublin, and
that of Erris *Domnann* in Mayo, where *Domnann* is
the genitive of *Domnu*, the name of an ancient
goddess, their eponymous ancestress. There were
Dumnonians among the auxiliaries at whose head
Labraid the Exile is supposed to have returned to
power in Leinster some five centuries before the
Christian era. The others were Fir Bolg, Galeóin
and Lagin, and it is to Labraid's initiative we are
possibly to trace the settlement of Brigantes and
other small tribes on the coast of Leinster from
Carnsore Point to the Liffey's mouth. They form a
secondary group of invasions partly Goidelic and
partly Belgo-Brythonic, not to mention the Cauci,
for instance, whose name suggests a Teutonic people
well-known on the Continent. These miscellaneous
tribes have no recognised place in the stock
genealogies of the Irish, and it is important to
distinguish them from the far earlier invasions by the
Goidels of the Eremonian group

DUNION, p. 219. If it be not an accident that the
MSS. of Ptolemy read Δούνιον and not Δούνον, the
i of the former is of importance, as showing that we
have here to do with a form differing from the Gallo-
Brythonic *dūnon*, which makes in Welsh *dîn*, a fort
or town. It could be explained only by the O. Irish
word *dún*, genitive *dúne* of the same meaning. Now
dūn has been ascertained to represent an early neuter
stem in *es*, nominative dūnos, genitive dūnesos, which,
when the *s* disappeared, would be *dūneo*, liable to
become *dūnio*. From *dūne* or *dūni*, which would
thus be the base for the oblique cases, nothing would
be more natural than for the word, seeing that it was

neuter, to take the form δούνιον and *dunium*, in the writings of Greek and Latin authors, in case it had not been Brythonicized into *dunon* before reaching them. The Peutinger Table gives the name of a town fifteen miles from *Isca Dumnoniorum* as *Ridumo*, to be read as an ablative *Ridunio ;* but the name is probably incomplete, and it is proposed to take it as standing for *Moridunio*, and as indicating the town of Seaton, a name which is a literal rendering of the Celtic one ; for *Moridunion* would mean the sea-fort, and that was probably also the name of the town of Carmarthen on the tidal part of the Towy, though it is only called *Maridunon* by Ptolemy.

DUROLIPONS, p. 229. This has been supposed to have been situated at one of the three places, Ramsay, Cambridge, or Huntingdon. The Antonine Itinerary gives it in the ablative as Duroliponte, so that there cannot be a doubt that the Romans thought they detected in the name their word *pons*, a bridge ; but it was quite possible that this was a bad guess ; and it is remarkable that the next station in the Itinerary has the name *Durobrivæ*, which, seeing that *briv-* meant a bridge (being, in fact, the Celtic cognate of that English word, An.-Saxon *brycg*, just as Welsh *wy* is in English *egg*), would have had, practically, the same meaning as *Durolipons*, for *duroli* would have to be regarded as a derivative from *duro ;* and *Durobriv-æ* is all but the same name as that mentioned in another route as *Durocobriv-is*, with a derivative *duroco* by the side of *duro :* compare *Domnoveros* and *Domnocoveros*. So it is quite possible that the Romans were mistaken, and that the name in question is to be divided *Duro-lipons*, with the same *lip* as in the personal name *Cunalipi*, a genitive in an early inscription discovered in Eivionydd in Carnarvonshire. The other element *duro*, so often

met with in Celtic names of places in Britain and
Gaul, appears to mean door, gate, or porch, and to
be of the same origin as the Welsh *dōr* and *drws*, Irish
dorus, a door, and the English word and its congeners.
Duroco in *Durocobrivis* is probably the same word as
the highly interesting *dvorico* of a Gaulish inscription,
in which it seems to have meant some kind of a
portico (De Belloguet's "Ethnogénie Gauloise," i.
p. 300). But, though the etymology of *duro* in Celtic
names is tolerably clear, it is not very evident what
it exactly meant : did it refer mostly to the gates or
entrances of strongholds, or to those of temples, as
in the case of the Gaulish Iron-Door mentioned in
the life of Eugendus (Act. SS., Jan. 1, vol. i., p. 50,
and "Lect. on Welsh Phil.," p. 26)? Lastly, the
etymology of the word suggests the possibility of
some of the *duro* names being of the same kind as
Forum Juli, *Forum Voconi*, and the like in Gaul,
Spain, and Italy.

DUROTRIGES, pp. 19, 219. The meaning of the
name is obscure, but the compound would seem to
resolve itself into *Duro-* and *trig-es :* it is remarkable,
however, that the name seems to admit of being
equated with that of the Irish people called *Dar-
traighi*, who have left their name to Dartry, in the
county of Leitrim.

EBUDÆ, p. 225. This name has been so treated in
later times that it has passed through *Hebudes* into
Hebrides, and attached itself to the islands north-west
of Scotland.

ECENI, p. 28, see *Cenimagni*.

EPATICCOS, p. 26. This name seems derived from
the Gallo-Brythonic word for a horse, which must
have been *epo-s*, whence the Welsh *ebol*, a colt ; but
the unexplained termination, with its double *c*, reminds
one of *Boudicca :* it is possibly diminutival or hypo-
coristic.

EPEIACON, p. 227. The affix *āc* would give the
name the force of a word meaning a place abounding
in, or in some way associated with, that which is
denoted by the preceding syllables. The base, which
we have here as *epei*, would imply a noun *epei-os, -a*,
or *-on* derived from *epo-s*, a horse; but whether the
derivative meant some kind of a horse or of a horse-
man, or else was a man's name, is impossible to
decide. The word *Vereda* (of which *Voreda*, the
other form in the MSS., would be a somewhat later
one) also referred to horses, as it cannot be severed
from the Welsh word *gorwydd*, a horse, which would
imply a masculine *verēdos*. Possibly *Vereda* stands
for an earlier *Veredas*, genitive *Veredotos* (to be compared with *Venedotos* mentioned under VENETI), and is
to be interpreted as meaning a place where cavalry
were collected. *Verēdos* is the word which became
in Late-Latin *verēdus*, whence the hybrid *paraveredus*,
the original of *palfrey* and the German *pferd*, a horse.

EPPILLOS, p. 23. It is remarkable that in this
name the *p* appears always double, though the name
is very probably a derivative from *epo-s*, a horse. The
double *l* in such names seems to stand for *li*. *Epillos*
(with one *p*) would be exactly the Welsh word *ebill*,
an auger, a chisel, the key of a harp, though literally
it ought to mean a little horse.

GALLI, pp. 2, 270. Here the double *l* is of the
same origin as in *Eppillos* and *Allobrox*: the nominative singular would be *Gallos* for *Galios* from *gal*,
which is a word met with in Irish in the sense
of valour, which it retains in Welsh in the compound
ar-ial (for *ar-gal*), "energy, courage."

GANGANI, p. 235. Ptolemy mentions the headland
of the Gangani as Γαγγανῶν ἄκρον, and this is to be
traced later in *Pentir Ganion*, or the headland of
Ganion, the home of a Goidel, mentioned in a pas-

sage in the "Mabinogion" (ii. pp. 208, 209), where
the MS. reads *Gamon*. The Goidel is spoken of
under the title of *arderchawg Prydein*, or prince of
Prydein. Here *Prydein* stands, as elsewhere, not
unfrequently for *Prydyn* or Pictland, but the name
can hardly have been applied to any part of Carnarvonshire. Besides the Gangani of Wales, Ptolemy
places a people of the same name in the west of
Ireland.

GERONTIOS, p. 96. This is the name which has
yielded in Welsh *Gereint* and *Geraint*, borne by the
man alluded to at p. 109. Compare *Ambrosius*
becoming *Emreis*, though more commonly *Emrys*.
A simpler form of the same origin as *Gerontios* occurs
in the Irish *gerat* or *gerait*, a champion.

ICTIS, p. 45 : see *Itius*.

ITIUS, p. 14. According to Holder, whose careful
edition of Cæsar *de Bello Gallico* (Freiburg, 1882) has
proved very valuable to the student of Celtic names—
the same remark applies on an extended scale to his
Altceltischer Sprachschatz still in course of publication
—the reading of the manuscripts is *Portum Itium* in
both the passages (v. 2 and 5) where it occurs. We
are, however, of opinion that the original name was
not *Itium*, but *Ictium*, and that the whole English
Channel was called *Mare Ictium*, or Ictian Sea. In
that case Portus Ictius would designate Cæsar's place
of embarcation, somewhat in the same way that
Dover might in English be termed the Channel
Harbour. The former probably had a Gaulish name
of its own, which may have become the Latin one
also as soon as the Romans began to be a little more
at home in the north of Gaul ; so that it would be
labour in vain to try to detect *Ictius* in any place-
name still current on the French coast. We infer
the term Mare Ictium, or Ictian Sea, from the fact that

the Irish used to call it *Muir n-Icht*, or the Sea of
Icht, which was probably a pre-Brythonic name, like
Albion or Alban.   It is, however, not to be supposed
that it had anything to do with the name of the Isle
of *Wight*, Welsh *Gwyth*, for an older *Vectis :* this
last might possibly become *Ficht* in the mouth of a
Goidel, but not *Icht*.   On the other hand, the *Ictis*
of Diodorus Siculus (v. 22) would just meet the case ;
and it was the same island, doubtless, that Timæus,
who was fond of quoting from the travels of Pytheas,
is supposed to have called *Mictis*.   The passage has
come down to us only in Pliny's " Natural History "
(iv. 30), where the words are *insulam mictim :* the
presence of the second *m* is presumably due to care-
lessness or caprice on the part of a copyist.   An
instructive article on the British peninsulas which
were islands at high tide, was published, with plans,
by Mr. A. Tylor, in " Nature," vol. xxix., pp. 84-6.

   IUDEU, pp. 134, 152.   The *Eidyn* of the Book
of Aneurin is supposed to have meant Edinburgh,
and   as   to   Carriden,   one   ancient   interpolator
of Gildas speaks of it as "*Kair Eden civitas anti-
quissima, duorum ferme milium spatio a monasterio
Abercurnig, quod nunc vocatur Abercorn, ad occidentem
tendens,*" &c., and as being also *supra mare Scotiæ*,
that is, the Firth of Forth. (See Mommsen's *Chronica
Minora*, iii. p. 18).   On the whole, we are inclined
to think, that Bede's *Urbs Giudi* or *Iudi*—for that is
said to be the reading of MS. C² (Plummer, ib. i. 12)—
was the same as Nennius's *Urbs Iudeu*, and that the
place   meant   was either Carriden or Edinburgh : we
are   inclined   to   the   former.   But   how   is   one   to
account for Bede placing it in the middle of the Firth
of Forth ? We are disposed to think that he has
confounded two names which were partly identical,
and that these were *Urbs Giudi* and *Insula Giudi* (if

not simply *Giudi*) respectively. The mistake would
be all the more natural if the island was, as at the
present day, fortified ; for undoubtedly Bede regarded
the place he had in view as a sort of counterpart to
Alclyde on the opposite estuary in the west.

IVERNA, p. 268. Dr. Neubauer, who looked for
the graffito a good many years ago, found that it had
been effaced by the weather ; but a few years before
it was carefully examined by the present Bishop of
Salisbury, who kindly communicated the following
reading to us :—*Bassus Cherronesiia et Tertius
Hadrumetinus et Concessus Iverna.* The names
appear to be those of three slaves, and the fact that
the one from Erin was called Concessus is remarkable ; for, though that name seems to have been
uncommon in Britain, it can be matched by a
Concessa, to the use of which in this country we have
testimony in the later form *Conchess*, the traditional
name of St. Patrick's mother, *Concessus, Concessa,
Concessanus*, and the like, were by no means unusual
names in other parts of the Roman world ; but the
only form of this group known in the Roman inscriptions of Britain is *Concessinius* on a stone found at
Hexham (C. I. L., vii. No. 481).

MÆATÆ, pp. 92-5, 158, 162, 166, 172. The name,
as it occurs in Reeves's Adamnan's Life of St.
Columba is *Miati* and *Miathi*. The meaning of the
word is unknown, but there is no reason whatever to
think that it has anything to do with the Goidelic
word *mag*, a plain or field, as some take for granted,
who have no notion of perspective in phonology. It
is probably not of Celtic origin at all, and the locality
of the Mæatæ is a matter of more importance : we
are now convinced that they were once in possession
of the country between the Firth of Forth and that
of Tay, between the Ochils and the sea, whatever

other districts they may have occupied, as, for instance, near the Northern Wall. Their name is perpetuated by the Ochil height called Dun-Myat, by Inver May and the May Water, which, rising in the Ochils, rushes down into the Earn near Forteviot, most of which it appears to have eaten away since the time when it was a Pictish capital, and lastly by the Isle of May, off the coast of Fife. It follows that the territory of the Mæatæ was, at least in part, that whose inhabitants appear in subsequent history under the name of Verturiones. In other words, Dion Cassius's Caledonians and Mæatæ are represented in Ammianus's pages by Dicalydones and Verturiones respectively. As to the latter, they may be regarded as Mæatæ with an admixture of Celts forming the leading or ruling element among them, such Celts being Goidels of Dumnonian stock who had probably adopted Brythonic speech. Lastly, the geographical position of the Mæatæ makes it improbable that the battle of Circinn was fought in the Mearns: the Circinn in point must have been nearer to the Wall, to which the territory of the Mæatæ reached, if we may trust Dion Cassius. It has been suggested to us that a writer of Dion's day cannot have meant the Northern Wall. In that case we can only say that Dion must have copied the words of some earlier writer who did mean the Northern Wall: to us the Southern Wall seems inadmissible. In case, however, a persistent push southwards was made soon after the Romans left Britain, it is but natural to suppose that such Picts as one reads of at different points between the Northern Wall and the neighbourhood, let us say, of Dunbar, came from the Mæatæ or Verturian country across the water.

MAGLOCUNOS, p. 122. This name has been successively softened down into Mailcon or Mailcun,

and Maelgwn, wrongly written Maelgwyn. It is not to
be confounded with the Irish Maelchon, for Brythonic
maglo-, is in Irish *mál.* a prince or hero, while Irish
mael, a tonsured (slave), is in Welsh *moel*, bald or
bare. The elements of this compound also made a
name *Cunomaglos :* the genitive *Conomagli* occurs
("Lect. on Welsh Phil.," p. 369), and the modern
Welsh is *Cynvael.*

MAPONOS, p. 230. The monument to Apollo
Maponos, found at Hexham, stands about four feet
high, and the lettering is said to be of the finest description ; but there are two other inscriptions which
refer to this god. The one was found in the parish
of Ainstable, in Cumberland (vii. No. 332), while the
other had been cut on a fine piece of sculpture,
made *pro salute* of the persons concerned, and discovered at Ribchester, near Blackburn, in Lancashire
(vii. No. 218). The name *Maponos* or *Mabon* is derived from *mapo-s*, in old Welsh *map*, now *mab*, a boy,
a youth, a son, and is formed like Welsh *gwron*, a hero
from *gwr*, a man. *Mabon* means a boy, and is best
understood by looking at the Greek representations
of Apollo, in which he was ever young and
vigorous, and by calling to mind that in Irish mythology the Ultonian hero Cúchulainn was always beard-
less, which his admirers of the other sex sometimes
excused by pretending to believe that he was too young.
Beside the youth of Maponos and his concern for the
health and safety of his worshippers, we learn the
following things of him as the Mabon of the "Mabinogion":—He was a great hunter, who had a wonderful
hound, and he rode on a steed swift as a sea-wave ;
when three nights old he had been stolen from
between his mother and the wall, no one knew
whither ; numberless ages afterwards it was ascertained by Arthur that he was in a stone prison at

Gloucester, uttering heart-rending groans and under-going treatment with which Apollo's bondage in the house of Admetus could not compare ; Arthur and his men succeeded in releasing him to engage in the great hunt of Twrch Trwyth, which could not take place without him (" Mabinogion," ii. pp. 225-6, 234-5, 286-7, 300-1). Lastly he is always called son of Modron, which was the name of his mother. Now *Modron* implies a stem *modr*, the reflex of the Latin *mater*, Eng. *mother ;* moreover, it is the exact equivalent of the Gaulish word *Matrŏna*, the name of the river (more correctly perhaps of the goddess of the river) now called the Marne. Apollo and Leto or Latona, with the corresponding Celtic duad Mabon and Modron may, perhaps, be regarded as a sort of pagan anticipation of the Madonna and Child. Welsh hagiology has very little to say about saints of the name of Mabon : it is quite possible that one or another of them is simply Apollo Maponos in a Christian garb. From the order in which *Maponi* comes in the lists of British places given by the anonymous Geographer of Ravenna, his temple would appear to have been somewhere in the south of Scotland or the north of England.

ORDOVICES, pp. 81, 220. The plural *Ordovices* seems to be an adjectival formation from a simpler word *Ordovo-s*, which is Latinized into *Ordous* in Corbalengi's epitaph : the plural would be Ordovi, which we seem to have in the name of a farmhouse, near Rhyl, in Flintshire, to wit, *Rhyd Orddwy* or the ford of the Ordovi. The further advance of the Ordovices is also marked by the strong position, now called Dinorwig in the neighbourhood of Carnarvon, having, as it seems, formerly been called *Dinorddwig*, the fortress of the Ordovices : see Duppa's " Johnson's

Tour in N. Wales," p. 198, where it is spelt *Dinorrddwig.* But still more significant is the fact learned from the fragment on boundaries in the " Iolo MSS.," pp. 86, 477, which gives the district between the Dovey and Gwynedd the name *Cantref Orddwyf* or the Hundred of the Ordovi : we have not succeeded in tracing the original, which Iolo calls a book of Mr. Cobb's of Cardiff ; but it speaks for the genuineness of the tract, that neither he nor his son, who undertook the translation into English, understood the passage. The addition of *f* to *Orddwy*, as it were after the analogy of *Dyfrdwyf*, is probably due to the father. The district appears to have been called *Y Cantref* or the Hundred *par excellence*, so that the distinctive word Orddwy ceased to be repeated. Others would explain these names by means of the Welsh word *gorddwy*, violence or oppression ; but violence was so general in former days as considerably to disqualify the word for topographical use. The etymon is probably to be found in the Welsh word *gordd*, a hammer or sledge-hammer, which was written in old Welsh *ord* as it has always been in Irish. The Ordovices were originally the hammerers, and the kind of hammer meant was probably the formidable axe-hammer of stone, of which specimens have been found in different localities in Britain : archæologists believe it to have been meant for war and used down to the Iron Age. It is not to be denied that the converse account of the words Ordovices and Ordous may prove to be the correct one, that is to say, that the former is a compound Ordo-vic- and that Ordous is a shortened form of it. In that case *Ordo-vic-es* might be interpreted as literally meaning "men who fight with battle-hammers, hammer warriors."

PARISI, p. 39.—According to Sir James Ramsay in his

"Foundations of England" (London, 1898), i., 61, the
proper seat of the Parisi seems fixed by the fact that
as late as the 13th century "Paris was still the name
of the district round Horncastle, to which we owe
our great chronicler, Matthew Paris." If so, it would
appear that the Parisi entered the Humber and took
possession of a very considerable tract of country on
both sides of that estuary. As to the Parisii of Gaul
M. d'Arbois de Jubainville conjectures that they
formed a part of the empire of Diviciacos, and that
some of them migrated to this country in his time :
see "Les Celtes," pp. 23-5.

PENNOCRUCION, p. 230. This name consists of
penno-s, head or end, and *crūcio-*, which became in Welsh
crūc, now *crūg*, a heap or mound : the whole would
mean the top or head of the mound or barrow, or
possibly the top mound. The name is now Penkridge,
and an intermediate form Pencrik occurs in the eighth
century charter of Æthilhard of Wessex ; see Kemble's
"Codex Diplomaticus," No. lxxvi. *Pencrik* represents
the Welsh pronunciation, which would then have
been *Pencrūc*, and is now *Pencrug* (as in the case of a
hill near Llandovery in South Wales), just as nearly
with regard to the narrow *ū* as Bede's *Dinoot* does
the personal name, which in his time was *Dūnōt*,
later Dunawd, Dunod, being no other than the Latin
Donatus in a Welsh form. The English having
eventually made *Pencrik* into *Penkridge*, nothing was
more natural than to divide the name in the wrong
place into Penk-ridge : hence it is that the river close
by Penkridge is said to be called the Penk. Dr.
Stokes suggests a connexion with the name of the
chief idol of ancient Erin, which is called *Cenn
Crúaich* in the "Tripartite Life of St. Patrick," Rawlinson, B. 512, fol. 22ª 2.

PETUARIA, pp. 39, 230. This would be the word

for fourth, agreeing with a feminine noun which is not given : the exact modern equivalent is the Welsh pedwaredd, *quarta*, which suggests that the old form was pronounced *petwariia*.

PICTI, pp. 160, 240. One of the latest views as to this word is that it represents a primitive form *quicto s* and that its meaning is a matter of uncertainty : see " Les Celtes," by M. d'Arbois de Jubainville, p. 22, where the author refers *Pictavi*, a form of the name of the people of Poitiers to the same origin : still more to the point would have been the earlier *Pictones*. On the other hand Mr. Nicholson in his " Keltic Researches " treats Pict as a Goidelic word. But there is a third possibility, nay an absolute certainty, that *Pictus*, *Picti*, are purely Latin, and it is possible that even the native name which suggested the Latin was not of Celtic origin either, though only found treated as Celtic. The first thing to do, however, is to have the forms classified : let us take them as follows in the plural :—1. *Pictones* comes first as applied to the people of Poitiers already mentioned ; but we find it also as a name of the peoples of North Britain : witness Tigernach's annals, published by Stokes in the " Revue Celtique," xvij., 251, 253, and see also Skene's "Chronicles of Picts and Scots," p. 76 ; Hennessy and MacCarthy's " Annals of Ulster, A.D. 749," and Reeve's " Adamnan," pp. 385, 386. It is further probable that *Pictores* is everywhere in the Chronicles to be corrected into Pictones. As to the genitive plural *Pictorum*, it is more difficult to decide whether it should be corrected into *Pictonum* or taken as belonging to the purely Latin form *Picti*. In any case the term Pictones, as occurring in Gaul in Cæsar's time makes it probable that it was also a name of long standing in Britain, many centuries before Tigernach's time. 2. *Pictones* with its *o* modified into *a* suggests

Goidelic treatment, of which we have an instance in
the Latin *Pictaneus*, of which the genitive plural
Pictaneorum occurs in the " Life of St. Cadroe " cited
in Skene's Chronicles, p. 108. He has also *Pictavi*
repeatedly in one of them, namely, the Pictish
Chronicle in the same volume, pp. 3-10 : he read
Pictauia, but we think the right reading is *Pictania :*
see " The Welsh People," p. 79. 3. There must have
been a more purely Goidelic form of the name,
to wit, *Pictiū*, genitive *Picten-a*(*s*), nominative plural
Pictin-e(*s*), and we have evidence of it in the Latin
creation *Pictinia* for Fortrenn: see Skene, loc. cit.,
p. 137, Reeves's " Chronicon Hyense," (A.D. 664,
866) in his " Adamnan," pp. 376, 391. 4. *Picti*,
meaning painted or tattooed, was the Latin name
suggested, partly, no doubt, by the first syllable of the
native *Pictones*, and partly by the fact that the peoples
of North Britain practised tattooing, which is proved by
Herodian's statement (p. 242 above) made long before
the term *Picti* appeared in literature referring to them.
This, however, does not prove that the word Pictones
itself had any reference whatsoever to the tattooing :
we must be content, with M. d'Arbois de Jubainville,
to regard it as of uncertain meaning ; only our
ignorance is greater than his, as we know not from
what language it comes. In any case we can discover
no certain use for *quicto-s* ; but it is true that an Irish
word *cicht* is given in Cormac's Glossary, and that it
looks like *Pictus*, borrowed and treated in the same
way as *pascha* made into *caisg*, " Easter or Passover,"
and as in the case of a few other well-known instances.
But it is to be noticed that the meaning given to *cicht*
is that of carver or engraver. 5. From *Picti*, current
doubtless in the latinity of the south and east of the
province towards the end of the Roman occupation,
the English settlers seem to have readily made their

Peohtas, which survives in Broad Scotch as *Pechts*, used more or less as meaning Fairies, or more correctly speaking, for the Picts and the Fairies confounded with one another. It is from such an English source that we have the comparatively late Norse *Petta*, as in Pettlandzfiorđr, "the Sea of Pictland," confined by modern geography to the Pentland Firth. For, as already mentioned (p. 153), the Pentland Hills derive their name from a Brythonic *Penn-llann*, whence *Pen-thland*, with the usual *thl* for the strong spirant *ll*: in fact the pronunciation with *thl* survives to this day in the neighbourhood of *Pencaitland*, the *tl* of which a Welsh friend of ours has heard as *thl*. The comparative prevalence of names beginning with *Peoht* in Anglo-Saxon seems to require explanation. Dr. Henry Bradley has supplied the writer with the following note : They are naturally most numerous towards the north ; there were bishops of Whithern named Peohthelm (730), Peohtwine (763-776), and the "Liber Vitæ" of Durham supplies Peohtgils, Peohthæth, Peohthun, Peohtwulf, while more southern examples are Peohthad (Middlesex, 704), Peohthæth (Worcester, 692), Peohtred (Kent, 863), Peohthan (moneyer, East Anglia), and Peohtwald (moneyer, Mercia, 8th century).

REMI, p. 29. *Rēmi* was the name of the leading Belgic people, and it would seem to be of the same origin as the Welsh word *rhwyf*, a king, Irish *riam*, before, and the Latin *primus*, first; compare the English *first* and the German *fürst*, a prince. The name of the Remi would thus be of the same flattering description as that of the Caturiges and others.

SCITLIVISSI, p. 254. Now and then Irish resolves its compound terms : thus, a field for athletic games is called *cluchimag*, or game-field, but also *mag in cluchi*, or a field for games ; both forms are found very near one another in the "Book of the Dun Cow," namely, at 59a, 59b, 60a, and 60b. So with the genitive *scitlivissi*, we have nowhere else met with the compound, but we would identify it with the resolved term in the same manuscript, fol. 55b, where it occurs as *fis scel*. Here *viss-* and *fis* are to be regarded as meaning knowledge, and as being of the same origin as the Irish *fess*, "was known," *fissi*, "sciendum," and the English word *wise*. The rest, *scitl-* and *scél*, meant a story, news, or tidings: compare *so-scéle*, good news, gospel. The Welsh equivalent is *chwedl*, for an older *chwedl* of the same meaning as the Irish *scél*. The two taken together prove the common Celtic stem to have once been *sqvedl*. If this last is to be treated as standing for *s(e)qvedl*, as suggested by Prof. Zimmer, we have to do with a word of the same origin as the English *say*, the German *sagen*, and Norse *saga*. The reduction by the Goidels of original *sqv* to *sc*, and by the Brythons to *sv* (whence Welsh *chw*) may prove of some use, if not confined to words borrowed from Irish, in distinguishing between the Celts of the two branches of the family; for we have it in other Welsh words, such as *chwydu*, to vomit, Irish *sceith*, *cy-chwyn*, to start, Irish, *scind*, flew, sprang, started; and *chwalu*, to scatter or disperse, Irish, *scáilim*, "I let loose, scatter, or disperse": compare the Scotch verb to *skail*, said of a congregation dispersing at the end of a meeting, exactly in the same way as *hwalu* in the Welsh of Cardiganshire. There remains the question of meanings, for while *scitlivissi* in the inscription referred to a man, *fis scél* meant news or information, —literally, knowledge of news or intelligence of tidings. So it may be surmised that *scitliviss-* might mean either a message or a messenger, news or a bringer of news. We need go no further than the passage referred to for a somewhat parallel case ; for there Maive says : *ráncatar mo thechta-sa cotucsat fis scél dam-sa ass*, "my scouts have come and brought me news from there." Here *techta*, scouts, is the plural of *techt*, a messenger or scout ; but the latter is also the same word as the verbal noun *techt*, the act of going. Compare the Welsh feminine *cennad*, which means not only a messenger, but also a message of permission or leave ; still better known is the double meaning of the Latin word *nuncius*. There is, however, a shorter and perhaps a better way of interpreting the word, to wit, as an adjectival formation *scitliviss-e*, genitive *scitliviss-i*, " relating to news, information," and hence " a person who acquires such information, a scout or emissary."

SEGONTIACI, p. 17. They came to make peace with Cæsar, and to their name must be added that of the Roman fortress near Carnarvon, called *Segontion*, which is made in Welsh into Seiont, and even into Seint, Saint in the name of the river flowing by. The syllable *seg* in these words is probably of the same origin as the German *sieg*, victory, and lends a presumption in favour of *Segeia* as against *Seteia* as the name of the divinity of the river. If, as Dr. Henry Bradley suggests, the Dee was meant, the name would appear still more appropriate : see *Deva*.

SELGOVÆ, p. 220. This is explained by the Irish word *selg*, hunting, the chase, as in *coin seilge*, a pack of hounds, Welsh *cwn hela:* the Old Welsh imperative for *hunt* was *helgha*, now *helia* and *hela*.

SENOTIGIRNIOS, p. 41. No coin gives more than *Seno* in one part and *tigir* (or *tigip*) in another. *Senotigirnios* would be in Welsh *hen-dëyrn*, from *hen*, old, O. Irish, *sen-* ; and *tëyrn*, a lord or prince, Irish, *tigerna*, lord.

SETANTII, p. 222. The alternative *Segantii* is given

in Ptolemy's Geography, and, similarly, the name of the river is either *Seteia* or *Segeia :* probably *Setantii* is to be preferred, as of the same origin as Setanta, the first name of Cúchulainn, the hero of Irish legend, which indirectly suggests British ancestry in his case.

SILURES, pp. 42, 81. The origin and meaning of this word are utterly unknown, but it is worth while noting that the name of the chief man connected with the temple of Nodens at Lydney Park on the western bank of the Severn in the country of the Silures has been there read SILVLANVS (Berlin, "Corpus Inscr. Brit. Lat.," No. 140), and that there is no need to make it into *Silvianus* or *Silvanus :* it should rather be read *Silulanus*, *silul-* being equated with the *silur-* of the word Silures. Probably the name given by Solinus as that of an island, Silura, whether he meant the land of the Silures or the Scilly Isles, is of the same origin. Sulpicius Severus, however, who flourished about the end of the fourth century, leads us to infer that the Scilly Islands did bear a name cognate with that of the Silures, for, in his "Chronica" (ed. Halm), ii. 51, he uses the words, *in Sylinancim insulam, quæ ultra Britannias sita est, deportatus*, and again, *in Sylinancim insulam datus.* The MS. which gives this reading is of the eleventh century, but the editors go their own way and print "*Sylinam insulam.*" *Sylinancis* is not an easy form to deal with, but it seems to be the only one attested, and it is possibly derived from some such a one as *Silulancis*, with the same *silul* as *Silulanus*. Some form of this name of the islands must have been in use when the Danes began to call them Syllingar, or Syllings, with which may be compared a passage in W. Smith's "Particular Description of England, 1588" (London, 1879), in which he speaks, p. 60, of "the Isles of Sorlingues, commonly called "the Sillies" : they are still Sorlingues in French.

TÆXALI, pp. 164, 234. The headland of the same name is called Ταίξαλον ἄκρον in Ptolemy's Geography, and I am persuaded that the *Trucculensis Portus* mentioned by Tacitus (Agr., 38) meant a place on the same part of the coast; but it is impossible to say which of the two, *Tæxal- Truccul-*, makes the nearest approach to the real name meant to be reproduced. The fleet may have wintered at Keith Inch, the small island at Peterhead.

TASCIOVANS, p. 26. Some of the various forms of the genitive on the coins are TASCIOVANI, TASCIIO-VANII, TASCIIOVANTIS, together with such abbreviations as *Tasciov, Tasciav, Tascio, Tascia, Taxcia Taxci.* The double *I* is probably to be read *E*, which is found to be one of the ways of representing the semi-vowel *i* in such Gaulish names as Ούιλλόιεος and the like; the vowel ε being perhaps the nearest approach to the semi-vowel which Greek spelling suggested. That this can, however, have been the value of the II at the end of TASCIIOVANII is doubtful; it probably argues a genitive corresponding to a nominative *Tasciovanios.* Whether the x in some of these forms had any value different from *s* is also doubtful; but the use here of *x* reminds one of the name of the Cantian king whom Cæsar calls Taximagulus. The hesitation between *Tasciovan-* and *Tasciavan-* shows that the formative vowel was but slightly pronounced, and ready to disappear; the old inscriptions of Wales give parallels in such names as *Senomagli* and *Senemagli, Trenegussi* and *Trenagusu.* Welsh pedigrees have *Teuhant* and *Tecwant,* and Geoffrey of Monmouth *Tenuantius* or *Teneuan,* which had as their common original probably an Old Welsh form Teheuant or Techuant, representing an early stem

Tacsi-vant- with *tacs* and not *tasc.* Possibly the name meant a brock-spearer or hunter of badgers : compare *Brohomaglos,* ' badger prince,' and see Holder, s.v. *taxea,* ' lard,' and *Taximagulus,* also " The Welsh People," p. 90. Geoffrey probably had his data in some Brythonic genealogy, but whose? I conjecture it was that of a northern family: the Nennian pedigree X in The Cymmrodor, ix., p. 174, derives Dyvnwal Moelmud from Coel Godebog, whose daughter Gwawl is said to have been Cunedda's mother (Iolo MSS., p. 121), and makes Coel himself son of Tecmant, son of Teuhant. Add to this that the 57th of the Englyns of the Graves (Evans's " Black Book of Carmarthen," p. 34ᵇ, Skene, ii. 33) mentions a Coel son of Kinvelin, a juxtaposition of names which suggests that Caratacos was not the sole warrior of his family who escaped to the North—that, in fact, there were others who succeeded in reaching the Brigantes, and in making their way farther, namely, to the princes of the Dumnonii, among whom they remained, perhaps, and flourished.

TINCOMMIOS, p. 23. This name looks as if compounded of *Commios* and another element *tin,* which is possibly the same word as the Welsh preposition, *tàn,* as in *tan y fainc,* under the bench, *tan y fory,* till to-morrow, literally, " under or up to the morrow." One cannot help identifying with this the Latin *tenus,* as far as, up to, and possibly the Irish word *tánaise,* second, also the tanist or heir-apparent in Goidelic succession. In that case Tincommios was not only a son of Commios, but bore a name meaning a " second Commios," a man like Commios, or Commios's representative. This would place the name within a well-known category of Welsh epithets or surnames with *eil* or *ail,* second, as in *Morvran eil Tegid,* and *Cadwallawn eil Cadfan,* " Cadwallon, second-

Cadvan,"—Cadvan was his father (see the "Mabinogion," ii. 206, and the "Myv. Arch.," ii p. 408,
triad 80). *Tin-commios* did not stand alone, for the
name accompanying that of Dubnovellaunos on the
Augustus monument at Ancyra begins with *Tim* or
Tin; nor is it improbable that such a Gaulish name
as *Tessignius* or *Teδδicnius* stands for an earlier
Tensignios, while the same initial element without
the *s* is to be detected in the feminine *Tenigenonia*,
of the same origin, and occurring in an inscription
from Cisalpine Gaul ("C. Ins. Lat.," v. No. 3345).
These forms would have, perhaps, to be interpreted
after the analogy of such Latin names as Secundinus,
Secundianus, Secundillus, and the like.

TOGODUMNOS, p. 35. At first compound names
doubtless had a definite and clear meaning; but, for
the purpose of multiplying those with a common
element in the same family, they were manipulated
freely, as in the case of a Carmarthenshire inscription
commemorating *Barrivendi* son of *Vendubari:* compare the Greek Δωρόθεος and Θεόδωρος, Ἵππαρχος and
Ἄρχιππος, and many more; also the Ang.-Saxon royal
names. Perhaps in this case the compound *Togodumnos* was suggested by the other, *Dumnotogos:* the
latter, according to what was surmised under *Domnoveros*, would mean the protection of the people or the
defender of the state, *togo* being of the same origin as
O. Welsh *to*, a cover or roof, Irish *tuige*, and the
English *thatch*, German *dach*, Latin *tegere*, to cover,
to protect. *Cogidumnos* would have to be explained
similarly, *cogi* being possibly the word which is in
Mod. Welsh *cae*, a fastening of any kind, such as a
brooch, a hedge or fence, and, in a secondary and later
sense, the area the fence encloses—that is, a field. It is
probably of the same origin (as well as meaning) as
the English *hedge*, German *hag*.

TRINOVANTES, p. 17. It is hard to decide whether we should write *Trinovantes* or *Trinobantes*, but *Tasciovant's* name, together with Ptolemy's Τρινόαντες, inclines us to prefer the former. In *trino-* we seem to have the Welsh word *trin*, a battle or conflict and the whole word *Trinovantes* would then mean battle-piercers, or men who penetrate the array of battle opposed to them.

TRUCCULENSIS or TRUTULENSIS, p. 89. See *Tæxali*.

UXELODUNON, p. 234. *Uxelodunon* is found written mostly with *ll*, which is, however, contrary to the evidence of the living words, Welsh, *uchel*, high, Irish, *uasal*, high-born, noble. But on a bronze cup this name, which should be in the ablative, is found engraved VXELODVMC, and it is best explained by supposing that the spelling meant to be written was *Uxelodunio* ("C. Insc. Lat.," vii. No. 1291 and p. 104). The anonymous Geographer of Ravenna wrote *Uxelludamo*, which in its *m* bears witness to an *ni*, while the MSS. of the *Notitia Dignitatum* point to one *l*, as they read *Axeloduno* and *Axdoduno*. As to *dunon* being Brythonic, and *dunion* more Goidelic than Brythonic, see *Dunion*. In either case the compound would mean the high town or the lofty fortress.

UXELLA, UXELLON, p. 234. These may be either inaccurately written for Uxela, Uxelon, which would be the adjectives in the feminine and neuter singular, agreeing with nouns not given ; or else they may be derived forms, standing for *Uxelia, Uxelion*. The stem *uxel-*, meaning high, is the same as that of the Greek ὑψηλός, high, and both are probably from the same root as the English word *up*, but the Celts have changed the labial into a guttural, as in Irish *secht*, "*septem*." Greek, however, has no parallel to ὑψηλόν, but the Celts have one in the Welsh adjective *isel*, Irish, *ísel*, low, from the old preposition *in* (in

Mod. Welsh *yn*), of the same origin and meaning as the English *in* and the Latin *in*, which in its derivative *īmus* (for *insmus ?*), lowest, comes to the same meaning as the Welsh superlative of *isel*, to wit, *isaf*, lowest, the comparative being *īs*, lower. This element enters possibly into the name of the *Insubres*, and of the British towns of *Isurion* and *Isubrigantion*. The *s* of the stems *up-s* and *in-s* implied in the Greek and Celtic words raises an interesting question which cannot be discussed here.

VACOMAGI, p. 163. It has been suggested to us that this name is an approximate reproduction of a Celtic compound meaning the inhabitants of the *open plains*, as contrasted with the adjoining tract covered by the Caledonian Forest. In that case *vaco-* is to be equated with the Welsh word *gwag*, "empty," and *mag-* with Welsh *ma*, Irish *magh*, "a plain or open field." Possibly the name is a shortened form of Vacomag-ii.

VENETI, p. 9. The word is most likely of the same origin as the Anglo-Saxon *wine*, a friend, and meant allies : the Irish *fine*, a tribe or sept, is probably related, and so may be the Welsh *Gwynedd ;* but the latter is inseparable from *Gwyndod*, which is of the same meaning. They probably represent an early Brythonic *Venedas*, genitive *Venedōtos*, *Gwynedd* being from the nominative, and *Gwyndod* from the stem of the oblique cases. *Venedōtos* is made in Latin into *Venedōtis* in an inscription at Penmachno, near Bettws y Coed : Hübner's *Inscr. Brit. Christ.*, No. 135. The Veneti have left their name to the part of Brittany called by the Bretons *Guened*, Vannes, and it is this name probably that laid the foundation for the tales which trace an army of Kymry from Gwynedd to Guened.

VEREDA, p. 230 : see *Epeiacon.*

VERGOBRETOS, p. 59. The analysis of the compound would suggest an adjective qualifying the name of the magistrate, and meaning *efficax judicii*, working or executing judgment. For the first part, *vergo*, seems identical with the Old Breton word *guerg* "efficax," and akin to Welsh, *cy-weirio*, to mend, to dress, or put in working order, Irish, *do-airc-i* or *tairci* "efficit, parat," a verb of the same origin and conjugation as the Greek ῥέζω, ἔρδω, I do or make, Gothic *vaurkjan*, to *work*. The other part *breto-* is identical with the Welsh *bryd*, mind, intention, *dedjryd*, a verdict; Irish, *breth*, judgment, *brithem*, genitive *brithemon*, a judge, Anglicised *brehon*. All these words are connected with the root *ber*, to bear, and the standing Irish law phrase for giving judgment is to " bear a *breth*," which literally means to *bear a bearing*, or *bear a birth*, and seems to point to some kind of supposed inspiration, brought about in a way similar, perhaps, to that whereby the Irish druids were believed to obtain visions of things to come. See Cormac's Glossary, s. v. *imbas forosnai*, and O'Donovan's " Battle of Magh Rath," pp. 46, 47, also Scott's " Lady of the Lake," canto iv. 5.

VERTURIONES, pp. 94, 224. This is usually written *Vecturiones*, which we tried in vain to understand, but on converting it into Goidelic, according to the usual rules of phonology, we found that it would yield *Fechtrenn* or *Fochtrenn*, which at once suggested the real name *Fortrenn*. On turning to Eyssenhardt's edition of Amm. Marcellinus, we were delighted to find that *Vecturiones* only comes from Gelenius, who lived in the sixteenth century, and that it has no manuscript authority whatever. The name is of the same origin as *Verteræ*, mentioned as one of the places where the Dux Britanniarum had some of his men quartered. It is found to have been at Brough-under-

Stanmore, in Westmoreland; and *Brough* (*i.e. burh*, a
fortress) is a translation, probably, of *Verteræ*, for the
latter is represented in Welsh by the word *gwerthyr*,
a fortification, and *Y Werthyr* occurs as the name
of a house in Anglesey, situated near the remains of
considerable earthworks and a large cromlech, also
of another in the parish of Llangïan in Lleyn.   Dr.
Stokes has pointed out to us the Sanskrit equivalent
in *vartra*, a dyke, German *werder*, an embankment.
The Chronicles usually speak only of the Plain of
Fortrenn or of the Men of Fortrenn ; so *Fortrenn*,
which is a genitive, is almost the only case of the
word which they give : the nominative in its old form
would probably have been *Fortriu* or *Foirtṛiu*, later
Foirtre, while the dative should, according to analogy,
have the optional forms *Fortrinn* ("Chronicon
Hyense," in Reeve's "*Adamnan*," p. 376), and
Fortriu like the nominative.   This latter is possibly
to be detected in the obscure place-name *Foircu* in
Todd's "Irish Nennius," p. 148 ; but Dr. Skene, in
his "Chron. of the Picts and Scots," p. 43, prints it
Foirciu, which may well have been somebody's mis-
reading of *Foirtriu*, seeing that *tri* would usually be
found contracted into a *t* (easily confounded with *c*)
with an *i* written above it.   The whole line is, *O chrich
Chath co Foirciu*, which has been rendered "from
the region of Cat to Forchu," whereby Dr. Skene
understood Scotland from Caithness to the Forth.
Here also, possibly, *Fothrev-e* belongs, comprising
approximately Kinross and Clackmannan.

VICTORIA, p. 161.   Such a name could hardly
have been expected beyond the limits of the Roman
province, and it is, perhaps, worth while to
suggest that it was possibly an approximate reproduction only of a native one which it bore.   Then
the question comes, what the latter may have been.

Evidently a repetition of *Verteræ* would hardly fit, and we cannot postulate a form *Vertōria* or *Virtōria;* but there seems to be no serious reason why we should not assume it to have been *Vĕrtŭria* or else *Vertŭrio*, the singular, in point of formation, of the plural *Verturiones.* Such a vocable would perhaps be sufficiently like *Victoria* in sound to have induced the Romans to treat it as the Latin word. The Sanskrit and German *vartra* and *werder* forbid our postulating *Vercturia*, which would approach still nearer, as well as supply an excuse for Gelenius writing *Vecturiones.*

Vortipori, p. 258. This name does not prove the bearer to have been a Brython, as it may have been a sort of metaphony or translation of a Goidelic vocable. This is forcibly suggested by the discovery in Dyved of a bilingual inscription in point, which reads in Latin *Memoria Voteporigis Protictoris* and in Ogam *Votecorigas*, the genitive of the name in Goidelic. The presence of the latter proves the man commemorated to have been a Goidel, though Brythonic was evidently the Celtic language in the ascendant in spite of its having to give way to Latin as the official idiom of the time. It is possible that the deceased was no other than the prince whom Gildas addressed as *Vortipori.* For more about these names see the " Archæologia Cambrensis " for 1895, pp. 307-313. The title of *protector* suggests that the bearer, whoever he may have been, was regarded as holding a position in the Roman army, though Rome had long since given Britain up.

Vriconion, pp. 234, 308. Ptolemy's Geography gives Οὐιροκόνιον, and the Itinerary has, among others, the forms *viroconio, uiriconio, uriconio, urioconio*, and *uriocunio ;* but when we take into account the modern

name, which is Wroxeter, and that of the neighbouring high ground, which is called the Wrekin, the preference must be given to *uriconio*, and the Celtic name
represented must be regarded as having been not
Uriconion, but *Vriconion*. It may have meant a spot
where rods and saplings grew, while it should in
modern Welsh be *Gwrygon*, which we doubtless have
in the *Caer Guricon* of Nennius. *Gwrygon* or
Guricon appears to have originally been the name of
the district in which that *caer* or town stood, and it
has been pointed out to us that it is called *Ureconn*,
that is to say, *Wreconn*, in a poem in the Red Book
of Hergest. It refers to another fortress situated
there, called Dinlle Ureconn, whereby it was meant
probably to distinguish that Dinlle from the Dinlle
near the Menai Straits : see Skene's " Four An. Books
of Wales," ii. p. 288.

INDEX.

Arthur, 73, 104, 108, 136, 236–239, 307

Arthuret, Knows of, 146

Artorius, 239

Assedomari, 279

Asser, 109

Atbret Iudeu, 134

Atecotti, 56, 91, 94, 113, 222, 235, 240, 279

Atrebates, 10, 23–25, 29, 43, 281, 282

Augusta, 102

Augustine, 127

Augustus Cæsar, 25-27, 32–34, 208

Aulerci, 292

Aulus Didius, 83

Aulus Plautius, 29, 35, 76, 77, 80

Aurelius Conan, 107

Avienus, 47, 268

BADONICUS, MONS, 108

Baetan mac Cairill, 158, 159

Banatia, 164

Barrivendi, 319

Beadwolf, 150

Bede, 97, 113, 130-139, 169, 171, 174, 223, 267, 275, 304

Belerion, 8, 45, 218

Belgæ, 4, 42, 44, 79, 217

Beli, 126

Beli, son of Benlli, 263

Belinos, 294

Belisama, 68, 282

Bellovaci, 23

Bergyon, 205, 287

Bericos, 37, 38, 76

Bernicia, 90, 114, 129, 133, 145, 146, 189 223

Bernicii, 113, 114

Berroc, 29

Beth, 267

Bibrax, 29

Bibroci, 17, 28, 29

Biceot, 266

Biturix, 65, 282

Blatobulgion, 233, 282, 283

Boia, 231, 258

Boresti, 89, 95, 163, 224, 283

Boudicca, 66, 85, 230, 284, 301

Bourges, 282

Boyd Dawkins, Prof., 21, 48, 262

Boyne, 67, 265

Bradley, Dr. H., 80, 283, 313, 315

Bran, 282

Bran Dub, 283

bratt, 212, 213

Branwen, 282

brecht, 211

Breennych, 113

Breiz, 215

Brennus, 284

Bret, Brettas, An.-Sax., 111, 138

Bretagne, 210

Bretain, 208, 293

Brethonec, 209

brethyn, 211

bretnais, 212

Βρεττανοί, 208

Brettones, 211

Bretwalda, 137, 138

Brezonek, 209

Brigantes, 30, 40, 63, 66, 81, 85, 90-2, 113, 118, 156, 221, 223, 284 285, 293, 299, 318

Brigit, 285

Britain, 137, 138, 204–10

—— Lesser, 209

—— Lower, 98, 101

—— Upper, 98, 100, 112, 115, 116

Britanni, 207–11

THE END.